PROJECT MANAGEMENT

PROJECT MANAGEMENT

Planning and Control Techniques

Fourth Edition

Rory Burke

Email (for orders and customer service enquiries): cs-books@wiley.co.uk
Visit our Home Page on www.wileyeurope.com or www.wiley.com

This publication is designed to provide accurate and authoritative information in regard to the subject matter covered. It is sold on the understanding that the Publisher is not engaged in rendering professional services. If professional advice or other expert assistance is required, the services of a competent professional should be sought.

Other Wiley Editorial Offices

John Wiley & Sons Inc., 111 River Street, Hoboken, NJ 07030, USA

Jossey-Bass, 989 Market Street, San Francisco, CA 94103-1741, USA

Wiley-VCH Verlag GmbH, Boschstr. 12, D-69469 Weinheim, Germany

John Wiley & Sons Australia Ltd, 33 Park Road, Milton, Queensland 4064, Australia

John Wiley & Sons (Asia) Pte Ltd, 2 Clementi Loop #02-01, Jin Xing Distripark, Singapore 129809

John Wiley & Sons Canada Ltd, 22 Worcester Road, Etobicoke, Ontario, Canada M9W 1L1

Wiley also publishes its books in a variety of electronic formats. Some content that appears in print may not be available in electronic books.

British Library Cataloguing in Publication Data

A catalogue record for this book is available from the British Library
ISBN: 0470851244

Typeset in Times New Roman 11/13pt by Mathematical Composition Setters Ltd, Salisbury, Wilts.
Printed and bound in Great Britain by Biddles Ltd, Guildford.
This book is printed on acid-free paper responsibly manufactured from sustainable forestry
in which at least two trees are planted for each one used for paper production.

To Sandra,
my best friend, partner, galley slave
and foredeck crew.

Twenty years ago I remember listening to an academic telling us that we professionally qualified engineers were our own worst enemies, in that anyone from a CEng to the lowest unskilled worker in an engineering company could, and did, call themselves engineers. To an outsider there was no distinction between the professional levels as, for example, there is in the medical world between doctors and nurses, and as a result engineers were not generally accorded the status our work and qualifications deserved.

Regrettably, the same can be said today for project managers in that anyone, from a social worker running a help desk to the manager running a major construction project, are called project managers. The main reason for this is because the term '*Project Manager*' is currently in vogue with regrettably not too many senior managers/ directors having the vaguest idea or understanding of what this really means.

So how do we project managers spread the word about our capability and the benefits that our profession can deliver? The only route is through education. That is the education of our peers, our bosses and all those who work with us and for us, until all the processes covered in this book become second nature. Rory's books on project management provide a clear understanding of what project management is all about and are widely used as standard text books in most colleges that teach the subject. If you think you are running a project but are not using the majority of the processes in this book then you are either running your project very badly or, more probably, you are simply not running a project.

Kirk Phillips
Hamble

This is a **techniques book** designed to take you step-by-step through the latest planning and control techniques, particularly those used by the **Project Management Software** and the Project Management **Body of Knowledge** (both APM and PMI).

Project management continues to grow as a profession through a wide range of projects (both large and small). The project management body of knowledge (PMBOK and bok) have both been revised and expanded into nine and 55 knowledge areas respectively. Employers are increasingly encouraging their managers to gain professional project management certification to comply with their quality management systems. Project management techniques are now used outside the traditional project industries, and a *management-by-project* approach has been adopted by many large companies in an effort to keep their work small, innovative and manageable.

Project Management Computing: Despite the advances in the project management software over the past twenty years (over 200 software packages are reported to be available), the project manager still needs to understand the basic principles of project management to apply the software successfully. Although there have been no new project management planning and control techniques introduced since the sixties, the communication field has developed through computer networking and the Internet - both enhancing the project's information and control system, and the mobile office.

Target Market: This book is widely used on university degree programmes, executive management training courses, planning software courses, and professional certification (PMP). The undergraduate degree programmes tend to focus on project management principles and calculations, while the postgraduate degrees and MBA modules focus on applying project management principles through case studies and academic projects.

The executive management training courses for practising managers focus on the practical planning and control techniques often using the delegates' projects as a live case study. The computer planning skills training courses teach clients how to use proprietary software (often having to explain basic planning techniques first). The professional certification examinations (project management professional [PMP]) are structured around the project management body of knowledge (PMBOK and bok) to give a formal qualification which is internationally recognised.

Academically there is a trend away from knowledge based assessment towards competency based assessment where you are not assessed on your knowledge alone, but on your ability to apply your knowledge. In this context project management competency is the application of project management planning and control techniques to your projects - developing a plan and guiding your projects towards a successful completion. An **accompanying website** with additional exercises, proformas and worked examples is available for lecturers using this book.

ACKNOWLEDGEMENTS

I have derived considerable benefit and ideas from lecturers, students, consultants and practising project managers who were willing to discuss the commercial application of project management techniques. The writing of this book was a team effort - I particularly wish to thank:

Book proposal: Particular thanks to Steve Hardman at John Wiley & Sons for co-ordinating feedback from lecturers in Britain and Australia, and Michael Hougham at Henley Management College.

Diagrams and DTP: Sandra Burke

Proof reading for content: Derek Archibald, Bob Burns, Peter Goldsbury, Steve Hinge, Mark Massyn, and Chris Naude (Chris and Derek also designed the computer screens).

Proof reading for grammar and spelling: Sandra Burke, Linda Logan, Renee Bampfield-Duggan, Tony Shapiro and Derek Archibald.

Sketches: Ingrid Franzsen and Buddy Mendis

Foreword: Particular thanks to Kirk Phillips.

Rory Burke
New Zealand

CONTENTS

C H A P T E R 1

Introduction To Project Management

Project management offers a **structured** approach to managing projects. The purpose of this book is to outline the latest planning and control techniques used by industry, commerce, sport and domestic projects, and particularly those used by the **project planning software** and referred to in the Project Management Institute's (PMI) **project management body of knowledge** (PMBOK), and the Association of Project Manager's (APM) **body of knowledge** (bok).

As the use of projects becomes more pervasive, so more managers are entering the field of project management. Their success will be helped by their ability to develop a fully integrated information and control system to plan, instruct, monitor and control large amounts of data, quickly and accurately to facilitate the problem-solving and decision-making process. To achieve these goals the project manager needs a comprehensive **toolkit** - as a plumber works with a bag of tools, so the project manager works with a computer producing organisation charts, work breakdown structures, barcharts, resource histograms and cash-flow statements.

Projects have traditionally been managed through a classic functional hierarchical type organisation structure, but with the increase of multi-disciplines, multi-departments, multi-companies and multi-national projects so there has been a move towards *management-by-projects*, project teams and matrix organisation structures. As the project manager is the **single point of responsibility**, it is the project manager's job to set up a management structure which not only meets the needs of the project, but the needs of the organisation, the needs of the stakeholders and the needs of the individuals working on the project as well (see figure 1.1).

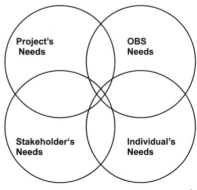

Figure 1.1: Intersecting Needs
(OBS = Organisation Breakdown Structure)

1. What is a Project? √

The main difference between project management and general management (or any other form of management for that matter) relates to the definition of a **project** and what the project intends to deliver to the client and stakeholders. Here are two well stated and eloquent definitions:

The PMBOK defines a project as: *".... a temporary endeavour undertaken to create a unique product or service. **Temporary** means that every project has a definite end. **Unique** means that the product or service is different in some distinguishing way from all similar products or services."*

Turner defines a project as: *"..... an endeavour in which human, (or machine), material and financial resources are organised in a novel way, to undertake a unique scope of work, of given specification, within constraints of cost and time, so as to deliver beneficial change defined by quantitative and qualitative objectives."*

Traditionally work in the construction industry and defence procurement were seen as projects, but in recent years most proactive companies are structuring their work as projects (*management-by-projects*) and using project management techniques to ensure successful completion.

Projects range in size, scope, cost and time from mega international projects costing millions of dollars over many years - to small domestic projects with a low budget taking just a few hours to complete. Consider the following projects:

- Career development (education and training courses)
- The transition period during which a change occurs.
- Designing and constructing a building, a house or a yacht.
- Designing and testing a new prototype (a car or a washing machine).
- The launch of a new product (advertising and marketing project).
- Implementing a new computer system (IT project, or upgrade).
- Designing and implementing a new organisational structure (human resource project).
- Planning and conducting an audit (quality management project).
- Improving productivity within a target period.
- Disaster recovery (limiting the damage of fires, floods or any type of accident).
- Olympics, or Springboks' tour of New Zealand (a sports project).
- Rolling Stones' world tour (an entertainment project).
- Moving house or going on holiday (a domestic project).

Other distinctive features of a project include:
- A **start and finish** (although they may be difficult to define - the start may have crystallised over a period of time and the end may be a slow phase out).
- A **life-cycle** (a beginning and an end, with a number of distinct phases in between).
- A **budget** with an associated cash-flow.
- Activities that are essentially unique and **non-repetitive**.
- Use of **resources**, which may be from different departments and need co-ordinating.

- A **single point of responsibility** (i.e. the project manager).
- **Fast tracking** - getting your product to market before your competitors.
- **Team roles** and relationships that are subject to change and need to be developed, defined and established (team building).

Within the context of this book a project may be defined as a beneficial change which uses the special project management techniques to plan and control the *scope of work* in order to deliver a product to satisfy the client's and stakeholder's needs and expectations.

2. Project Management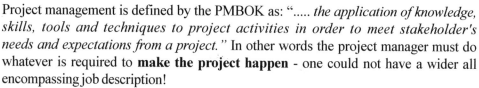

Project management is defined by the PMBOK as: "..... *the application of knowledge, skills, tools and techniques to project activities in order to meet stakeholder's needs and expectations from a project.*" In other words the project manager must do whatever is required to **make the project happen** - one could not have a wider all encompassing job description!

This definition clearly identifies that the purpose of the project is to meet the stakeholders needs and expectations. It is therefore a fundamental requirement for the project manager to establish who are the stakeholders (besides the client) and analyse their needs and expectations to define, at the outset, the purpose of the project, its *scope of work* and objectives (this will be developed in the *Feasibility Study* chapter).

The discipline of project management can be described in terms of its component processes, conveniently defined by the PMBOK as nine knowledge areas:

• Integration	• Scope	• Communication
• Time	• Cost	• Procurement
• Quality	• HRM	• Risk

See page 7 for a brief description of the nine knowledge areas.

The APM bok defines project management as '*the most efficient way of introducing change .... achieved by:*

- *Defining what has to be accomplished, generally in terms of time, cost, and various technical and quality performance parameters;*
- *Developing a plan to achieve these and then working this plan, ensuring that progress is maintained in line with these objectives;*
- *Using appropriate project management techniques and tools to plan, monitor and maintain progress;*
- *Employing persons skilled in project management - including normally a project manager - who are given [single] responsibility for introducing the change and are accountable for its successful accomplishment.*'

Peter Morris describes project management as: '*..... the process of integrating everything that needs to be done* (typically using a number of special project management techniques) *as the project evolves through its life cycle* [from concept to handover] *in order to meet the project's objectives.*'

3

Companies performing projects will generally subdivide their projects into several phases or stages to provide better management control. Collectively these project phases are called the ***project life-cycle***. Along with the *project life-cycle* some of the other special project management techniques that form part of the project management integrative process are:

- Work breakdown structure (WBS)
- Critical path method (CPM)
- Resource smoothing
- Earned value
- Configuration control.

3. Management-by-Projects

Many organisations are changing in nature as more of them are accomplishing their business through projects. This *management-by-projects* approach has been used in engineering, construction, aerospace and defence for many years, and now we see other organisations buying into the process; pharmaceutical, medical, telecommunications, software development, systems development, energy, manufacturing, educational and service organisations. The *management-by-projects* approach encourages:

- organisation flexibility
- decentralised management responsibility
- holistic view of problems
- goal-orientated problem solution processes.

Time Magazine identifies these profound changes happening in the job market. '*Full-time, full-year workers are no longer as dominant as they were. There is more self-employment, more part-time employment and the beginnings of what might be called task employment.*' I would call this project employment. Therefore for employer and employee to make the most of the new employment patterns a working understanding of *management-by-projects* and project team dynamics is essential.

Oracle: '*The business world is moving increasingly towards projects orientation operation to measure the true costs and perfectibility of any business endeavour.*' It is very difficult, if not impossible, to quantify costs if they are grouped together and shared - the only way would be a sharing percentage.

The importance and acceptance of the trend towards *management-by-projects* was endorsed by the International Project Management Association (IPMA) Project Management Conference in Vienna (1990) that adopted *management-by-projects* as its theme.

Programme Management: Where the project office is managing a large capital project (e.g. Channel Tunnel), it may be subdivided into a number of smaller related projects to achieve a single common goal.

Portfolio Management: Defines a project office that is running a number of unrelated projects. This could be managing the repairs and maintenance of; a large telecom type company, a power station or a water utility.

Small Projects: Managing small projects have their own unique problems, although they may appear to be simple, they are often associated with a lack of definition (no drawings, no specifications and no contact), instructions are given verbally, and minimum standards are not established. There are no arbitration mechanisms, no exit strategies and the small projects may only be for a short duration that does not give you time to establish a management system.

General Management: Although this book is about project management, the successful project manager must also be competent in a wide range of general management skills in addition to the nine knowledge areas. These would include:
- recruiting and personnel
- economics
- computer systems
- legal contracts
- personnel and human resources
- sales and marketing
- accounts and salaries.

The project manager would obviously not be expected to be an expert in all these fields, but for a project to be successful they may all need to be addressed at one time or another and as the *single point of responsibility*, the project manager will be responsible for either performing the work, or delegating it (see figure 1.2).

Production Management: Although projects are deemed to be unique, in reality they usually consist of groups of repetitive tasks. Henry Ford emphatically showed years ago that production lines are the quickest, and most cost effective way to manufacture a car. The same applies to projects, if there are repetitive tasks, then setup a production process to carry them out at the same time.

Technical Management: The technical aspects of the project also need to be managed. On smaller projects the project manager may be expected to be the technical expert as well as the manager. In fact early on in your career you will probably only be appointed as project manager if you are a technical expert.

There is usually a certain amount of overlap between project management, general management and technical management. This can be simply presented as intersecting circles (figure 1.2).

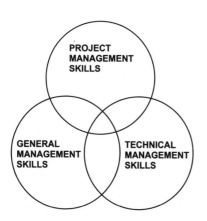

Figure 1.2: Intersecting Management Skills

Project Management Environment: The project environment directly affects the project and how it should be managed. Projects are not carried out in a vacuum, they are influenced by a wide range of stakeholders and issues. Consider the following:

- Stakeholders (all interested parties)
- Client / sponsor's requirements
- Your own company's organisation structure
- Market requirements
- Competitors
- New technology
- Rules and regulations (Health and safety)
- Politics (both internal and external)
- Economic cycle.

For project managers to be effective they must have a thorough understanding of the project environment which may well be changing and so continually shifting the goal posts. The project environment consists of the numerous stakeholders and players that have an input or are effected by the project. All must be managed as any one person could derail the project (see stakeholder analysis in the *Feasibility Study* chapter).

4. Project Management Software

Today, powerful but inexpensive project management software is readily available for the personal computer. This availability has essentially moved project management computing away from the data processing department to the project manager's desk. This represents a major shift in the management of information.

Whilst project planning software will certainly help the project manager plan and control their projects, its application will only be effective if the planning and control techniques are clearly understood. The purpose of this text is therefore to develop these techniques through manual exercises, but with the assumption that computer systems will be used later - see the project management computing chapter.

ONE COMPUTER

MANY
DISCIPLINES

5. Project Management Associations

A number of project management associations and institutions have formed chapters around the world to encourage the development of project management as a profession. These chapters organise regular meetings and newsletters to keep their members informed about project management issues:
- body of knowledge
- certification of project managers (PMP)
- unit standards
- ethics
- global forum.

Body of Knowledge: Over the past fifty years a considerable body of knowledge has built up around project management tools, skills and techniques. This database of information has been developed into the following:
- The APM's bok - Association of Project Managers (UK)
- The PMI's PMBOK - Project Management Institute (USA)
- The IPMA's BOK - International Association of Project Managers (formerly called INTERNET)
- The AIPM's Competency Standards for Project Management (Australia)
- ISO 10006 '*Guideline to Quality in Project Management*' - this will assist clients evaluating the effectiveness of the project management system
- South African unit standards.

The purpose of the body of knowledge is to identify and describe best practices that are applicable to most projects most of the time. There is widespread consensus about their value and usefulness. They are also intended to provide a common lexicon and terminology within the profession of project management - locally and internationally. As a relatively young international profession there is still a need to converge on a common set of terms. The PMBOK describes project management under the following nine knowledge areas:
- **Project Integration:** integrates the three main project management processes of planning, execution and control - where inputs from several knowledge areas are brought together.
- **Project Scope Management:** includes the processes required to ensure that the project includes all the work required, and only the work required, to complete the project successfully. It is primarily concerned with defining and controlling what is or is not included in the project, to meet the sponsors' and stakeholders' goals and objectives. It consists of authorisation, scope planning, scope definition, scope change management and scope verification.
- **Project Time Management:** includes the process required to ensure timely performance of the project. It consists of activity definition, activity sequencing, duration estimating, establishing the calendar, schedule development and time control.

- **Project Cost Management:** includes the process required to ensure that the project is completed within the approved budget. It consists of resource planning, cost estimating, cost budgeting, cash-flow and cost control.
- **Project Quality Management:** includes the process required to ensure that the project will satisfy the needs for which it was undertaken. It consists of determining the required condition, quality planning, quality assurance and quality control.
- **Project Human Resource Management:** includes the process required to make the most effective use of the people involved with the project. It consists of organisation planning, staff acquisition and team development.
- **Project Communications Management:** includes the process required to ensure proper collection and dissemination of project information. It consists of communication planning, information distribution, project meetings, progress reporting and administrative closure.
- **Project Risk Management:** includes the process concerned with identifying, analysing, and responding to project risk. It consists of risk identification, risk quantification and impact, response development and risk control.
- **Project Procurement Management:** includes the process required to acquire goods and services from outside the performing project team or organisation. It consists of procurement planning, solicitation planning, solicitation, source selection, contract administration and contract closeout.

The body of knowledge can be subdivided into four core elements which determine the **deliverable** objectives of the project:
- Scope
- Time
- Cost
- Quality

The other knowledge areas provide the **means of achieving** the deliverable objectives, namely:
- Integration
- Human resources
- Communication
- Risk
- Procurement and contract.

APM bok: The APM bok takes a much broader approach than the PMBOK, by subdividing project management into 55 knowledge areas. It incorporates not only inward focused project management topics (such as planning and control techniques), but also broader topics in which the project is being managed (such as social and ecological environment), as well as specific areas (such as technology, economics, finance, organisation, procurement and people, as well as general management). The topics are described at an outline level, leaving the details to recommended texts (on their book list) to explain the working of the knowledge areas (see www.apm.org.uk).

Certification of Project Managers (PMP): The certification process offers a means for experienced project managers to gain a formal qualification in project management. There is a trend away from the knowledge based examinations which assess a person's knowledge, towards competence based examinations which assess a person's ability to perform. The PMI's certification is called the Project Management Professional (PMP). There is an increasing recognition of certification and for some projects it is being made a mandatory pre-qualification.

Competency is a mixture of explicit knowledge derived from formal education, tacit knowledge and skills derived from experience. For young professionals, explicit knowledge is more important, but the other competencies will become increasingly important as they progress in their careers. The PMI's (PMP) is a single level certificate programme, which measures explicit knowledge directly through a multi-choice test, and tacit knowledge and skill indirectly by assessing the candidate's work experience. It is therefore aimed at an early to mid-career professional.

The IPMA and AIPM (Australia), on the other hand, have developed a multi-stage programme. At the first stage explicit knowledge is measured directly through a multi-question test. This is aimed at the professional managers starting their careers. At the second stage tacit knowledge and skill are measured directly. This is early to mid stage certification, equivalent to PMP. At the third stage, the programme measures performance of senior project managers directly, and IPMA has a fourth stage to measure the performance of project directors.

The key issue is ensuring equivalence, so that client organisations can compare the competence of project managers against different programmes. In Europe the integration of the EU is encouraging a growing number of cross-border projects, which not only require collaboration, but a need to converge on common practices, legal systems and, not least, a common business language.

Global Project Management Forum: Project management has been an international profession for many years, but only recently have the global issues of project management been discussed. The first global project management forum was held in New Orleans in 1995 where 30 countries were represented. Some of the key topics discussed at the forum included:

- What industries or types of projects are the main users of modern project management in your country?
- What industries or areas of application in your country have the greatest need for more or better project management?

9

- What industries or organisations offer the greatest opportunities for growth of professional project management in your country?

The answers to these and other questions relating to standards, certification, a global PMBOK and advancing the project management profession were published by the PMI as *The Global Status of the Project Management Profession.*

6. Benefits of Project Management

The benefits of using a project management approach, obviously follows on from addressing the needs of the project. The project manager is responsible for developing a plan through which the project can be tracked and controlled to ensure the project meets preset objectives. To do this effectively the project manager requires accurate and timely information. This information should be supplied by the planning and control system, which outlines the scope of work and measures performance against the original plan.

Although the planning and control systems will incur additional management costs, it should be appreciated that lack of information could be even more expensive if it leads to poor management decisions, mistakes, rework and overrun. Listed below are some of the main benefits associated with a fully integrated project planning and control system:

- **Client:** The project manager is the project's *single point of responsibility* and the company's representative to the client (and other stakeholders). During meetings with the client the planning and control system will provide information about every aspect of the project. Clients prefer to deal with one person - the project manager - who is accountable. This gives them confidence that problems will be addressed and the project will be completed on time.
- **Single Point of Responsibility:** With the project manager responsible for the complete project, this should limit scope overlap and scope underlap.
- **Estimating:** The estimate forms the basis of the project plan. If you cannot estimate and measure it, how can you manage it?
- **CPM:** The critical path method calculates all the activities start dates, finish dates and floats. Activities with zero float form the critical path which determines the duration of the project - delaying a critical activity will delay the project.
- **Fast Track:** Bring a new product to the market quickly before your competitors.
- **Schedule Barchart:** Communicates the what, where, when and who.
- **Project Integration:** Co-ordinates and integrates the contribution of all the project participants.
- **Reporting Interfaces:** The planning and control system's database can be structured around the work breakdown structure (WBS) for project reporting and around the organisation breakdown structure (OBS) for corporate reporting. Without an integrated system the two reporting requirements would have to be processed separately.

- **Response Time:** Timely response on project performance is essential for effective project control. The project planning and control system can adjust the content and frequency of the feedback to address the needs of the project, while the corporate systems may be less flexible. Consider the accounts department for example - they generally use a monthly reporting cycle where feedback on invoices may be four to six weeks behind timenow.

- **Trends:** Projects are best controlled by monitoring the progress trends of time, cost and performance. This information may not be available to the project manager if the trend parameters are derived from a number of different functional sources and not communicated.

- **Data Capture:** If the project progress reporting is based on information supplied by the functional departments, the project manager cannot control the accuracy of this information. The problem here is that it may only become obvious towards the end of the project, that the reporting is inaccurate, by which time it may be too late to bring the project back on course to meet the project's objectives (see *Project Control* chapter).

- **Procedures:** The planning and control system enables the project manager to develop procedures and work instructions which are tailored to the specific needs of the project.

- **Project Office:** Offers a centre for project management excellence.

- **Closeout Report:** The performance of the current project will form the estimating database for future projects. If this data is not collected by the planning and control system it may be lost forever and you will live to repeat your mistakes. The closeout provides an effective mechanism to learn by mistakes, and strive for continuous improvement.

- **Marketing:** Vendors can distinguish themselves by marketing their project management systems. If two vendors are offering similar products at similar prices - then their selection may be based on the vendor who can demonstrate they can effectively manage the project.

Although there are many benefits from using project management techniques, senior management should tread carefully if the project management culture is not already established within the company, because the resistance to change could derail the project.

7. Role of the Project Manager

It is appropriate to conclude this chapter with a few words on the role of the project manager. Experience has shown that the selection of the project manager is a key appointment which can influence the success or failure of the project. As the *single point of responsibility*, it is the project manager who integrates and co-ordinates all the contributions, and guides them to successfully complete the project.

The role of the project manager should be outlined in the **project charter** (see *Scope Management* chapter) along with the purpose of the project. The following lists some desirable project manager attributes:

- Ability to select and develop an operational team from a standing start
- Leadership and management ability
- Ability to anticipate problems, solve problems and make decisions
- Ability to integrate the project stakeholders
- Operational flexibility
- Ability to plan, expedite and get things done
- Ability to negotiate and persuade
- Understand the environment within which the project is being managed
- Ability to review monitor and apply control
- Ability to administer the contract, the scope of work and scope changes
- Ability to manage within an environment of constant change
- Ability to keep the client happy.

We are witnessing a silent revolution - the transition from conventional functional management to project management. It is *Goodbye MBA* - hello *M.Sc Project Management*. I hope you are on-board!

Key Points:

- The project management body of knowledge (PMBOK) and APM (bok) define project management under a number of knowledge areas.
- Project management has become a recognised profession with international accreditation of its members.
- Many companies are adopting a *management-by-project* approach with the project manager as the *single point of responsibility*.

Further Reading:

Morris, Peter, *The Management of Projects,* Thomas Telford
Oosthuizen, Pieter, *Goodbye MBA*, International Thomson
Project Management Institute (PMI)., *The Global Status of the Project Management Profession*, PMI publication
Turner, R., *Handbook of Project Based Management*, McGraw-Hill

Global PM Forum <www.pmforum.org>

PMI <www.pmi.org>

APM <www.apm.org.uk>

IPMA <www.ipma.ch>

APM <www.apm.org.uk>

Australian AIPM <www.dab.uts.au/aipm/competencystandards/index.html>

SA Qualifications Authority <www.saqa.org.za>

Case Study and Exercises:

You have been appointed by the CEO of an international telecommunications company to make a short presentation to the board of directors about the benefit of using a ***management-by-projects*** approach on the company's next project. Your short presentation (written and/or verbal) should consider the following:

1. Explain what project management is, and why it is different to other forms of management.
2. Explain how project management can be applied to your company's projects.
3. Point out the trend towards professional project management and your local project management society / association who are supporting certification.
4. Outline the role of the project manager.
5. Suggest a small pilot project on which you can develop your project management systems.

History of Project Management

The history of project management is often associated with the construction of the massive Egyptian Pyramids and the Great Wall of China. They were certainly large complex structures, built to high standards, that have stood the test of time and must have required an enormous workforce. But with no documented evidence the management techniques used can only be based on conjecture. Although archeologists are starting to suggest that the construction of the pyramids were the largest fill-in job the world has ever seen - when the River Nile flooded annually the workforce would move off the land to work on the pyramids. They were not slaves as Hollywood suggests, but willing workers who were probably paid. And when the annual floods subsided they would return to their farms.

Modern day project management is associated with Henry Gantt's development of the barchart (early 1900s), and special project management techniques developed during the military and aerospace projects of the 1950s and 1960s in America and Britain. It is these special distinctive project management tools and techniques which are referred to in the body of knowledge, used by the planning software and developed in this book.

Traditionally the management of projects was considered more of an art than science, but with the growing number of project management institutions, associations and academic establishments, project management has become more of a **science and discipline** as accepted practices are captured and formalised in the global body of knowledge and certificate programmes.

Today, rapidly changing technology, fierce competitive markets and a powerful environmental lobby have all encouraged companies to change their management systems - in this sink or swim, adopt or die environment, project management and *management-by-projects* are offering a real solution.

1. Gantt Chart - 1900s

The history of the barchart can be traced back to World War 1 when an American, **Henry Gantt** (1861 - 1919), designed the barchart as a visual aid for planning and controlling his shipbuilding projects. In recognition, planning barcharts are often called after his name - **Gantt charts**. The Handbook of Industrial Engineers (1982, p.11) acknowledges the Gantt chart for significantly reducing the time to build cargo ships during World War 1.

Figure 2.1 indicates the format of a Gantt chart, where the top line is a calendar time-scale in days [1] and the activities [2] are listed on the left hand column. The scheduling of each activity is represented by a horizontal line [3], from the activity's start to finish date. The length of the activity line is therefore, proportional to its estimated duration.

Gantt further used this barchart to track progress by drawing a second line alongside the planned schedule to indicate work done [4]. The relative position of the progress line to the planned line indicates percentage complete and remaining duration, while the relative position between the progress line and Timenow [5] indicates actual progress against planned progress.

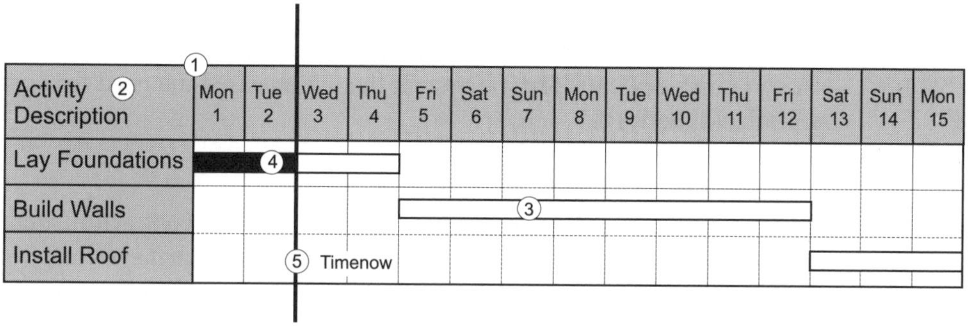

Figure 2.1: Gantt Chart

The Gantt chart has stood the test of time and is widely acknowledged today as the most effective method of communicating planning information - people find them easy to use and understand. A survey by Microsoft Project users found that 80% of managers preferred the barchart to the network diagram for planning and controlling their projects.

Henri Fayol: In 1916 Fayol, a French industrialist, presented a management process that consisted of:

- Planning (forecasting)
- Organising (staffing)
- Commanding (motivation)
- Directing (co-ordinating)
- Controlling (monitoring).

Fayol's principles are fundamentally universal and apply to all types of management, whether ongoing or project, and if you add initiation and closing, then you have the key components of the planning and control cycle developed in chapter 7.

2. Project Management 1950s and 1960s

Nearly all of the special project management techniques we use today were developed during the 1950s and 1960s by the US defence-aerospace industry (DoD and NASA) - this includes *program evaluation and review technique* (PERT), *earned value* (EV), *configuration management, value engineering* and *work breakdown structures* (WBS). The construction industry also made its contribution to the development of the *critical path method* (CPM) and the *precedence diagram method* (PDM), using *network diagrams* and *resource smoothing* - the motivation was scheduling urgency and engineering management. During this period large scale projects were effectively shielded from the environment, society, and ecology issues. The Apollo space programme and the construction of nuclear power stations typified projects of this period. Some of the key achievements during this period are chronologically listed below:

1950s - Development of PERT and CPM.

1950s - Development of the concept of a **single point of responsibility** for multi-disciplined projects where one person is made responsible for completing the project. Coupled with this approach came the project team, secondment and resource sharing through a matrix organisation structure.

1960 - NASA experiments with **matrix** organisation structures.

1962 - NASA introduces a PERT type system that emphasised the need for cost control and the WBS.

1963 - *Earned value* adopted by the USAF.

1963 - *Project life-cycle* adopted by the USAF.

1963 - Polaris was the first British project on which the sub-contractors were required contractually to use advanced project management systems.

1964 - *Configuration management* adopted by NASA to review and document proposed changes.

1965 - DoD and NASA move from cost-plus contracts towards incentive type contracts such as firm fixed price or cost plus incentive fee.

1965 - The mid 1960s saw a dramatic rise in the number of projects in the construction industry that used modern project management techniques.

1965 - The TSR-2 (swing-wing bomber) highlighted the problems of **concurrency**, i.e. starting the development and production before the design was stable. Increasing the *scope of work* led to cost overrun and delays - eventually the project was scrapped.

1966 - A report in 1966 stated that not enough time was spent on front-end definition and preparation (of the *project life-cycle*); there were wide variations in standards of cost and schedule control; and inadequate control over design changes.

1967 - International Project Management Association (IPMA) founded (formerly called INTERNET). Grouping of over 20 international associations.

1969 - Project Management Institute (PMI) formed, certification and the PMBOK (1987, 1996, 2000) were to follow.

3. Network Diagrams

For a project plan to be effective it must equally address the parameters of activity time and activity logic. This logical relationship is required to model the affect schedule variance will have downstream in the project. As projects became larger and more complex, the Gantt chart was found to be lacking as a planning and control tool because it could not indicate the logical relationships between activities. Although the linked barchart does show logical relationships, it soon becomes cluttered as the number of activities and logical relationships increase.

In the 1950s feedback from industry and commerce indicated that project cost and time overruns were all too common. It was suggested at the time that the project estimates were on the optimistic side in order to gain work, however a more important reason emerged which indicated that the planning and control techniques available to manage large complex projects were inadequate. This encouraged the development of scheduling methods which integrated project procurement, resources and costs.

With these shortcomings in mind, network planning techniques were developed by Flagle, the US Navy and Remington Rand Univac. Flagle wrote a paper in 1956 on *'Probability based tolerances in forecasting and planning'*. Although it was not published in the Journal of Industrial Engineers until April 1961, it was in a sense the forerunner of the US Navy's *program evaluation and review technique* (PERT). Both PERT and Remington Rand Univac's *critical path method* (CPM) used a similar network format, where the activities were presented in boxes and the sequence of the activities from left to right showed the logic of the project (see figure 2.2).

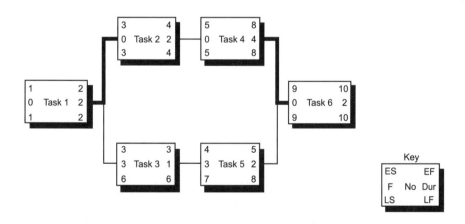

Figure 2.2: Network Diagram (showing logical relationships)

Network diagrams were also being developed in other countries. In France Professor Roy developed *Graphes et Ordonnacements* (networks and schedules). In Russia a technique which translates to 'Lattice Planning' was developed, and in the UK the CEGB developed a CPM system for a maintenance overhaul at Keadby Power Station.

4. Critical Path Method (CPM)

The main difference between CPM and PERT is how they addressed activity time duration. The accuracy of an activity's time estimate usually depends on the information available from previous projects. If an activity has been performed before, its duration can be reasonably accurately estimated. However, activities with a new scope of work, which are difficult to measure or dependent on other uncertain variables, may have a range of possible time duration.

CPM uses a deterministic approach, which suits a project where time duration can be accurately predicted, e.g. a construction project. While PERT on the other hand uses a probabilistic approach, which suits a project where time duration may vary over a range of possibilities, e.g. a research project.

The *critical path method* (CPM) also called *critical path analysis* (CPA) was developed around 1957 by Remington Rand Univac as a management tool to improve the planning and control of their turnaround time (production to sales) - the benefits were quickly recognised and they soon paid back their development costs.

CPM was initially setup to address the **time cost trade-off** dilemma (crashing) often presented to project managers, where there is a complex relationship between project *time-to-complete* and *cost-to-complete*. If the duration of the project is shortened, will the project cost more or less? Some costs will reduce (plant hire), while others will increase (overtime). On large complex projects you need a model like CPM to work out the overall affect of these types of changes.

The initial growth of CPM in the industrial market was slow. This was partially due to the lack of project management education and CPM training offered at the time by the universities and colleges. Also, as with the PERT application, the computer hardware and software facilities were limited compared with the personal computers of today. Further, the systems were not interactive. They required a batch card input through a hands-off data processing department, which often led to an inherently slow response.

5. Program Evaluation and Review Technique (PERT)

In the late 1950s the US Navy set up a development team under Admiral Red Raborn with the Lockheed Aircraft Corporation, and a management consultant Booz Allen & Hamilton - to design PERT as an integrated planning and control system to manage the hundreds of sub-contractors involved in the design, construction and testing of their Polaris Submarine missile system.

The PERT technique was developed to apply a statistical treatment to the possible range of activity time duration. A three time probabilistic model was developed, using pessimistic (p), optimistic (o) and most likely (m) time duration (see figure 2.3). The three time duration were imposed on a normal distribution to calculate the activity's expected time.

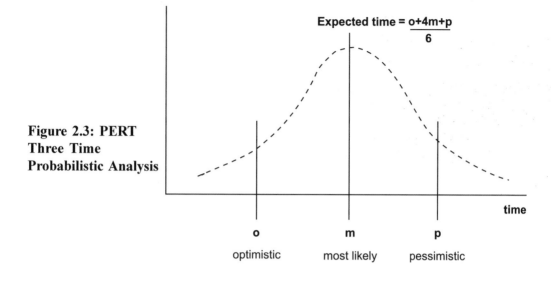

**Figure 2.3: PERT
Three Time
Probabilistic Analysis**

In practice one would estimate around the *most likely* time. The *optimistic* time would be slightly shorter, if everything went better than planned. While the *pessimistic* time would be extended if everything went worse than planned (late delivery, or a machine breakdown).

The success of the Polaris Submarine project helped to establish PERT in the 1960s as a planning tool within many large corporations. At the time PERT was believed to be the main reason the submarine project was so successful, meanwhile CPM was not receiving anywhere near as much recognition even though it also offered a resource allocation facility.

There were, however a number of basic problems which reduced PERT's effectiveness and eventually led to its fall from popularity. Besides the computer limitations previously mentioned, statistical analysis was not generally understood by project managers - they must have been pleased to see the end of standard deviations and confidence limits.

Other features of PERT, however, are seeing a renaissance as the benefits of milestone planning is becoming more widely used. By defining a series of milestones you can simplify the planning process at your level and make your sub-contractors responsible for achieving their key dates. Even with the powerful planning software available today there is still a need to empower an increasingly educated workforce.

The early differences between CPM and PERT have largely disappeared and it is now common to use the two terms interchangeably as a generic name to include the whole planning and control process.

6. Activity-on-Arrow / Activity-on-Node

Network diagrams were originally developed as both *activity-on-arrow* and *activity-on-node*. The *activity-on-arrow* wrote the activity details on the arrow, while the *activity-on-node* wrote the activity details in the node. *Activity-on-arrow* was initially preferred by engineers in the 1960s, but with the transition from manual calculations to computers so the preference changed to *activity-on-node*.

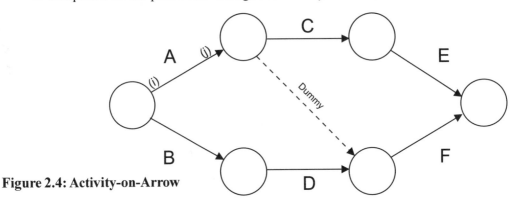

Figure 2.4: Activity-on-Arrow

The benefits of *activity-on-arrow* (AOA):
- The activity (i, j) identification indicates the preceding and succeeding activities, this is very useful walking through a large network. However, it does mean that when an activity is inserted its neighbouring activities numbers will have to change - not so on AON as inserting an activity only changes the logical links.

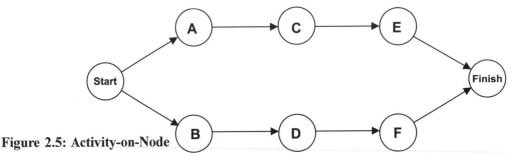

Figure 2.5: Activity-on-Node

The benefits of *activity-on-node*: (AON)
- AON offers a number of logical relationships between the activities, such as *start-to-start, finish-to-finish* and *lag*. This overcomes the AOA's need for dummy activities (see Lockyer, 1989).
- The AON also offers a professional presentation, which is generally known today as a *network diagram*.
- AOA uses a dummy activity to clarify the logic, but it is possible to have a double dummy that is illogical.

There are many other management tools that present information in a box; WBS, OBS and *flow charts*. After carrying out the activity calculations, both methods should produce exactly the same result.

7. Project Organisation Structures

Up to the mid 1950s projects tended to be run by companies using the traditional functional hierarchical organisation structure, where the project work would be passed from department to department. There were also examples of pure organisation structures where everyone worked on the same project (e.g. The Manhattan Project). But as projects became more complex (particularly the aerospace and military projects), meeting budgets became more important, delivering the project on time was more crucial and working with many disciplines, departments or companies became a fact of life - so out of necessity '*project focused*' organisation structures started to develop.

In the 1950s Bechtel was one of the first companies to use a project management organisation structure to manage their oil pipeline project in Canada where responsibility was assigned to an individual operating in a remote location with an autonomous team. This is a good example of an organisation structure with the project manager as the *single point of responsibility* with autonomous authority over a pool of resources. The norm during this time (and still is for many companies) would be for the head of department or functional manager to be responsible for the project as it passed through their department. The project approach is to assign responsibility to one person who would work on the project full-time through the *project life-cycle* from initiation to completion. In due course this person was called the **project manager**.

As the project responsibility shifted from the functional managers to the project managers so the functional departments were increasingly seen as a pool of company resources that could be used on any project. This new organisation structure where the project lines of responsibility and authority overlaid the functional lines of responsibility and authority became known as the *matrix organisation structure* (see the chapter on *Project Organisation Structures*). This enabled companies to work on many projects at the same time, share resources, address scope overlap and underlap, and most importantly have one person communicating with the client. *Matrix organisation structures* were soon to become synonymous with project management (see figure 2.6). The matrix structure answers the question - "*If the project manager is not co-ordinating the project who is*???".

Figure 2.6: Matrix Organisation Structure

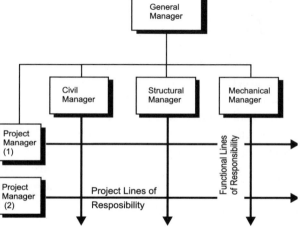

8. Project Management in the 1970s

The Vietnam war, the OPEC oil embargoes and environmental pressure groups all featured in the 1970s to constrain projects across a wide range of industries and commerce. Environmental matters became a project issue impacting on: pollution (oil spills), nuclear waste, noise pollution (Concorde), and roads (impact on the countryside).

Project management continued to grow and develop into a multi-disciplined profession with its distinctive tools and techniques. High technology companies outside the defence and construction industries were starting to use project management systems effectively enabling them to design to cost.

This was a period of refinement as the problems of using the distinctive tools and techniques became apparent. During this period, public sector projects experienced a high failure rate. This could be attributed in part to poor project definition (scope management), poorly defined project organisation structure (matrix structure), and failure to consider the impact of external factors (stakeholders).

Project management associations in America (PMI) and Britain (APM) were establishing project management as a profession, as project experience was beginning to supersede ideas, project results were starting to reinforce concepts and the distinctive tools and techniques were being refined.

9. Project Management in the 1980s

In the 1980s there was a significant increase in the influence of external stakeholders, the green issue and CND - this put increasing pressure on designers to find acceptable solutions for all the stakeholders.

As project management tools and techniques proliferated in the 1960s, were refined in the 1970s, so they were integrated in the 1980s into accepted practices. The integration of time, cost and quality was initially presented as a triangle of balanced requirements - where a change in one parameter could affect the others (see figure 2.7). This was later joined by scope and the organisation breakdown structure (OBS) to indicate that the scope of work was performed through an organisation structure. There was also an increasing awareness of external issues, so the project environment was included (see figure 2.8).

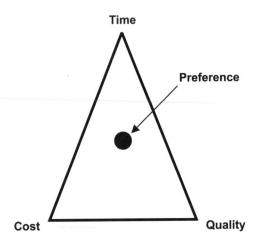

Figure 2.7: Time, Cost and Quality Triangle (trade-off)

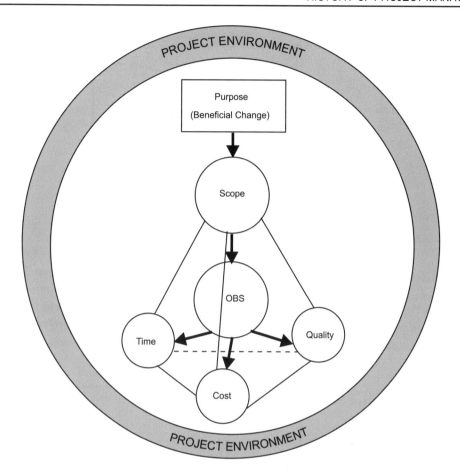

Figure 2.8: Project Environment Model (encourages project managers to look at the bigger picture and consider all the stakeholder's needs)

Project Life-Cycle: In the 1960s and 1970s project management tools and techniques tended to focus on the **implementation phase** of the *project life-cycle* (see figure 2.9). The implementation phase certainly accounted for the greatest level of effort where the majority of the expenses were incurred, but in the 1980s the emphasis was beginning to shift and focus more on the front-end of the project that had the greatest opportunity to add value (see figure 2.10). This is where the stakeholder's needs were analysed, *feasibility studies* conducted, *risk and uncertainty* assessed and the product or facility designed. The front-end approach further emphasised that the cost of making any changes due to design errors or the client changing the scope were becoming increasingly more expensive as the project progressed.

The *product life-cycle* encouraged the designers to look at the bigger picture and consider the trade-off between construction costs and maintenance costs. They were also encouraged to consider how upgrades, expansions, half-life refits, decommissioning and disposal would be carried out (see *Project Life-Cycle* chapter).

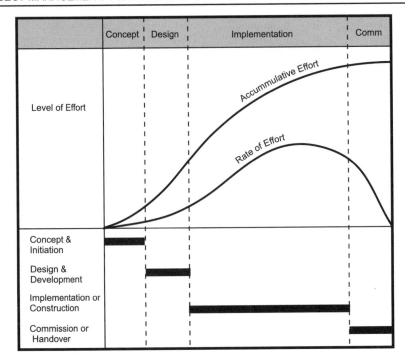

Figure 2.9: Project Life-Cycle (showing barchart and level of effort)

Figure 2.10: Project Life-Cycle (showing potential to add value and cost of changes)

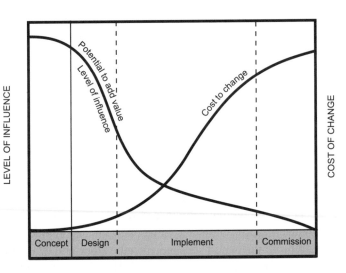

The 1980s saw a proliferation of personal computers and an explosion of software, both for business applications in general and project management specifically. The project manager with a computer, which began as the exception, soon became the norm. The pressure was now on for the project manager to become computer literate.

PMBOK: Professionalism was developed through ethics, standards and accreditation, which led to the first project management body of knowledge (PMBOK) in 1987. This offered an integrated and structured approach rather than an ad-hoc collection of tools and techniques.

10. Project Management 1990s and 2000s

In the 1990s fierce competition from the Far East encouraged leaner and meaner, flatter and more flexible organisation structures, together with a more efficient systems approach. Large companies found that by using a *management-by-projects* approach they could assign their work to many small project teams, which were able to quickly respond to innovation, new ideas and market competition and keep the spirit of the small entrepreneurial company alive even in large corporations. The nineties saw increasing deregulation, GATT agreements, reduced tariff barriers and expanding IT facilities communicating through the Internet.

Total quality management (TQM) emerged as a comprehensive project management technique, emphasising the importance of the client, continuous improvement, team work, and management through the *project life-cycle*. However, the adoption of TQM within project management initially proceeded relatively slowly, but with the introduction of ISO 9000 Quality Management System, TQM gained wider acceptance.

Another development of the 1990s was the **project office** not only to manage projects, but as a centre of excellence to develop a project management culture within the company.

11. History of Project Management Computing

The development of *schedule barcharts, network diagrams* and other distinctive project management tools were originally developed for manual calculation. These tools were gradually computerised during the 1960s and 1970s using mini and mainframe computers, but it was the introduction of the personal computer (PC) that ushered in a dramatic explosion and proliferation of project management software. Some of the key dates to note are:

1977 Launch of Apple 11, the first PC.

1979 Launch of VisiCalc, the first spreadsheet. Lotus and Excel were released a few years later.

1981 Launch of the IBM PC - this established the market standard.

1983 Launch of Harvard Project Manager, the first planning software package.

1990s Launch of Windows, networks, Internet and email

2000s Mobile communication (with Iridium you can communicate anywhere on the planet). Development of web site facilities; B2B (business-to-business) procurement, and real-time progress reporting.

The introduction of the PC in the late seventies (Apple 11) and the IBM PC (1981) in the early eighties with accompanying business software encouraged the growth of project planning software and the use of project management techniques.

The history of PC based project management computing dates back to 1983 with the launch of the **Harvard Project Manager** a planning software package. Although this may be an isolated event it does reflect the general development of a broad range of management software taking place at the time.

The sequence of dates indicates that the project management techniques were developed first, followed by hardware and software. However, the situation has changed in recent years with the computer facilities now leading the development of the management techniques, for example, B2B is changing procurement management. The limiting factor now is project management education and training. This more than any other factor holds the key to successful implementation of the latest project management technology.

This concludes the chapter on the *History of Project Management* - the following chapter will introduce the *Project Life-Cycle* which is widely used as a model to visualise the whole project from the cradle to the grave.

Key Points:

- Henry Gantt developed the barchart in the early 1900s.
- Most of the planning and control techniques used today were developed in the 1950s and 1960s on US defence and aerospace projects.
- The personal computer (PC) ushered in a dramatic explosion and proliferation of project management software.

Further Reading:

Fayol, Henri, *Administracao Industrial e Geral,* Sao Paulo, Brazil: Editora Atlas SA., 1967, p.12

Flagle, *Probability based tolerances in forecasting and planning,* Journal of Industrial Engineers, April 1961

Lockyer, Keith, *Critical Path Analysis,* Financial Times Pitman

Morris, Peter, *The Anatomy of Project's,* Thomas Telford

Morris, Peter, *The Management of Projects,* Thomas Telford

Case Study and Exercises:

Project management techniques were originally developed to plan and control large capital military projects, particularly the US military projects in the 50s and 60s. Since then project management has expanded to all sectors of industry and commerce. Give a brief presentation (written or verbal) on:

1. How project management was introduced to your industry and your company.
2. How project management computer systems were introduced to your industry and your company.
3. Henry Gantt developed the barchart, and Henri Fayol developed a management process. Discuss how adoptions and improvements on these original systems are used on your projects.
4. The time, cost, quality trade-off clearly shows a relationship between the three parameters. Give examples how these trade-offs apply to your projects.
5. The project environment model encourages us to look at the bigger picture. Give examples of how external stakeholders have influenced your projects.

"In they went, two by two"

Project Life-Cycle

The *project life-cycle* and the *work breakdown structure* (WBS) have come to the forefront in recent years as key frameworks or structures for subdividing the project's scope of work into manageable phases or work packages. Where the WBS is a hierarchical subdivision of the scope of work, the *project life-cycle* subdivides the scope of work into sequential project phases.

The PMBOK states; '*... because projects are unique and involve a certain degree of risk, companies performing projects will generally subdivide their projects into several project phases to provide better management control. Collectively these project phases are called the project life-cycle.*'

When I first heard the term *project life-cycle*, it struck me as an odd expression, I had previously only heard of a life-cycle being applied to tadpoles and butterflies! But on closer inspection all projects do pass through a number of recognisable stages from initiation to completion. And, as these stages are interrelated and dependant on each other, so it is reasonable to say the project passes through a *project life-cycle*.

1. Project Life-Cycle (4 phases)

There is general agreement that most projects pass through a four phase life-cycle under the following headings (see figure 3.1):

- **Concept and Initiation Phase:** The first phase starts the project by establishing a need or opportunity for the product, facility or service. The feasibility of proceeding with the project is investigated and on acceptance of the proposal moves to the next phase.
- **Design and Development Phase:** The second phase uses the guidelines set by the *feasibility study* to design the product, outline the build-method and develop detailed schedules and plans for making or implementing the product.

- **Implementation or Construction Phase:** The third phase implements the project as per the *baseline plan* developed in the previous phase.
- **Commissioning and Handover Phase:** The forth phase confirms the project has been implemented or built to the design and terminates the project.

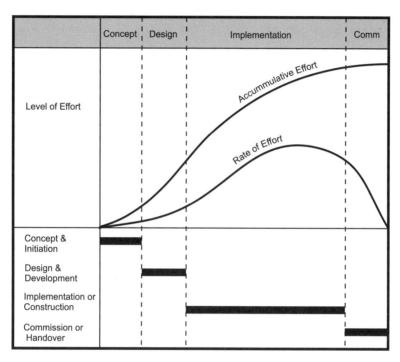

Figure 3.1: Project Life-Cycle (this is a typical presentation showing barchart, project phases, level of effort and rate of expenditure)

Project Life-Cycle (example): Consider a simple house building project which passes through the following four phases:

Concept and Initial Phase: The desire for a new house develops into a need. The options and alternatives are considered, and the feasibility of the best options are evaluated.

Design and Development Phase: The preferred option is now designed and developed in detail, together with all the associated planning of schedules, procurement, resources and budgets. The land and long lead items may be bought in this phase.

Implementation or Construction Phase: The contracts are let and the house is built to the detailed plans developed in the previous phase. Changes may be made to the original *baseline plan* as problems arise or better information is forthcoming.

Commissioning and Handover Phase: The building is inspected and approved. The house is now ready to be handed over to the owner.

Taking the *project life-cycle* model a step further, consider some other interesting characteristics:

- The project phases take their name from the **deliverables** of the phase, e.g. initiate, design, construct or handover.
- The sequence of the project phases generally involves some form of technology transfer or handover from one phase to the next phase, such as:
  - Project brief to design and development
  - Detailed design to manufacture
  - Construction to commissioning
  - Commissioning to operation.

This has also been called *over-the-wall* transfer if it is not accompanied with appropriate discussions and explanations.

- The end of a project phase is generally marked by a review of both the deliverables and performance in order to determine if the project should continue into the next phase.
- Each phase can be planned and controlled as a mini project.
- Each phase may be performed by different departments or contractors.
- As the project progresses through the phases, if the goals and objectives change so the project management process should reflect these changes.

Some other characteristics of the *project life-cycle* that will be developed in the following sections include:

- Inputs, processes and outputs within each phase.
- Key activities, milestones, hold-points and approvals within each phase.
- Overlaps between phases (fast tracking).
- Plotting level of effort (labour or cash-flow) against the project life-cycle.
- Plotting level of influence against the cost of changes (to show front-end importance).
- Project life-cycle costing.

2. Input, Process and Output Format

The *project life-cycle* subdivides the project into a number of definable project phases or stages and these phases in turn can be further subdivided into an input, process and output format. This is consistent with the body of knowledge's approach to describing the project management process in terms of input, output, tools and techniques (see figure 3.2).

3. Key Activities, Milestones, Hold-Points and Approvals

Within each phase there may be a number of key activities, milestones and hold-points which help to focus the project team and impose control. The following proforma would be a useful document for capturing and presenting this information (see figure 3.2 and 3.3).

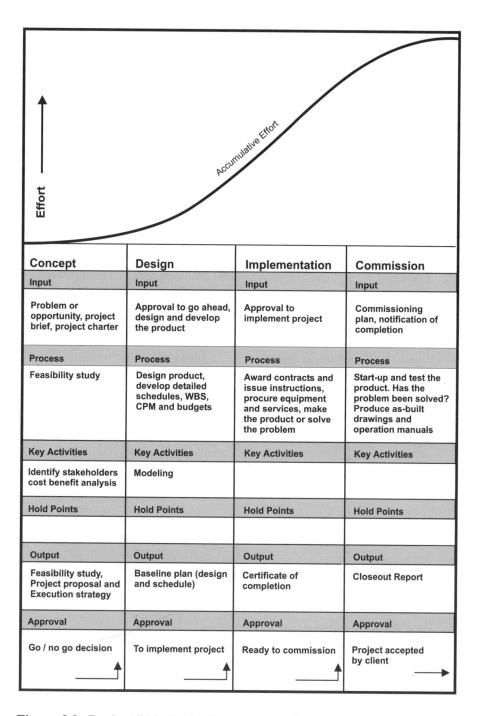

Concept	Design	Implementation	Commission
Input	**Input**	**Input**	**Input**
Problem or opportunity, project brief, project charter	Approval to go ahead, design and develop the product	Approval to implement project	Commissioning plan, notification of completion
Process	**Process**	**Process**	**Process**
Feasibility study	Design product, develop detailed schedules, WBS, CPM and budgets	Award contracts and issue instructions, procure equipment and services, make the product or solve the problem	Start-up and test the product. Has the problem been solved? Produce as-built drawings and operation manuals
Key Activities	**Key Activities**	**Key Activities**	**Key Activities**
Identify stakeholders cost benefit analysis	Modeling		
Hold Points	**Hold Points**	**Hold Points**	**Hold Points**
Output	**Output**	**Output**	**Output**
Feasibility study, Project proposal and Execution strategy	Baseline plan (design and schedule)	Certificate of completion	Closeout Report
Approval	**Approval**	**Approval**	**Approval**
Go / no go decision	To implement project	Ready to commission	Project accepted by client

Figure 3.2: Project Life-Cycle Components (for a typical project, using this as a standard proforma relate the components to one of your projects)

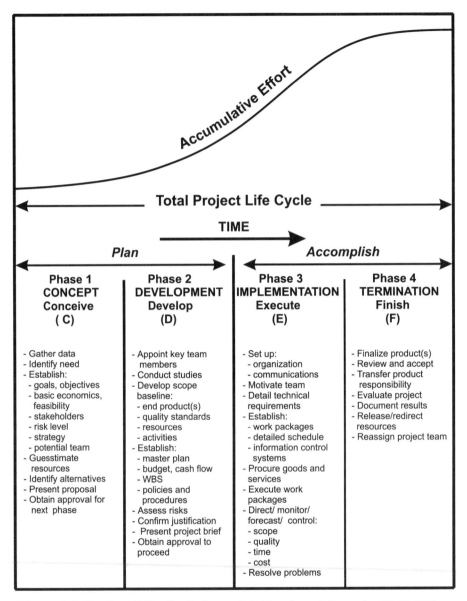

Figure 3.3: Project Life-Cycle [generic] (developed from the PMBOK)

4. Overlap Between Phases (fast tracking)

The project phases are shown here in sequence, but in practice there may be some overlap between the phases. Deliverables from the preceding phase are generally approved before work starts on the next phase. However, if the deliverables are approved progressively and work begins on the following phases before the previous phases are totally complete, this practice would be called *fast tracking*. For example on a ship building project the construction of the hull may start progressively as the drawings are available and similarly be commissioned progressively as the work is completed.

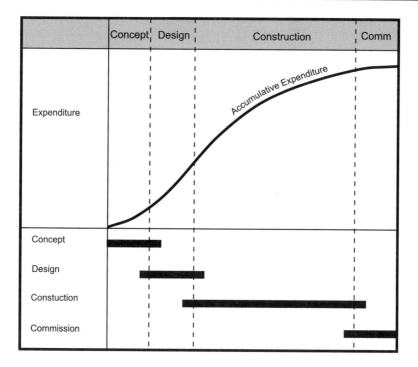

Figure 3.4: Project Life-Cycle (showing the barchart of the four main activities overlapping the project phases)

5. Level of Effort

The *project life-cycle* is often presented with its associated level of effort. This level of effort could be any parameter that flows through the project that can be measured, but it is most commonly expressed as manhours or costs. These parameters can be presented as a line graph of *'rate of expenditure'* and/or a line graph of *'accumulated expenditure'* (see figure 3.1).

The *'accumulated expenditure'* profile clearly shows a slow build-up of effort during the initial phases as the project is being designed and developed. The build-up of effort accelerates during the implementation phase to a maximum as the work faces are opened-up, before a sharp decline as the work is completed and commissioned and the project draws to a close.

From this curve one would naturally assume that as the greatest level of effort occurs during the implementation phase - this is after all where the product is made. Certainly the tools and techniques developed in the 1960s (PERT, CPM, WBS) were all focusing on this phase. But we need to consider the difference between efficiency and effectiveness - efficiency is doing activities right, while effectiveness is doing the right activity (see next section).

6. Level of Influence vs Cost of Changes (front-end importance)

In the 1960s and 1970s project management tools and techniques tended to focus on the implementation phase of the *project life-cycle* which certainly accounted for the greatest level of effort where the majority of the expenses were incurred, but in the 1980s the emphasis began to shift and focus more on the front-end of the project where the design and development decisions were made. This is where the stakeholder's needs are analysed, feasibility studies conducted, value management encouraged, project risk assessed and the product designed. Therefore the initial phases offer the greatest potential to add value, whereas the implementation phase, even though it has the greatest expenditure, should do no more than implement the product as designed. Further the cost of making any changes due to design errors or the client changing the scope, were recognised as becoming increasingly more expensive as the project progressed (see figure 3.5).

As projects become more involved and complex, together with time pressures to shorten the implementation phase (fast track to bring the product to market), so the need to get the design right from the outset becomes more important. Consider a shipbuilding project, where the cost of changing the engine room arrangement at the concept and design phases would be the cost of design hours for reproducing a number

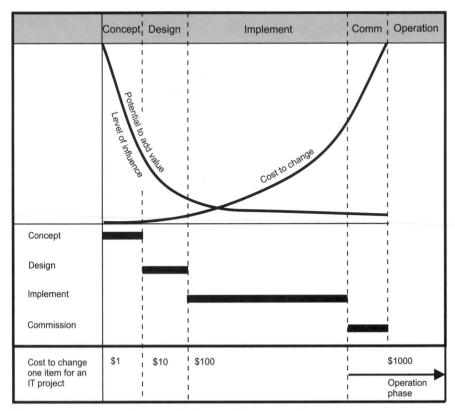

Figure 3.5: Potential to Add Value / Cost of Changes
(showing typical cost of changes in the IT industry)

of drawings. However a change at the implementation phase would not only incur design costs, but also the cost to remove machinery already fitted, together with the cost of new equipment, additional labour and maybe time penalties for late delivery. This cost profile encourages model testing and computer aided simulation where ideas and options can be developed and tested cost effectively before the implementation phase.

The stakeholders level of design influence, or potential to add value to the project reduces as the project progresses. As the design develops, so design freezes must be imposed progressively for the design to progress. For example, if the foundations are changed after the building has been designed, then all the design figures must be recalculated.

This is clearly illustrated in figure 3.5 where the level of influence and cost of changes are plotted against the *project life-cycle*. At the outset of the project the potential for adding value and cost savings are at their highest, but steadily reduce as the project progresses - loosely mirroring this curve are the associated cost of any changes. **The financial encouragement is therefore, to spend proportionally more time and effort during the initial phases to get the design right before implementation.**

From Henley MBA notes:
- Hitachi claim that 75% of the production costs are determined by the design.
- Mazda find that more than 50% of a product's quality is determined in the design phase.
- In the software industry it has been found that the cost of correcting an error when the software is in use is at least 250 times greater than finding and correcting it at design stage.
- It is estimated that over 40% of software errors occur during the requirement specification and design phases.

In the IT industry a rule of thumb for the cost to make changes increases by a factor of ten. For example, if it costs $1 in the concept phase, it will be $10 in the design phase, $100 in the implementation phase, and a $1000 during operation (see figure 3.5).

The opportunities for improving performance and results on all types of projects are at the front-end. The ability to influence the project, to reduce project costs, build-in additional value, improve performance and increase flexibility is highest at the very

early conceptual and design stages. But by the time the construction or implementation gets under way, the ability to influence the costs has reduced considerably. It therefore follows that the project manager should be appointed during these early phases to ensure that the maximum advantage is taken to influence the project effectively.

7. Level of Detail

The project management philosophy of subdividing the scope of work into a number of smaller units to increase the level of detail and control can also be applied to the *project life-cycle*. Each phase can be subdivided into a further four phases and run as mini projects (see figure 3.6):

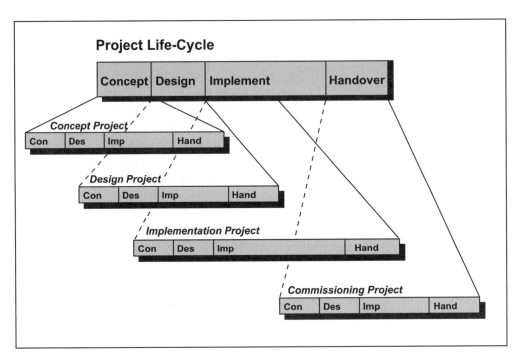

Figure 3.6: Project Life-Cycle (showing how each phase can be subdivided into its own life-cycle of four phases)

The concept phase could be subdivided into a *feasibility study* project:
- **Concept:** should we carry out a *feasibility study*
- **Design:** plan the *feasibility study*, select the team
- **Implement:** carry out the *feasibility study*
- **Commission:** closeout the *feasibility study* and present the report.

The same type of subdivision can be applied to the other three project phases, and if required, these sub-phases in turn can be further subdivided until an appropriate level of subdivision is achieved. The *project life-cycle* can also be subdivided along the lines of the stakeholders, designers, contractors and suppliers with each having their own four phase *project life-cycle* that integrates with the client's *project life-cycle*.

Another method of subdividing the *project life-cycle* is to integrate it with the *work breakdown structure*, where each work package can have its own four phase life-cycle (see figure 3.7).

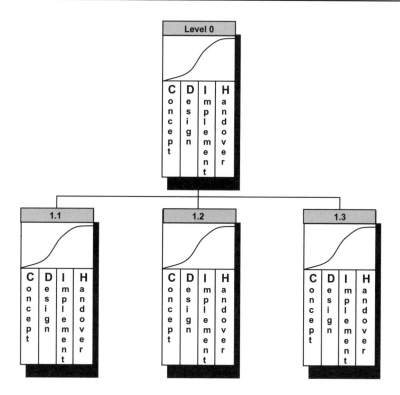

Figure 3.7: WBS / Project Life-Cycle Subdivision (each work package can be subdivided into their own four phase life-cycle)

8. Product Life-Cycle (8 phases)

The classic *project life-cycle* only considers the project from concept to handover. However if the project was to build a facility, a factory, a computer system or sports stadium then (looking at the project from the client's perspective) the efficient operation of the facility and the return on investment should also be considered. To look at the wider picture we use what is termed the ***product life-cycle***, which considers the facility from ***the cradle to the grave*** (figure 3.8).

This view highlights why decisions made during the initial phases can have a large impact during later phases even though they may be many years away and the facility may be operated by another company. It is important to look at the project as a whole from conception to disposal, to ensure that all the interrelated activities are identified. Seemingly simple decisions made during the initial phases of the project (equipment selection, for example) could have a major impact on future equipment maintenance and upgrading. By looking at the *product life-cycle* as a whole these issues can be highlighted.

Pre-Project Phase: Projects usually evolve from the work environment or market within which your company operates. There is usually some event which **triggers** the project, consider the following:

- Your R&D generating new ideas, innovation and creativity
- Upgrade a system (computer system) to take advantage of new technology
- Market research identifies market changes
- Responding to your competitor's new product
- Expand your facilities to meet increased demand
- Output from quality circles, improving efficiency and effectiveness
- Disaster recovery, accident, or cyclone damage.

Managing the pre-project environment is the key for your company's survival in a changing world.

Project Life-Cycle: (four phases already discussed)

Operation Phase: Although the operation phase may be the whole purpose of the project, it usually falls outside the project manager's sphere of influence. However the project manager would interface with the operation's manager with respect to:

- Handover
- Upgrade and expansion
- Maintenance
- Disposal

Maintenance Phase: The maintenance phase(s) are embedded in the operation phase to keep the facility functioning. Ease of maintenance and minimum impact on production are important design considerations.

Up-Grade, Expansion Phase: Also called *half-life refit*. At some point the facility will require a major upgrade, refit or expansion to keep it running efficiently and competitively. New technology, competition, market requirements, rules and regulations are all factors influencing this phase. Consider managing this change as a mini project - these type of projects are characterised by tight time scales to get the facility up and running again with minimum disruption of their markets and clients.

Ease of upgrade or expansion is a consideration here - was it allowed for in the initial design? A good example of where expansion was incorporated in the design is the dual-carriageway to Southampton (UK). Although only two lanes were initially built, the bridges were constructed to span four lanes, so that when they need to build the additional two lanes they will not have to rebuild the bridges as well.

A good example where expansion was not planned for is the Auckland harbour bridge (NZ). Originally built with four lanes, but within ten years the volume of traffic demanded another four lanes. Fortunately the bridge supports were over designed and could accommodate additional lanes *'clipped-on'* to the outside.

Any company working in a high technology environment will be well aware of the short life-cycle of their products. Upgrading and the ability to accommodate new technology are essential to extend the life of the computer system and stay competitive in the market place.

Your company's organisation structure will also change with time, particularly if the company has adopted a *management-by-projects* approach. The organisational structure should consider this at the design stage creating flexible; organisation structures, office space, computer facilities and car parking.

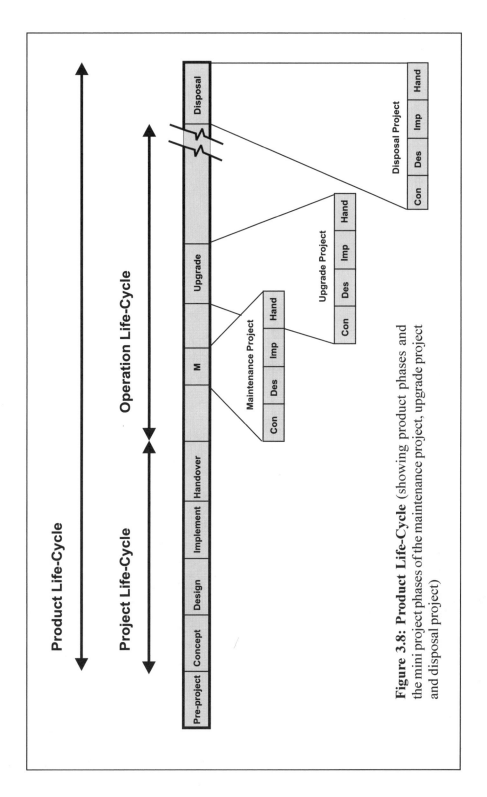

Figure 3.8: Product Life-Cycle (showing product phases and the mini project phases of the maintenance project, upgrade project and disposal project)

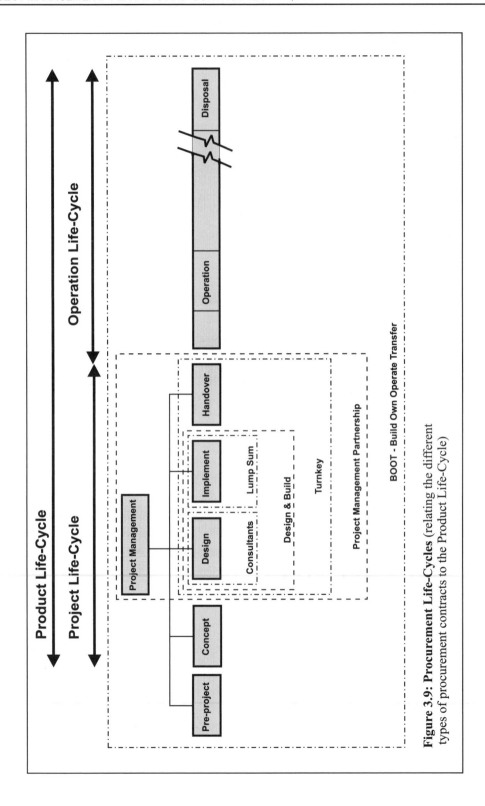

Figure 3.9: Procurement Life-Cycles (relating the different types of procurement contracts to the Product Life-Cycle)

Decommission and Disposal: The final part of the *product life-cycle* is decommissioning and disposing of the facility. As people become more aware of the environment, so the impact of disposing of a facility needs to be considered at the design phase. A good example of where disposal would appear not to have been thought through is the decommissioning of nuclear power stations. It is reported that Britain has budgeted over £10 billion pounds to decommission their Magnox power stations. Another environmental issue is the decommissioning of offshore oil rigs. Recently an oil company had to abandon plans to dispose of an oil platform at sea after bowing to the environmental lobbing.

9. Life-Cycle Costing (procurement life-cycle)

Projects are often implemented to provide a facility or to produce a product that will give the client a return on their investment. By looking at the bigger picture the designers are able to trade-off the cost of the construction with the cost of maintenance, upgrading, expansion and disposal over the life of the facility. The extreme case would be a cheap construction which turned out to be expensive to maintain, difficult to upgrade and expand, and an environmental disaster to dispose of.

One of the methods of addressing this problem is to make one company responsible for all aspects of the *product life-cycle*, thus eliminating any short term construction gains. These are often called **BOT** contacts (Build, Operate and Transfer), or **BOOT** contracts (Build, Own, Operate and Transfer), or **ROT** contracts (Refurbish, Operate and Transfer) where a company is given a licence to finance, build, operate and sell a product (see figure 3.9). Governments find these contracts attractive as they are seen to provide facilities without having an impact on their budget. The facility could be a power station, bridge or tunnel and the investors would receive a return by selling their product through electricity bills, or tolls.

Using the project life-cycle can be compared to how we drive a car, a learner driver looks no further than the car in front, but with maturity and experience a driver looks further afield and takes in the whole picture and makes their decisions accordingly.

Key Points:

- Most projects can be subdivided into four generic phases; concept, design, implement and commission.
- The product life-cycle looks at the bigger picture from the cradle to the grave.
- The level of influence curve and cost of changes curve clearly shows the importance of getting the design right before implementation.

Further Reading:

Barnes, N., & **Wearne**, S., *The Future for Major Project Management*, International Journal of Project Management, Vol 11, No 3, August 1993, pp 135-142
Wideman, Max, *A Framework for Project and Program Management Integration*, PMBOK Handbook Series - volume 1, 1991

Case Study and Exercises:

The project life-cycle enables the project manager to look at the total picture (from the cradle to the grave). Prepare a short presentation (written or verbal) on how the project life-cycle can be applied to a book publishing project. Consider the following:

1. The phases of the life-cycle, particularly if they are different to the classic four phase model.
2. The product life-cycle from concept to disposal. Outline how design considerations at the outset influence how upgrades and refits (new editions) happen down stream in the life-cycle.
3. As a design develops, design freezes have to be imposed to constrain the options and focus on an optimum solution.
4. The value / changes model indicates that the cost of changes increase as the project progresses.
5. Each phase of the project life-cycle can be subdivided into its own mini life-cycle, and further, each phase of this life-cycle can also be subdivided, and so on. Give an example how this can be applied to your project as a method of subdivision leading to planning and control.

Vision-see the big picture!

Feasibility Study

Ideas, needs and problems crystallise into projects in different ways. The process of project formulation varies in different companies and on different types of projects. However, whichever way your projects develop there should at some point be a *feasibility study* to not only ensure the project is feasible, but also ensure it is making the best use of your company's resources.

1. Feasibility Study Initiation

The lead up to the *feasibility study* (from the client's perspective) is the formalising of the project with the *project charter*. The *project charter* outlines the purpose of the project and what it is meant to achieve. Likewise the *feasibility study* should be formalised with requirements, boundaries and expected outcomes:

- Who is responsible
- Project brief to be analysed
- Who should be involved
- Level of detail
- Budget for the feasibility study
- Report back date.

At this point senior management have only made the decision to proceed with the *feasibility study*. The decision to proceed with the implementation of the project will be made later - presumably based on the *feasibility study's* recommendations.

It is a senior management responsibility to select the project manager for the *feasibility study*. It is then the project manager's responsibility to select the feasibility study team. It is most important that the team membership should include a representative of the future operators. This will encourage them to have an input into the design and a certain amount of control over their destiny. The company should make sure that the team members have sufficient time to develop the new product. This may mean releasing them from part or all of their present duties.

2. Plan the Feasibility Study

The *feasibility study* should be managed as a mini project using the planning and control techniques outlined in this book. It will also have its own *project life-cycle* (see figure 4.1).

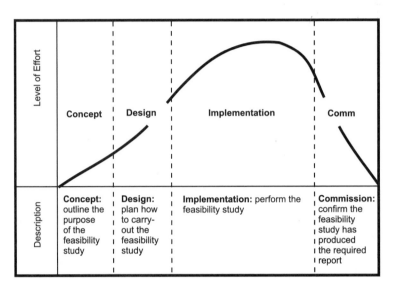

Figure 4.1: Project Life-Cycle (of feasibility study)

3. Stakeholder Analysis

The purpose of the needs analysis is to determine the needs and expectations of all the stakeholders. Project stakeholders are people and organisations (both internal and external) who are either actively involved in the project, or whose interests may be affected by the project being implemented. It is the project manager's responsibility to identify all the stakeholders and determine their needs and expectations. These needs and expectations should then be managed, influenced and balanced, to ensure project success. The project manager should create an environment where the stakeholders are encouraged to contribute their skills and knowledge as this may influence the success of the project. Consider the following headings:

- **Originator:** The person who suggests the project.
- **Owner:** The person whose strategic plan creates the need for the project.
- **Sponsor:** The company or client who authorises expenditure on the project - this could also be an internal client or venture capitalists.
- **Project Champion:** The person who makes the project happen. Often a person with influence in high places.
- **Users:** The people who will operate the facility on behalf of the owner when the project is completed.

- **Customers:** The people who receive and pay for the benefit from the facility. For example we are all customers for electricity, telephones and commercial travel facilities. Customers may prefer a wide range of fashionable products - this would encourage short production runs and quick turnaround times.
- **Project Team:** The team members who plan, organise, implement and control the work of the sub-contractors to deliver the facility within the constraints of time, cost and quality (also consider the affect on their families).
- **Senior Management:** Within your company who you **need** to support your project (mentor support and coaching).
- **Functional Managers:** Within your company who will be supplying the workforce for your project (matrix structure).
- **Boss:** Your boss, the person you report to, can play an important role in establishing your working environment, the support you receive and your career prospects within the organisation.
- **Colleagues:** Although they may not be working on your project, indirectly they can supply useful information and offer moral peer support, or conversely peer pressure.
- **Sub-contractors:** The external companies or people offering specialist expertise to supplement the company's resources.
- **Suppliers and Vendors:** The external companies or people who supply materials and equipment. They have a wealth of experience about their products which you should try and tap.
- **Supporters:** The parties who provide goods and services to enable the facility to be built, for example the suppliers of telephones, electricity, the postal service and even the corner shop. Financial support through the banking system could also be included here.
- **Legal Requirements:** Rules and regulations both nationally and internationally that must be complied with.

There are other external stakeholders who, although they may not be directly involved with the project, they can still influence the outcome:

- Regulatory authorities - health and safety
- Trade unions
- Special interest groups (environmentalists) who represent the society at large
- Lobby groups
- Government agencies and media outlets
- Individual citizens.

Some stakeholders are interested in the outcomes of the project, while others are only interested in the project while it is being implemented. Stakeholders can be further classified into those who are *positively* affected and those who are *negatively* affected by the project. In this situation can the positively affected compensate the negatively affected parties? (See the dam project example in the *Cost-Benefit Analysis* section later in this chapter, to quantify the stakeholders risk tolerance as this will influence their reaction to the project). Where possible identify the key decision makers (those with power) and focus your attention on their needs. Any differences between the stakeholders should be resolved in favour of the client and customers, but not necessarily at the expense of the other stakeholders.

Some stakeholders will support the project, while others will oppose the project. It is important to address those who oppose the project and discuss their fears, because it is these stakeholders that could derail your project particularly if they have power. Some of their concerns may be valid and with some flexibility could be accommodated. At the end of the day you may not be able to please all your stakeholders and in this conflict environment you will need to establish the **priority** of your stakeholders' needs and make your decisions accordingly.

Stakeholder	Needs and Expectations	Priority

Table 4.1: Stakeholder, Needs, Expectations, and Priority (proforma)

It is the project manager's responsibility to build coalitions among the various stakeholders - this is a way of gaining power. The project manager must negotiate authority to move the project forward, so the success of the project may depend on the project manager's ability to build a strong team from the internal and external players.

4. Define the Client's Needs

The starting point for a project is usually to address a problem, need, or business opportunity that may be internal or external to your company. The sponsor may start a project to implement a change, make a product, enter a new market or solve a problem. The evolution of needs from something quite vague to something tangible that serves as the basis of a project plan is the project manager's challenge. Some of the objectives may be stated as:

- The product must carry out a certain function at a predefined rate.
- The product must operate in a specific environment.
- The product must have a working life of so many years.
- The project's budget must not exceed $ x.
- The project must meet certain specifications and standards.
- The product must achieve reliability requirements - these may be quantified as mean time between failures (MTBF).
- The product must be energy efficient. A car would quantify this requirement as miles per gallon or kilometres per litre.
- The product must meet statutory health and safety regulations.
- The ergonomics must be consistent with the latest accepted practice.
- Ease of maintenance and repair must be incorporated into the design.
- A predetermined level of system redundancy and interchangeable parts must be achieved.

- The operational requirements must achieve predetermined manpower levels and automation.
- The product must be manufactured with a predefined value of local content.
- The product must provide opportunities for future expansion.
- The project must be operational by a predefined date.
- The product must be manufactured by approved and accredited suppliers, if necessary pre-qualified by an audit.
- All suppliers must have implemented an approved quality management system.
- All suppliers must have a good track record, supported by references.
- All suppliers must be flexible to accommodate any reasonable changes made by the sponsor during the manufacturing phase.
- All suppliers must be financially stable, supported by a bank reference.
- The end product must be marketable and profitable.

Many of the above items may be mutually exclusive, which means there will have to be a trade-off. For example, it is generally not possible to achieve both a minimum construction cost for a machine that also has minimum maintenance cost. These items of conflict need to be discussed and resolved during the early stages of the project, with all decisions recorded to form the basis of the design philosophy. This key document must be structured in such a way as to facilitate an audit trail of the decisions. If the field of the project is specialised the client may employ consultants and specialists to assist defining the scope - on small projects this task may fall to the contractor's project manager.

Project Viability Check: The client may also need assistance checking the viability of the proposal. Will the product technically and commercially be fit for the purpose? Has the client kept away from wish lists and pipe dreams? These questions will form the basis of the client's *feasibility study* to which the contractor, as a practising specialist, can have a valuable input:

- Consider the effect location has on the project. Can the logistic requirements during the project and subsequent operation be met through existing roads and ports? Large infrastructure projects (power stations) often have to widen roads for their abnormal loads.
- Consider how the environment will affect the product, for example, a hotel in a hot country will require air-conditioning for a five star rating.
- Consider how the product will affect the environment - will the product deplete the ozone layer, or increase global warming?
- Calculate the optimum size of the end product. Economies of size are not always a straight line extrapolation, but pass through plateaus of optimum production.
- Are the aesthetics and style commensurate with current fashions - modern office blocks and museums need to be stylish on the outside, to attract people to the inside?
- Define the target market. Who will buy the product? These questions can be quantified by market research.
- Assess the market supply and demand curve. What is the demand for the product now and forecast demand in the future?

- Assess the competition from other players in the market. How will an increase in your rate of production affect market share?

At the outset of the project it may not be possible to answer all of these questions. The unanswered questions will, however, indicate areas that need more research to gain a better understanding of the project and reduce risk.

5. Evaluate Constraints

Project constraints can be considered as internal or external restrictions that may affect the achievable scope of the project. These anticipated limitations can be quantified under three subheadings:

- Internal project constraints
- Internal corporate constraints
- External constraints

Internal Project Constraints: The internal project constraints relate directly to the scope of the project and ask basic questions about the product.

- Can the product be made? Can the company meet the specifications? Consider the Rolls Royce RB111 carbon fibre turbine blades which led to the company's liquidation in the 1970s.
- Does the company have the technology? If not, can the technology be acquired through a **technology transfer**, and if so with whom? South Africa took this approach to develop their offshore gas fields.
- Should we start the project now with the present technology or wait until new and better technology is available? (See figure 4.2).

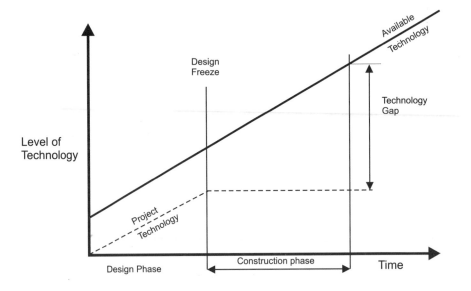

Figure 4.2: Technology Change Against Time (at some point you will have to implement a design freeze so you can build the product)

- At what point in the development should a design freeze be imposed? This will affect the technology gap at the end of the project (see figure 4.2).
- Is the new technology component greater than 10%? Practitioners recommend the amount of innovation should be kept below 10% to reduce risk and uncertainty.
- Can the resources be trained up to the required level of ability, or should contractors be employed to meet the forecast skills requirement?
- Will the multi-project resource analysis consider the effect other projects will have on the supply of internal resources?
- Are there any special design requirements?
- Are special machines and equipment required? If yes, are they available?
- Are there special transport requirements? Can the product be transported to where it is required or does it need to be made piece-small and assembled on site?
- If new management systems are introduced will they be compatible with existing systems they need to interface with?
- Can the project be completed within the budget?
- What is the quality assurance requirement? For example, is accreditation to ISO 9000 required? Is the present quality management system sufficient?
- Are there company and project procedures in place? If not allow time to develop them?
- Is the project office established? Has the project manager been appointed, the project team selected, the office space allocated and are the equipment and information systems available?
- Can the project meet the client's completion date and any intermediate key dates?
- Can the company accept the time penalties?
- Are the project risks and uncertainties acceptable?
- Can the company accept the terms and conditions outlined in the contract document?

All these questions relate directly to the project. The next section will show how the company itself can impose further constraints.

Internal Corporate Constraints: The company itself can impose further quasi constraints on the project. Corporate umbrella policy and strategy usually relates to long term issues that indirectly (and unintentionally) may impose limitations on the project.

- **Financial Objectives:** The project selection criteria may be based on a financial feasibility study quantified as, payback period, return on investment (ROI), net present value (NPV), internal rate of return (IRR) and a cost-benefit analysis.
  - The company may wish the project to maintain a positive cash-flow.
  - The progress of the project may be encouraged or delayed to meet the company's annual budget.
  - The company's share price may have an effect on the project's ability to borrow.

- **Marketing:** The company may wish to diversify its products and enter new markets. Your project may be implementing the technology transfer for the company to operate in this market, or be a loss leader to enter a new market. The project must therefore accept subnormal profits to get a *'foot in the door'*.
- **Estimating:** Due to a down turn in the economy, the company's main priority may be to keep the workforce intact. The lower the bid the greater the probability of being awarded the next contract. The lowest a company can bid is to cover direct costs, with the overheads being written-off. If this is the case, will the project's budget be based on the estimated cost or the sales price?
- **Partner:** The company may wish to take on a partner who has previous experience in the field of the project (**technology transfer**) and also to spread the risk.
- **Industrial Relations:** Industrial unrest is often caused by conflict over pay and working conditions. The project manager may have little power to influence these conditions.
- **Training:** Your project may become the training ground for new recruits, in which case the learning curve will be an expense to your project.
- **Exports:** The company may influence the quotation in an effort to acquire exports to enter new markets or take advantage of export incentives (buy work).

Where these company objectives are in conflict with project objectives the company objectives usually take preference. This could lead to increased project costs and delays that must be included in the *baseline plan*.

WBS	Activity	Internal Project Constraints	Internal Corporate Constraints	External Constraints

Table 4.2: Table of Constraints (proforma to capture and present information)

External Constraints: External constraints are imposed by parties outside the company and the project's sphere of influence. Many of these constraints may not be negotiable.
- National and international laws and regulations.
- Material and component delivery lead times.
- Unavailable resources; finding carpenters after floods or storm damage, welders while there are offshore projects, computer programmers leading up to the year 2000 (Y2K).
- Logistic constraints, availability of transportation.
- Availability of foreign currency and currency fluctuations.
- Environmental issues, Government legislation and pressure group activities, for example, Green Peace and CND. The nuclear, chemical, mining and transport industries have been particularly affected in the past.
- Climatic conditions, rain, wind, heat and humidity (El Nino).

- Market forces, supply and demand curve.
- Political unrest.
- Construction site in a residential area - may not be allowed to work a night shift, because of the noise.
- Planning permission, licenses, permits, clearances, right of way, insurance.

These headings should not be seen as comprehensive, but as the forerunner of a company checklist that ensures all the appropriate questions are asked, which in turn should reduce the level of risk and uncertainty (see table 4.2).

6. Evaluate Alternatives and Options

The alternative analysis is the process of breaking down a complex product into its component parts before identifying different, and hopefully more effective methods of achieving the desired result. The process should start with a checklist to structure the thought process. This can be achieved through; the *work breakdown structure* (see *WBS* chapter), the project constraints (see table 4.2), or the project objectives (see table 4.3).

The technical definition should aid the direct comparison between alternatives. With a machine for example the capital costs should be compared with the operating costs. Although this process should be ongoing during the project, the design freeze would usually signal the end of this phase. Once the manufacturing phase starts the emphasis would shift to consider manufacturing alternatives. The following check list outlines a number of the basic questions to be asked:

- **Time:** Can the project be completed quicker?
- **Cost:** Can the budget be reduced?
- **Quality:** Can the project be made to more cost effective level of quality which would be acceptable to the client and quicker to produce?
- **Resources:** Can the work be cost effectively automated to reduce the manpower requirement?
- **Technical:** Is there a simpler design configuration and simpler build method?
    - Can cheaper materials be used?
    - Has the latest technology been considered?
    - Has the use of different equipment and machines been considered?
    - Has the trade-off between cost, delivery schedule and technical performance been quantified?

WBS	Activity	Alternatives and Options

Table 4.3: Table of Alternatives and Options (proforma)

7. Gather Information

Without the latest information on the product's technical and market issues the alternative analysis will be self-limiting (see figure 4.3). Information is a prerequisite for effective problem-solving and decision-making. Information may be found in:

- Books and periodicals
- Technical reports
- Bureau specifications
- Sales and marketing brochures (product information)
- Market research (market trends and fashions)
- Internet (data base search)
- Stakeholders (interviews and questionnaires)
- Closeout reports.

Closeout Reports: Closeout reports from previous projects offer a valuable source of historical information. It cannot be over stressed how important it is for a company to learn from its previous experience - not only should the mistakes be noted, but also what went right, together with any recommendations for future projects (see *Scope Management* chapter).

The size of the company will influence how and where information will be available (or hidden)! In a small company, information may be collected by individual managers, while a large company may have a corporate library. The responsibility for setting up a data base of information should lie with either the project office or the company's general manager.

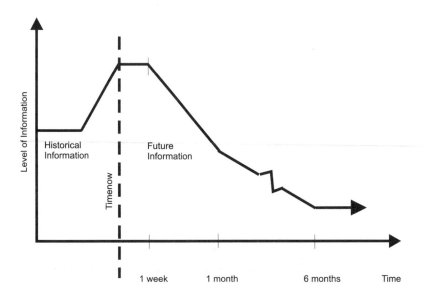

Figure 4.3: Level of Information against Time (this shows how the level of accurate information varies with time. The highest level of information is required around timenow, with this requirement moving forward like a wave as the project progresses)

8. Value Management

Value Management is a structured, systematic and analytical process that seeks to achieve value for money by providing all the necessary functions at the lowest total cost, consistent with required levels of quality and performance. Underlying the *value management* theory is that there is always more than one way of achieving a function and that examination of alternatives should produce the most acceptable option. *Value management* looks at the project or product as a whole. It considers the relationship between function, cost and worth. Its purpose is to ensure value for money over the *product life-cycle*. Consider the following points:

- Identify unnecessary expenditure
- Challenge assumptions
- Generate alternative ideas
- Promote innovation
- Optimize resources
- Save time, money and energy
- Simplify methods and procedures
- Eliminate redundant items
- Update standards, criteria and objectives.

Value management is about:

- Clarifying and satisfying customers' needs
- Creating ideas as to how a system can best do its job at appropriate levels of quality and performance
- Challenging assumptions and maximising returns on investment
- Participation by clients, end-users and stakeholders
- Seeing the purpose of the system itself
- Seeking the lowest total cost of providing the clients' needs - it is not about seeking the cheapest solution.

The process is one of participatory planning in which the project design team work closely with stakeholders in a workshop format seeking to identify those functions which the project must perform, consider:

- Identifying appropriate quality and performance criteria
- Creating alternative ways of performing these functions
- After analysis and evaluation, selecting the lowest total life-cycle cost option that satisfies those requirements.

During the *value management* workshop considerable advantage is gained by capitalising upon the synergy that is developed and upon the potential constructive overlap of expertise and knowledge within the project team. Team members are able to ask questions and generate ideas (brainstorming) about issues outside their specific area of expertise. Traditional design processes do not encourage overlap and rely upon specialists to work exclusively within their own areas.

9. Cost-Benefit Analysis

A cost-benefit analysis may be performed at this stage to establish the financial feasibility of the project. A cost-benefit analysis is generally based on the following economic principles:

- Pareto improvement criteria
- Hicks-Kaldor test
- Willingness-to-pay test

The basic concept is simply to express the costs and benefits in money terms. If the financial benefits exceed the costs, then the project passes the test. The **Pareto** improvement criteria is expressed as; *'The project should make some people better off without making anyone worse off'*. This situation may be difficult to achieve in reality.

The **Hicks-Kaldor** test seems more realistic. This states that; *'The aggregate gains should exceed aggregate losses.'* This framework will enable the people who gain, to compensate the people that lose. For example, a dam project may have many benefits to the community, but might cause the silting up of the river. If the financial benefits of having a dam exceed the costs of dredging the river, this project will satisfy the Hicks-Kaldor test.

The **willingness-to-pay** test is simply to determine how much your clients are prepared to pay for your product. Have you ever considered how airlines manage to charge a range of fares for the same seats. The economists model this test using the following techniques:

- The supply and demand curve (see Begg)
- Monopolies and Oligopolies (see Begg)
- Product elasticity (see Begg).

These techniques will model the relationship between supply, demand and prices. With the presentation of the *feasibility study* to senior management, so ends this mini project. This concludes the *Feasibility Study* chapter, the following chapter will discuss *Project Selection*.

Key Points:

- Identify all your stakeholders - assess, quantify and prioritise their needs and expectations.
- Identify all the constraints, both internal and external.
- Consider alternative options to produce a better product.

Further Reading:

Begg, David, *Economics*, McGraw-Hill
Meredith, J., and **Samuel**, J., *Project Management A Managerial Approach*, Wiley

Case Study and Exercises:

The feasibility study offers the project manager and management student a framework to assess the feasibility of a project against predefined parameters. Consider a Public Private Partnership (PPP), or BOOT (Build Own Operate and Transfer) project to (select a project):

- Refurbish and operate the London Underground.
- Build and operate a toll road or tool bridge.
- Build and operate a power station.

For your selected project structure your presentation (written or verbal) to include the following:

1. Identify your key stakeholders and determine their influence on the project.
2. Your client is the key stakeholder, identify their needs and how the project will fulfil them.
3. A key function of the feasibility study is to confirm that you can make the product or perform the service. If appropriate outline the build method.
4. Identify any internal and external constraints that will affect your project.
5. The economists say if the *'aggregate gains exceed the aggregate losses'* then the project passes their test. How can this test be applied to your project?

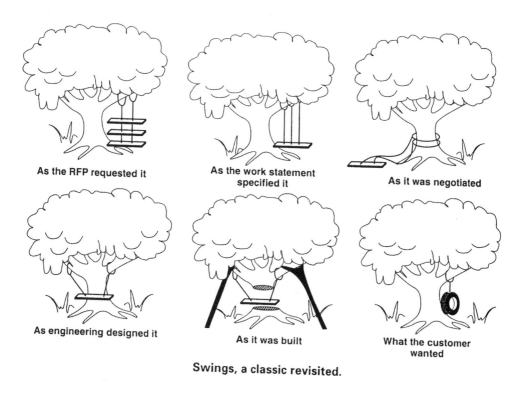

Swings, a classic revisited.

Project Selection

The selection of the right project for future investment is a crucial decision for the long-term survival of a company. The selection of the wrong project may well precipitate project failure leading to company liquidation. This chapter on project selection will outline a framework for evaluating and ranking prospective projects using numeric methods.

The project selection process is developed here as a separate chapter, but it should be recognised as a subsection of other knowledge areas, namely; scope management (scope initiation), project life-cycle (concept phase) and the feasibility study.

Project selection is making a commitment for the future. The execution of a project will tie up company resources and, as an opportunity cost, the selection of one project may preclude your company from pursuing another (more profitable) project. We live in a world of finite resources and therefore cannot carry out all the projects we may want or need. Therefore a process is required to select and rank projects on the basis of beneficial change to your company.

1. Project Selection Models

A numeric model is usually financially focused and quantifies the project in terms of time to repay the investment (*payback*) or *return on investment*. While non-numeric models look at a much wider view of the project considering items such as; market share, client retention, move to a new field, or environmental issues.

The main purpose of these models is to aid decision-making leading to project selection. When choosing a selection model the points to consider are; realism, capability, ease of use, flexibility and cost effectiveness. Most importantly the model must evaluate projects by how well they meet a company's strategic goals and corporate mission. The following subheadings indicate the type of questions to ask:

- Will the project maximise profits?
- Will the project maximise the utilisation of the workforce?

- Will the project maintain market share, increase market share or consolidate market position?
- Will the project enable the company to enter new markets?
- Will the project maximise the utilisation of plant and equipment?
- Will the project improve the company's image?
- Will the project satisfy the needs of the stakeholders and their political aspirations.
- Is the project's risk and uncertainty acceptable?
- Is the project's scope consistent with company expertise?

This list can be developed further by weighting the evaluation items. The weighting indicates the value of the contribution to the company's strategic goals and objectives. With a numeric value for each project, the projects can be ranked in line with their contribution to the success of the organisation.

The relationship between a project's expected results and the company's strategic goals, needs to be established. In general the kind of information required can be quantified under the following headings as developed by **Meredith**:

- Production
- Marketing
- Financial
- Personnel
- Administration

Consider a project to introduce a new computerised information and control system. For this exercise the system is intended for both in-house use and a consultancy service.

Production Considerations (for new information and control system):

- Method of implementation
- Time to be up and running
- Other applications of the system
- Learning curve - time until the product is saleable
- Amount of double processing and waste
- Extent of outside consultants required
- Cost of power requirements
- Interfacing equipment required
- Period of disruption
- Safety of system

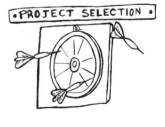

Marketing Considerations (for new information and control system):

- Number of potential users
- Market share
- Time to achieve proposed market share
- Impact on current system
- Ability to control quality of information
- Customer acceptance
- Estimated life of new system
- Spin-offs
- Enhanced image of company
- Extent of possible new markets.

Financial Considerations (for new information and control system):

- Cost of new system
- Impact on company cash-flow
- Borrowing requirement
- Time to break-even
- Payback period, NPV and IRR
- Size of investment required
- Cost of implementation
- Cost of training
- Cost of mistakes
- Level of financial risk.

Personnel Considerations (for new information and control system):

- Skills requirements and availability
- Training requirements (technology transfer)
- Employment requirements
- Level of resistance to change from current workforce
- Impact on working conditions
- Ergonomics, health and safety considerations
- Effect on internal communication
- Effect on job descriptions
- Effect on work unions
- Effect on morale.

Administration and other Considerations (for new information and control system)**:**

- Compliance with national and international standards
- Reaction from shareholders and other stakeholders
- Cost of maintenance contract
- Disaster recovery planning
- Cost of upgrading the system to keep pace with new technology
- Vulnerability of using a single supplier
- Customer service
- Effect of centralised databases
- Extent of computer literacy
- Legal considerations.

This list is by no means complete, and you will notice that each heading has been conveniently subdivided into ten items, there could be more! The main **advantage** of this type of list is that it considers a wide range of factors which greatly helps to present a fuller picture of the project. However, the main **disadvantage** of the list approach is that all items are viewed with equal importance. Others are:

- Unknown level of error
- Different level of effect and importance
- Different level of risk and uncertainty
- Frequency of occurrence not known
- Threshold of rejection not quantified
- The list may contain redundant items
- Some items are intangible and therefore difficult to quantify
- The list could be incomplete.

Although the limitations seem to outnumber the benefits, the most important feature is that the checklist approach asks questions that encourage the managers to think about a wide range of possible problems.

2. Numeric Models

The numeric selection models presented here may be subdivided into financial models and scoring models. The financial models are:

- *Payback period*
- *Return on investment* (IOR)
- *Net present value* (NPV)
- *Internal rate of return* (IRR)

Companies tend to prefer financial models and often select solely on profitability. This may not be as drastic as it sounds because subconsciously the managers will be considering a wider scope of selection criteria.

In an investment appraisal only the incremental income and expenses attributed directly to the project under consideration should be included. Costs that have already been incurred (sunk costs) should be ignored as they are irrelevant to decisions effecting future projects. It should be noted that all the appraisal techniques discussed in this chapter have a limiting factor, they are based on a forecasted cash-flow.

3. Payback Period

The *payback period* is the time taken to gain a financial return equal to the original investment. The time period is usually expressed in years and months. Consider this example where a company wishes to buy a new machine for a four year project. This example will be used extensively in this chapter. The manager has to choose between machine A or machine B, so it is a mutually exclusive situation. Although both machines have the same initial cost ($35,000) their cash-flows perform differently over the four year period due to different labour, material and maintenance costs. To calculate the *payback period*, simply work out how long it will take to recover the initial outlay (see table 5.1).

Year	Cash-Flow Machine A	Cash-Flow Machine B
0	($35,000)	($35,000)
1	$20,000	$10,000
2	**$15,000**	$10,000
3	$10,000	**$15,000**
4	$10,000	$20,000
Payback period	2 years	3 years

Table 5.1: Payback Period (Machine A 2 years, Machine B 3 years)

Machine A will recover its outlay one year sooner than machine B. Where projects are ranked by the shortest *payback period*, machine A is selected in preference to machine B. The **advantages** of the payback method are:
- It is simple and easy to use.
- It uses readily available accounting data to determine cash-flows.
- It reduces the project's exposure to risk and uncertainty by selecting the project that has the shortest *payback period*.
- The uncertainty of future cash-flow is reduced.
- It is an appropriate technique to evaluate high technology projects where the technology is changing quickly and the project could run the risk of being left holding out of date stock.
- It is an appropriate technique for fashion projects where the market demand tends to change seasonally.
- Faster payback has a favourable short-term effect on earnings per share.
- The *payback period* quantifies the selection criteria in terms the decision-makers are familiar with.

The **disadvantages** of the *payback period* calculation are:-
- It does not consider the time value of money. The *payback period* is indifferent to the timing of the cash-flow. The project with a high, early income (cash-inflow) would be ranked equally with a project that had a late income if their *payback periods* were the same (see figure 5.1).

- It is not a suitable technique to evaluate long term projects where the effects of differential inflation and interest rates could significantly change the results.
- The figures are based on project cash-flow only. All other financial and non-financial data are ignored.
- Although *payback period* would reduce the duration of risk, it does not quantify the risk exposure.
- The *payback period* calculation does not look at the total project. What happens to the cash-flow after the payback period is not considered. A project that built up slowly to give excellent returns (project F in figure 5.2) would be rejected in favour of (project E in figure 5.2) with lower early returns if the payback period was shorter.

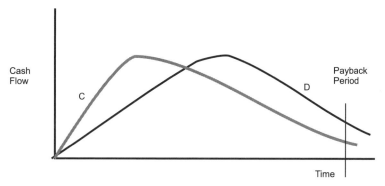

Figure 5.1: Payback Period (project C and project D have the same payback period even though their cash-flows are different)

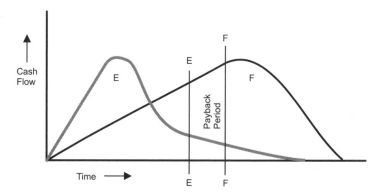

Figure 5.2: Payback Period (does not consider the cash-flow after payback period. In this case project F may be a better option even though project E has a shorter payback period)

The *payback period* is the most widely used project selection calculation, even if this is only an initial filter. Its main strength is that it is simple and quick (it can almost be worked out in your head).

4. Return on Investment (ROI)

Another popular investment appraisal technique that does look at the whole project is *return on investment* (ROI). This method first calculates the average annual profit, which is simply the project outlay deducted from the total gains, divided by the number of years the investment will run. The profit is then converted into a percentage of the total outlay using the following equations:

$$\text{Average Annual Profit} = \frac{(\text{Total gains}) - (\text{Total outlay})}{\text{Number of years}}$$

$$\text{Return on investment} = \frac{\text{Average Annual Profit}}{\text{Original investment}} \times \frac{100}{1}$$

Using the machine selection project calculate the return on investment (see table 5.2).

Year	Cash-flow Machine A	Cash-Flow Machine B
0	($35,000)	($35,000)
1	$20,000	$10,000
2	$15,000	$10,000
3	$10,000	$15,000
4	$10,000	$20,000
Total gains	$55,000	$55,000

Table 5.2: Return on Investment (ROI) Cash-Flow

Profit (A & B)   = $55,000 - $35,000
Annual Profit   = $\frac{$20,000}{4 \text{ yrs.}}$ = $5,000 per year (same for both machines)

Return on investment   = $\frac{$5,000}{$35,000} \times \frac{100}{1} = 14\%$

The *return on investment* method has the advantage of also being a simple technique like the *payback period*, but further, it considers the cash-flow over the whole project. The total outcome of the investment is expressed as a profit and percentage return on investment, both parameters readily understood by management.

The main criticism of *return on investment* is that it averages out the profit over successive years. An investment with high initial profits would be ranked equally with a project with high profits later if the average profit was the same. Clearly the project with high initial profits should take preference.

This point is shown in the above example, where, although machine A and machine B have different cash-flows, their profit and return on investment come out the same. To address this shortcoming of both *return on investment* and *payback period*, the time value of money must be considered using a *discounted cash-flow* technique. This is particularly desirable where interest rates and inflation are high.

5. Discounted Cash-Flow (DCF)

The *discounted cash-flow* (DCF) technique takes into consideration the time value of money, for example, a $100 today will **not** have the same worth or buying power as a $100 this time next year. Our subjective preference to $100 now is quite rational because we have seen the cost of goods rise with inflation. There are two basic DCF techniques that can model this effect, *net present value* (NPV) and *internal rate of return* (IRR).

These discounting techniques enable the project manager to compare two projects with different investment and cash-flow profiles. There is, however, one major problem with DCF, besides being dependent on the accurate forecast of the cash-flows, it also requires an accurate prediction of the interest rates.

6. Net Present Value (NPV)

To assist the understanding of NPV let us first look at compound interest which is commonly used in saving accounts. If we invest $100 at 20% interest, after one year it will be worth $120 and after two years compounded it will be worth $144. Now NPV is the reverse of compound interest.

If you were offered $120 one year from now and the inflation and interest rate was 20%, working backwards its value in today's terms would be $100. This is called the present value, and when the cash-flow over a number of years is combined in this manner the total figure is called the *net present value* (NPV). This calculation is best set up in a tabular form using the following headings (see table 5.3).

Years	Project Cash-Flow	Discount Factor	Present Value
0			
1			
2			
3			
Total			NPV

Table 5.3: Net Present Value (NPV) (tabular format)

Where the cash-flow timing is expressed in years from the start date of the project, the inflation effect is assumed to act at the end of the first year or beginning of the second year, therefore all cash-flows in the first year are at present value.

Project cash-flow = income - expenditure
Present value   = discount factor x cash-flow

The discount factor is derived from the reciprocal of the compound interest formula.

Discount factor $= 1 / (1 + i)^n$

where i = the forecast interest rate

n = the number of years from start date

The discount factor is usually read from a table, see table of discounting factors (table 5.4). Using the formula above, calculate a few of the discount factors to satisfy yourself of their origin. You can then forget the calculation and work straight from the tables.

Years	10%	11%	12%	13%	14%	15%	16%	17%
1	0.9091	0.9009	0.8929	0.885	0.8772	0.8696	0.8621	0.8547
2	0.8264	0.8116	0.7972	0.7831	0.7695	0.7561	0.7432	0.7305
3	0.7513	0.7312	0.7118	0.693	0.675	0.6575	0.6407	0.6244
4	0.683	0.6587	0.6355	0.6133	0.5921	0.5718	0.5523	0.5337
5	0.6209	0.5935	0.5674	0.5428	0.5194	0.4972	0.4761	0.4561

Years	18%	19%	20%	21%	22%	23%	24%	25%
1	0.8475	0.8403	0.8333	0.8264	0.8197	0.813	0.8065	0.80
2	0.7182	0.7062	0.6944	0.683	0.6719	0.661	0.6504	0.64
3	0.6086	0.5934	0.5787	0.5645	0.5507	0.5374	0.5245	0.512
4	0.5158	0.4987	0.4823	0.4665	0.4514	0.4369	0.423	0.4096
5	0.4371	0.419	0.4019	0.3855	0.37	0.3552	0.3411	0.3277

Table 5.4: Table of Discounting Factors

The NPV is a measure of the value or worth added to the company by carrying out the project. If the NPV is positive the project merits further consideration. When ranking projects, preference should be given to the project with the highest NPV. Consider the machine selection example again, this time using NPV. Assume the discounting factor is 20%, set up the NPV format. The steps are as follows:

- Insert the cash-flow
- Transfer the discounting factors from the table
- Calculate present value - multiplying cash-flow by discount factor
- Aggregate the present values to give the NPV (see tables 5.5 and 5.6).

The NPV for machine A is $2692 and for machine B is ($1396). NPV analysis would select machine A in preference to machine B because it has a higher NPV. Machine B would be rejected in any case because it has a negative NPV. A negative NPV indicates the company would lose money by carrying out this project.

Column (1)	Column (2)	Column (3)	= (2) x (3)
Years	Project Cash-Flow	Discount Factor 20%	Present Value
0	($35,000)	1	($35,000)
1	$20,000	0.8333	$16,666
2	$15,000	0.6944	$10,416
3	$10,000	0.5787	$5,787
4	$10,000	0.4823	$4,823
Total NPV			$2,692

Table 5.5: Machine A - Net Present Value Calculation (DF 20%)

Column (1)	Column (2)	Column (3)	= (2) x (3)
Years	Project Cash-Flow	Discount Factor 20%	Present Value
0	($35,000)	1	($35,000)
1	$10,000	0.8333	$8,333
2	$10,000	0.6944	$6,944
3	$15,000	0.5787	$8,681
4	$20,000	0.4823	$9,646
Total NPV			($1,396)

Table 5.6: Machine B - Net Present Value Calculation (DF 20%)

The **advantages** of using NPV are:
- It introduces the time value of money.
- It expresses all future cash-flows in **today's values**, which enables direct comparisons.
- It allows for inflation and escalation.
- It looks at the whole project from start to finish.
- It can simulate project what-if analysis using different values.
- It gives a more accurate profit and loss forecast than non DCF calculations.

The **disadvantages** are:-
- Its accuracy is limited by the accuracy of the predicted future cash-flows and interest rates.
- It is biased towards short run projects.
- It excludes non financial data e.g. market potential.
- It uses a fixed interest rate over the duration of the project. The technique can, however, accommodate a varying interest rate, this will be explained later in this chapter.

Although NPV quantifies the profit this is expressed in absolute terms. Managers tend to prefer profitability expressed as a percentage. This can be addressed by using another DCF method called *internal rate of return* (IRR).

7. Internal Rate of Return (IRR)

The *internal rate of return* is also called *DCF yield* or *DCF return on investment*. The IRR is the value of the discount factor when the NPV is zero. The IRR is calculated by either a trial and error method or plotting NPV against IRR. It is assumed that the costs are committed at the end of the year and these are the only costs during the year. Consider the machine selection example again. Looking at machine A first, to reduce the NPV increase the discounting factor in small steps until NPV becomes negative.

Column (1)	Column (2)	Column (3)	= (2) x (3)
Years	Project Cash Flow	Discount Factor 22%	Present Value
0	($35,000)	1	($35,000)
1	$20,000	0.8197	$16,394
2	$15,000	0.6719	$10,079
3	$10,000	0.5507	$5,507
4	$10,000	0.4514	$4,514
Total NPV			$1,494

Table 5.7: Machine A - Discount Factor 22% (The NPV is still positive, therefore increase the DF by 2%)

Column (1)	Column (2)	Column (3)	= (2) x (3)
Years	Project Cash-Flow	Discount Factor 24%	Present Value
0	($35,000)	1	($35,000)
1	$20,000	0.8065	$16,130
2	$15,000	0.6504	$9,756
3	$10,000	0.5245	$5,245
4	$10,000	0.423	$4,230
Total NPV			$361

Table 5.8: Machine A - Discount Factor 24% (NPV still positive increase DF by a further 1%)

Column (1)	Column (2)	Column (3)	= (2) x (3)
Years	Project Cash-Flow	Discount Factor 25%	Present Value
0	($35,000)	1	($35,000)
1	$20,000	0.8	$16,000
2	$15,000	0.64	$9,600
3	$10,000	0.512	$5,120
4	$10,000	0.4096	$4,096
Total NPV			($184)

Table 5.9: Machine A - Discount Factor 25% (NPV is now negative, therefore IRR must lie between 24% and 25%)

As the discount factor increases the NPV is reducing. The NPV becomes negative between 24% and 25%, therefore the IRR is between 24% and 25% for machine A. For machine B the NPV is already negative at 20%, so decrease the discounting factor until NPV becomes positive - try 18% to start with.

Column (1)	Column (2)	Column (3)	= (2) x (3)
Years	Project Cash-Flow	Discount Factor 18%	Present Value
0	($35,000)	1	($35,000)
1	$10,000	0.8475	$8,475
2	$10,000	0.7182	$7,182
3	$15,000	0.6086	$9,129
4	$20,000	0.5158	$10,316
Total NPV			$102

Table 5.10: Machine B - Discount Factor 18% (the NPV is now positive - try 19%)

Column (1)	Column (2)	Column (3)	= (2) x (3)
Years	Project Cash-Flow	Discount Factor 19%	Present Value
0	($35,000)	1	($35,000)
1	$10,000	0.8403	$8,403
2	$10,000	0.7062	$7,062
3	$15,000	0.5934	$8,901
4	$20,000	0.4987	$9,974
Total NPV			($660)

Table 5.11: Machine B - Discount Factor 19% (NPV is now negative again)

The IRR for machine B must lie between 18% and 19%. These values can now be presented in a tabular or graphic form.

Interest Rate	NPV Machine A	NPV Machine B
18%	-	$102
19%	-	($660)
20%	$2,692	($1,396)
21%	-	-
22%	$1,494	-
23%	-	-
24%	$361	-
25%	($184)	-

Table 5.12: Internal Rate of Return (IRR) (plot A and B against interest rate)

67

Figure 5.3: Plot NPV for Machine A and B against IRR

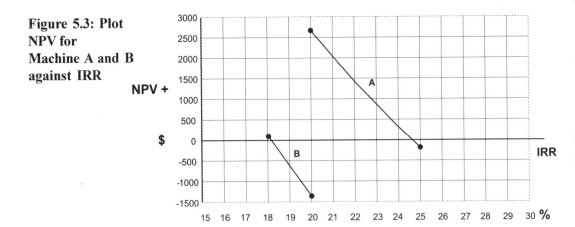

The IRR analysis is a measure of the *return on investment*, therefore, select the project with the highest IRR. This allows the manager to compare IRR with the current interest rates. One of the limitations with IRR is that it uses the same interest rate throughout the project, therefore as the project's duration extends this limitation will become more significant. This problem can be addressed, however, using a modified version of the DCF method which will be outlined in the next section.

8. Net Present Value (NPV) Using Variable Interest Rates

In the DCF examples discussed the discounting factor was kept constant for the duration of the project. This unfortunately is not a true reflection of the world markets which are quite volatile. Interest rates can fluctuate considerably over a two to three year period. Consider the following example which starts with $100, compound forward using different interest rates, then discount backwards using the same interest rates:

Year	Cash Flow	Interest Rate	Compound Interest	Discount Factor Yearly	Total Discount Factor	Present Value
1	100	10%	110	0.9091	0.9091	100
2		20%	132	0.8333	0.7576	100
3		15%	152	0.8696	0.6588	100

Table 5.13: Net Present Value (NPV) Using Variable Interest Rates

- The cash-flow for the first year is $100.
- The forecast annual interest rates are 10%, 20% and 15% respectively.
- Using these annual interest rates the compound interest for the three years will be $110, $132 and $152 respectively.

- The annual discounting factor is taken straight from the discounting factor tables. Enter year 1 and the interest rate in each case.
- The total discount factor for the second year is the total for year 1 [0.9091] times the annual discounting factor for year 2 [0.8333], giving 0.7576. (This is the most complicated step, the rest is easy).
- The present value is the total discount factor times the compound interest value, for example, in year 3, the total discount factor is [0.6588] times the compound interest value [$152], giving, $100. This is what you would expect, each year should be discounted to $100.

Which DCF Method?: The text has outlined five financial selection acceptance models. Which method or methods should you employ? If the cash-flow data can be set up on a computer spreadsheet there is no reason why you should not use all the methods outlined. Certainly *payback period* should be used as an initial filter, then two more calculations will give IRR.

For the DCF methods accountants suggest NPV should be used in preference to IRR, because NPV allows the user to vary the interest rate over the years whereas IRR employs one rate for all the cash-flows. NPV is a measure of profitability depending on the ingredients of a particular transaction, whereas IRR is dependent upon the opportunity cost of capital, which is a standard of profitability established by the capital markets.

In the absence of capital rationing, all projects that have an IRR above the opportunity cost should be considered and so should all projects that have a positive NPV. Whichever test is employed, the same decision should be reached.

However, where capital shortages exist, the two approaches may indeed give conflicting results. In this situation NPV must be employed because the fundamental objective of financial analysis is not to measure profitability but to maximise the present value of the company's investment portfolio.

9. Scoring Models

The numeric models discussed so far all have a common limitation, they only look at the financial element of the project. In an attempt to broaden the selection criteria a scoring model called the factor model, which uses multiple criteria to evaluate the project will be introduced.

The **factor model** simply lists a number of desirable factors on a project selection proforma along with columns for Selected and Not Selected. The following list shows a development of a rating sheet from Meredith.

A weighted column can be added to increase the score of important factors while reducing the scoring of the less important. The weighted column is calculated by first scoring each factor, then dividing each factor by the total score. The total of the weighted column should always add up to one. The factors can be weighted simply 1 to 5 to indicate; 1 "very poor", 2 "poor", 3 "fair", 4 "good" and 5 "very good". Three, seven and ten point scales can also be used.

Factors	Select	Do not select	Weighting
Profit > 20%	X		
Enter new market		X	
Increase market share	X		
New equipment required		X	
Use equipment not being utilised	X		
No increase in energy requirements	X		
No new technical expertise required	X		
Use underutilised workforce	X		
Manage with existing personnel		X	
No outside consultants required		X	
No impact on workforce safety	X		
No impact on environmental issues		X	
Payback period < 2 years	X		
Consistent with current business	X		
Offer good customer service	X		
Total	10	5	

Table 5.14: Scoring Model

The **advantages** of using a scoring model include:
- Encouraging objectivity in decision making.
- Using multiple selection criteria to widen the range of evaluation.
- Simple structure, therefore easy to use.
- Selection factors are structured by senior management. This implies that they reflect the company goals and objectives.
- Easy to change factors.
- Weighted scoring reflects the factor's differential importance.
- They are not biased towards short run projects favoured by financial models.
- Very low weightings can be removed from the list as they have little to no influence. This will reduce the number of questions.
- The weighted model can also be used as a flag to improve projects by identifying the variance between the factor score and the maximum possible score.

The **disadvantages** of using a scoring model are:
- If the factors are not weighted they will all assume equal importance.
- A simple model may encourage the development of long lists that could introduce trivial factors and therefore waste management time.

10. Cost Break-Even Analysis

The *cost break-even* analysis should not be confused with the cost-benefit analysis. The separation of costs into **fixed** and **variable** will be discussed in the *Project Estimating* chapter. This section on *cost break-even* analysis will take this technique a step further to model how these costs change with increasing production and determine the break-even point.

Example: A company makes a product which sells for $15 each. The variable cost per unit is $5, this covers labour and material, leaving $10 per unit as a contribution towards fixed costs. The fixed costs total is $75,000 per annum, which covers all the overhead costs. The break-even point is reached when the contribution equals the fixed costs.

Break-even point = $\dfrac{\text{Fixed costs}}{\text{Contribution per unit}}$

$\qquad\qquad\qquad =\quad \dfrac{\$75,000}{\$10} \quad = \quad 7,500 \text{ units}$

The break-even point is 7,500 units, when sales income exactly balances the total cost of $112,500 (labour and material 7,500 x 5 = $37,500 + fixed costs $75,000). Output less than this amount would result in a loss, while greater output would make a profit. This profit or loss situation can be easily read off a graph, or calculated directly.

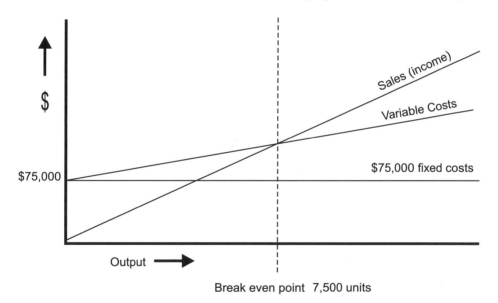

Figure 5.4: Cost Break-Even Analysis

This technique allows the project manager to see at a glance how profit varies with change in volume. It can also be used to show the effect on the cost structure by switching from manual to automatic machinery.

Cost break-even analysis can also be used to aid decision-making where two mutually exclusive projects present a different cost structure. Consider a project to install a heating system for an office block where project G has a high installation cost but low maintenance, while project H has a low installation cost but high maintenance costs. The *cost break-even* analysis will indicate which system is the most cost effective for a given period of time.

11. Project Life-Cycle Cash-Flow

Another way to model the project is to plot the cash-flow and break-even point against the project (or product) life-cycle. Initially the cash-flow will be increasingly negative until the product goes into service and a return is achieved on your investment. In the long term you need to make allowances for a decline in income and profit, and do not forget the cost to decommission and dispose of the facility.

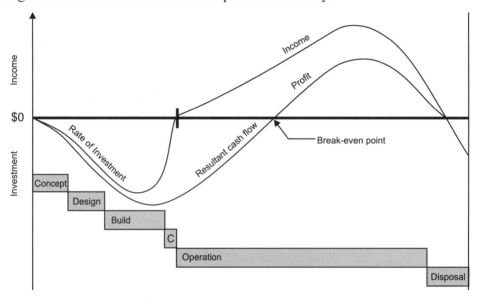

Figure 5.5: Project Life-Cycle Cash-Flow (from the cradle to the grave)

This concludes the chapter on *Project Selection*. The following chapter will discuss *Project Estimating*.

Key Points:

- Selecting the '*right*' project is crucial for your long term profitability.
- Payback period is the most commonly used selection technique
- The time value of money is addressed using discounted cash-flow techniques.

Further Reading:

Meredith, J., **Samuel**, J., *Project Management A Managerial Approach*, Wiley
Mott, G, *Investment Appraisal for Managers*, Pan

Case Study and Exercises:

The selection of the right project may be the single most important consideration which determines success or failure. Outline how your company selects projects, and give an example of how the following are considered:

1. Departmental considerations.
2. Payback period (relate to project risk).
3. Discounted cash flow using the present forecast rate of interest.
4. Scoring models, considering as wide a net as possible.
5. Break-even analysis.

"You don't think it's too flash?"

Project Estimating

For the project manager to effectively plan and control a project, accurate estimating is essential. The estimator's task is to predict the project's parameters by building a model of the project on paper. The quality and accuracy of the estimate should be seen as the best approximation based on:

- Time available
- Information available
- Techniques employed
- Expertise and experience of the estimator

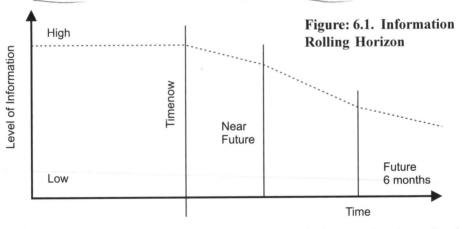

Figure: 6.1. Information Rolling Horizon

The quality and accuracy of the estimate can be continually improved as the project is progressively executed as more detailed and accurate information becomes available. Unfortunately, the project manager may have to commit the company financially and contractually at the tender or quotation stage when the amount of data and information may be limited. For this reason alone it is important to be able to provide accurate estimates based on incomplete information at the tender stage.

Although estimating usually focuses on the financial aspects of the project, it is important to remember that the costs cannot be accurately established until the other factors of scope, specifications, time, resources, materials, equipment and risks have been quantified.

Estimating is an integral part of the project management process, which should be based on past experience together with market norms and standards. Although the estimate will have an input into all areas of the project the investigation here will be restricted to **financial estimating**.

1. Estimating Terminology

In industry and commerce it is common to label the estimate according to its level of detail and accuracy. The following estimating terms; concept, feasibility, definitive and costing, relate quite closely to the *project life-cycle* phases. This classification depends on the quality of information available and the amount of effort put into compiling the estimate. The text will identify three types of estimate according to their purpose, scope of work, detail and level of accuracy.

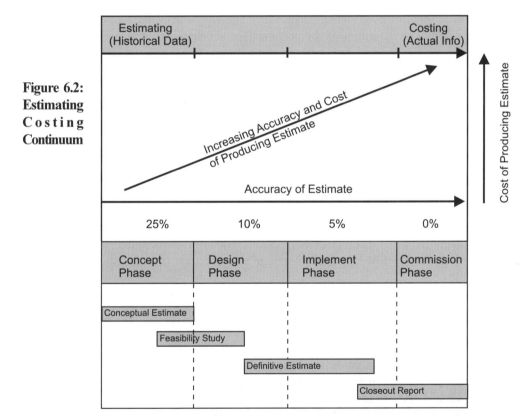

Figure 6.2: Estimating Costing Continuum

1.1 Conceptual Estimate

Also called **order of magnitude**, **budget figure**, **ball-park figure** or **thumb suck**. The conceptual estimate addresses the needs of senior management who are presented with a number of possible projects. They need an initial filter to select those projects that warrant further investigation. This would occur in the concept and initiation phase.

The conceptual estimate will be based on a limited scope of work using scale factors or capacity estimates to give a low level of accuracy +/- 25%. A conceptual estimate would not be a legally binding document, however, professional competence could be questioned if the estimates were too far adrift. If the conceptual estimate looks promising, senior management will then allocate funds to finance a more detailed *feasibility study*.

1.2 Feasibility Study

Also called **preliminary estimate** or **comparative estimate**. Irrespective of how the project has evolved and crystallised the *feasibility study* investigates the feasibility of pursuing with the project within the defined boundaries and answers the question "*Should we go ahead with this project?*" (See *Feasibility Study* chapter).

The *feasibility study* should be managed as a highly structured mini project as set out in your company's procedure manual. It is essential at the outset to determine the needs and expectations of all the stakeholders. This can be achieved through a structured needs analysis to determine if the proposal (or alternatives) offer a real solution to address the project's brief. Although the *feasibility study* is characterised by information gathering, processing and reporting, the accuracy of the estimate may still be somewhat limited at about +/-10%.

1.3 Definitive Estimate

Also called **detailed estimate, project control estimate, quotation** or **tender.** When the decision has been made to proceed to the next phase, the design and development phase, or planning phase, this will initiate another mini project to provide detailed designs and plans to build and manage the project.

The definitive estimate will be based on a considerable amount of data incorporating a developed *scope of work*, detailed WBS, detailed drawings, specifications, vendor quotations (that are now legally binding) and site surveys to give an improved accuracy of +/- 5%.

1.4 Costing

If estimating is defined as a quick method for pricing a project based on incomplete data, then costing may be defined as a detailed price based on a complete bill of materials (BOM) and parts lists. Costing requires the following items to be complete:

- Design and calculations
- Scope of work, bill of materials (BOM) and parts list
- Detailed planning
- Firm prices from subcontractors and suppliers, manhours and labour costs.

Almost every aspect of the project must be quantified, and with this high level of information and effort, accurate quotations of +/- 1% can be achieved. There is, however, a time and cost penalty, as costing is expensive and time consuming to produce.

1.5 Accuracy of Estimate

In figure 6.2 the level of accuracy is presented as a continuum from conceptual estimate at 25% to closeout report at 0%. As the graph moves from estimating to costing so the data moves from historical to actual information, and the level of accuracy increases, but so does the time to produce the estimate and the associated cost to produce the estimate.

Figure 6.2 shows the relationship between a higher level of accuracy and the increasing cost of producing it. Although it is not the project manager's function to set the company's profit margin, the project manager does need to know what the profit margin is, as this will influence the accuracy of the estimate and subsequent level of control. As a guide, the level of accuracy should be at least equal to, or greater than, the profit margin so that in the worst case a cost overrun would be accommodated by the profit margin.

2. Project Costs

A project estimate can be subdivided into a number of different **costs**, consider the following:
- Direct costs
- Indirect costs
- Time related costs
- Labour costs
- Material and equipment costs
- Transport costs
- Preliminary and general (P&G) costs
- Project office costs
- Project team costs.

2.1 Direct Costs

As the term implies, direct costs are those costs that can be specifically identified with an activity or project. The current trend is to assign as much as possible, if not all costs to direct costs, because direct costs can be budgeted, monitored and controlled far more effectively than indirect costs.
- Direct management costs refer to the project office running costs. Salaries for the project manager, project engineer, planner, accountant, secretary and QA.
- Direct labour costs refer to the people working on an activity, e.g. boilermakers, welders, fitters, computer programmers, etc.
- Direct material costs are for the materials, consumables, components which are used for completing an activity and an allowance for scrap and wastage.
- Direct equipment costs refers to machinery, plant and tools.
- Direct expenses include bought-in services that are specific to the project, for example, plant hire, surveyor, designer and subcontractor fees.

The distinctive nature of direct costs is that the total expense can be charged to an activity or project.

2.2 Indirect Costs

Indirect costs, also called **overheads**, are those costs that cannot be directly booked to an activity or project, but are required to keep the company operational.

- Indirect management costs refer to senior managers, the estimating department, sales and marketing, accounts, IT, general office staff, secretarial, administration and the personnel department.
- Indirect labour costs refer to the reception, maintenance, security and cleaners. Basically it includes all the employees who are required to keep the company functioning.
- Indirect materials include stationery, cleaning materials and maintenance parts.
- Indirect equipment includes computers, photocopiers and fax machines.
- Indirect expenses include training, insurance, depreciation, rent and rates.

Indirect costs are usually financed by an overhead recovery charge added to the earned man-hour rate and if not properly managed will eat away at the company profits. The acid test for the project vis-a-vis indirect costs and overheads, is to compare internal costs with the same services available outside the company.

2.3 Time Related Costs

Critical path method (CPM) was originally developed to address the time / cost trade-off (crashing). If a project's duration is reduced or extended how will the costs change? To do this calculation you need to determine how costs are affected by time. Consider the following:

- Rent increases with time.
- Running costs - water, electricity and gas would increase with time.
- If the project's duration is reduced, employee labour rate will increase if the workers have to work overtime.
- Contract labour on a fixed rate is not affected by time, but their productivity may reduce if they work long hours.
- Fixed price contracts may not be affected by time.

Simulating all the costs will give you the overall effect of time changes on project costs. This technique can also be used for project acceleration where you need to know the trade-off between the cost of accelerating a project to meet certain milestones compared with the penalties of failing to achieve them.

2.4 Labour Costs

This section will explain how to determine your labour charge-out rate. The labour costs considered here are for the project workforce and thus a direct cost. Although the salaries of a workforce may be clearly identified there are also a number of other associated costs which form part of the labour rate.

The labour rate is calculated by aggregating the various costs and dividing them by the number of manhours worked (in this case per month). This process is explained in the following worked example. Here the costs are subdivided into four main headings:

[1] Salary (see table 6.1)
[2] Associated labour costs (see table 6.1)
[3] Contribution to overheads
[4] Contribution to company profit.

		Cost per month	Days lost per month
1	**Salary**	**$2,000**	
2.1	Medical insurances	$50	
2.2	Sickness benefit		1
2.3	Annual holiday		1
2.4	Training courses	$30	1
2.5	Protective clothing	$20	
2.6	Car allowance	$250	
2.7	Housing allowance	$50	
2.8	Subsistence allowance	$100	
2.9	Pension	$100	
2.10	Tool allowance	$20	
2.11	Private jobs	$20	
2.12	Productivity bonus	$100	
2.13	Standing time		1
2.14	Inclement weather		1
	Total	$740	5 days

Table 6.1: Labour Cost

[3] Contribution to overhead: 30% of salary = $600

[4] Company profit: 25% of salary = $500

Labour rate = $\dfrac{\text{Total monthly costs}}{\text{Total number of normal working hours per month}}$

Where the total monthly costs are (salary + associated costs + contribution to overheads + company profit). And the working hours per month are (21 days less 5 days lost, times eight hours per day).

Labour rate = $\dfrac{2000 + 740 + 600 + 500}{(21 - 5) \times 8}$

= $ 30/ hr.

Some of the above items may be difficult to quantify without access to statistical analysis, for example, days lost due to sickness and standing time. They should be recognised as potential costs and a figure assigned if only as a contribution to an unknown amount. The end product of this analysis should be a labour rate per hour.

Overtime: This brings us to an interesting question, based on the above calculations, how do you cost out overtime? If all the associated costs have been paid for by the contribution during normal working hours, can you assume they do not need to be paid for again? If yes, then you need only assign costs to the following headings:

- Labour wages overtime rate (time and a half or double time)
- Contribution to indirect variable costs
- Contribution to company profit.

You can also assume there will be no lost time, because you are either working overtime or not. In industry and commerce, however, the overtime rate to the client usually increases as a multiple of the employee overtime rate (time and a half, or double time).

2.5 Procurement Costs

This section will determine the procurement costs to acquire all the required bought-in goods and services. The simplest method is to add a percentage to the buying price to cover all the procurement costs, consider the following (table 6.2):

Department	Scope of work	Cost
Drawing office	Bill of materials, Specification	
Buying office	Source suppliers and vendors	
Quality department	Pre-qualify suppliers	
Buying office	Tender cycle, adjudication and selection	
Planning office	Procurement schedule	
Buying office	Place order, expedite	
Quality department	Goods inwards inspection	
Warehouse	Material handling, Inventory and stock control	
Accounts department	Pay invoice	
Production	Scrap and waste	
Shareholders	Profit	
Total Costs		

Table 6.2: Procurement Costs

$$\text{Procurement percentage} = \frac{\underline{\text{Procurement costs}}}{\text{Total cost of materials}} \times 100$$

Many of the above costs may be covered by another budget, for example the inspection and pre-qualifying suppliers could fall under the QA budget, in which case they must not be included here (double accounting). The procurement costs would generally be developed at the company level and apply to all the company's projects. Typical percentages would be between 10% to 20%.

Old Stock: How does the estimator price material and equipment that has already been paid for on a previous project. What is the value of surplus material and equipment that has already been written-off? The estimator obviously has scope to price the old material and equipment from free issue to current market price. If the material is priced as free issue this will make your quotation more competitive. Company policy will determine stock rotation, which could be a mixture of:

LIFO - Last in first out
FIFO - First in first out

The material and equipment estimate usually allows the procurement manager the scope to save 5% to 10% on material and equipment costs through negotiation with the suppliers. In a competitive market this saving would significantly enhance the project's profit.

2.6 Transport Costs

It is important to appreciate the additional costs that may be incurred delivering the goods from the suppliers factory to client's premises or site, consider the following terms:

Ex-Works: It is the purchaser's responsibility to organise and pay for delivery, loading, transport and insurance from the factory gate.

FOB (Free on Board): The supplier will arrange for the goods to be loaded on board a ship, plane, train or truck at an agreed place. The supplier will pay for the port duties and export clearances, while the client is responsible for the transport, insurance and any import duties. It is important to clarify when the change of ownership and responsibility takes place. This is usually when the goods have been loaded.

CIF (Cost, Insurance and Freight): The supplier pays for the delivery of the goods to their final destination plus the insurance. The client pays for import duties.

DDP (Delivered Duty Paid): The goods will be delivered to the purchaser's front door. All the risks and costs relating to transport, insurance and duty will be the supplier's responsibility.

In order to compete successfully on the world market and convert quotations into orders it may not be sufficient to simply quote ex-works - at a minimum the quote should be 'per container load'. To quote in these terms will require the estimator to establish the weight and volume of the product needed to fill a container. A more useful quote to an international client would be FOB, for this it would be necessary to establish the cost of transport to the coast. But why not go further and quote CIF, or better still match other international exporters and quote DDP and delivery to the buyer's front door and quote in their own currency?

To offer these enhanced facilities will require the estimator to establish a data base of the 'total cost breakdown', so that they can respond quickly and accurately to an inquiry. DDP will also have the added benefit to the exporting country of earning additional foreign currency from the insurance and freight.

2.7 Project Office Costs

The project office costs or **project management fee** are often separated out and may form a separate contract within the total project. The project office costs not only include the management fee, but also many other associated costs. Many of the costs vary as the project passes through the project phases, there may be a number of part time team members either on contract or seconded from another department. Watch out for Parkinson's law (1957): *"Work expands so as to fill the time available for its completion."* Once you have a data base of historical costs you may be able to relate this project management fee as a percentage of the project's value, about 6% to 10% would be typical.

Table 6.3: Project Office Costs

Cost Breakdown Structure		Costs
Project Team's salary	Project Manager	
	Project Engineer	
	Project Planner	
	Project Accountant	
	Procurement Manager	
	Quality Manager	
	Configuration Manager	
	Project Estimator	
	Project Secretary	
Project Office costs	Rent, water, electricity	
	Office equipment	
	Stationery	
	Telephone, internet	
Travel	Car pool	
	Air flights	
	Accomodation, meals	
Security	Reception, guards	
Training	Project management, quality TQM, computer skills	
Marketing	Entertaining clients	
Total Costs		

2.8 Preliminary and General (P&G) Costs

If the project requires work on site, on location, or away from your office (virtual office), these costs are often separated out and called P&G's in the construction industry. A typical construction project would use the following headings: (Note, many of these headings have been identified already under indirect costs).

- Site establishment
- Site supervision
- Insurance and performance bonds

- Plant-hire, equipment, cranage, tools, vehicles and generators
- Site establishment, huts, toilets and fencing
- Site security, which would include the night watchman and guard dogs to protect the site from theft and vandalism
- Site services, which include telephone, electricity and water
- Temporary access roads and sign posts
- Scaffolding and ladders
- Temporary lights and power supply
- Accommodation for the workforce
- Special travelling expenses to site
- Special training and testing of tradesmen
- Material handling, which would include receiving inspection, off-loading, storage and inventory control
- Removal of rubbish, waste and scrap.

The costs assigned to these headings should include the normal recovery percentage for overhead costs and profit. Check that these costs are not being recovered elsewhere in the estimate, for example, site services and security may be provided by the client.

3. Estimating Methodology

This section will discuss some of the estimating techniques that can be used to predict the project's parameters quickly with reasonable accuracy. The estimating techniques used by industry and commerce can vary tremendously from one company to another, consider the following:

- Jobbing
- Factoring
- Inflation
- Economies of scale
- Unit rates
- Day work.

3.1 Jobbing

Also termed **job costing** or **operational estimating**. Jobbing is the process of including all the operations that go into executing an activity or task. Consider the following example (table 6.4) where the job is subdivided into its component parts. Once the activity has started, operational estimating enables the progress to be quantified:

- It provides a cost estimate for all the WBS work packages and activities.
- Progress can be measured as percentage complete or remaining duration.
- When the activity is complete the profit or loss can be calculated. This data can also be used to ensure that the estimating data base is kept up-to-date.

Task	Description	Labour	Material	Plant hire	Transport	Total
100	Mark-out foundations	$1,000	$500			$1,500
200	Dig foundations	$5,000	$500	$1,000	$500	$7,000
300	Lay foundations	$3,000	$10,000	$3,000	$2,000	$18,000

Table 6.4: Operational Estimating Format

The operational estimating technique is a prerequisite for *critical path method* (CPM) planning and control. At the tender stage, however, there may not be sufficient time or need to produce an estimate with this level of detail. Certainly on award of contract, operational estimating must be carried out as it is part of the CPM process. We therefore need to look at other estimating techniques that are quicker to produce, but still provide a reasonably accurate estimate. The accuracy of the estimate can be improved by subdividing the WBS into more detailed work packages.

3.2 Factoring

Also called **component ratio** or **parametric method**. Factoring can be used when historical data from previous projects indicates that an item of the project can be expressed as a percentage of a known or calculated core cost (see table 6.5).

Management fee	5% of contract price
Quality assurance	1% of contract price
Engine beds	2% of engine
Pipework	20% of generator price
Consumables	10% of material price
Profit	20% of construction price

Table 6.5: Factoring

Once the core costs have been established the associated ratios can be calculated very quickly. These ratios should be confirmed progressively as performance data becomes available.

3.3 Inflation

Also called **time based indices**. The project costs will change with time due to the non-reversible effect of inflation on the economy. If the current project is similar to a previous project completed a few years ago, the financial figures from the previous project can be used as the basis for the current estimate (see table 6.6).

	2000	2001		2002	
	Base cost	Inflation rate	New price	Inflation rate	New price
Labour	$500,000	10%	$550,000	8%	$594,000
Material	$400,000	15%	$460,000	5%	$483,000
Total	$900,000	12.2% average	$1,010,000	6.6% average	$1,077,000

Table 6.6: Inflation

The upward effect of inflation can be established using a Cost Price Index (CPI) and inflation indices. One of the problems with this method is that different commodities tend to escalate at different rates. This can however, be addressed by subdividing the project into its component costs by a CPI category, then applying an escalation factor to each, separately (see table 6.6).

3.4 Economies of Scale

Also called **cost capacity factor**. The cost capacity factor mathematically relates similar jobs of different sizes. If a job is twice as big as the previous job, will it cost twice as much? Usually not, for the following reasons:

Indivisibility: In a production process there may be certain indivisibilities, or fixed costs that are required just to be in business, but not related to output. For example, a firm may require a manager, a telephone and a secretary. These costs are indivisible because you cannot have half a manager merely because you want to operate at a lower output.

Specialisation: In a small business people have to be flexible and become a *Jack of all trades* to survive, but as companies grow in size so they are able to group work and assign repetitive tasks to one person. It is obviously more efficient (if not a little boring for the operator) to setup jigs to perform the same task repetitively.

Technical: Large scale production is often able to take advantage of automated machinery. The high capital expenditure can be written off over large production runs, thus reducing the unit cost, e.g. car production lines.

Scaling: There is not always a linear relationship between dimensions and volumes, e.g. on an oil tanker, the surface area increases at two-thirds the rate of the volume. Thus the tankers require proportionally less steel per cubic metre of cargo as they increase in volume. These economy of scale effects show that as projects get larger their unit cost reduces and the production becomes more efficient, however, there can be another side to the coin.

Diseconomies of Scale: As the output increases there are some **Diseconomies of scale** that are usually associated with the management function. When the organisation structure becomes large and bureaucratic the co-ordination between the management levels and departments becomes increasingly more complex, costly and inefficient. Not only are the lines of communication longer, but inevitably the number of unproductive meetings increases and internal memos proliferate.

These economies of scale which have a non-linear relationship can be quantified through a simple equation:

$$\$E = \$K \times (q1/ q2)^p$$

where $\$E$ is the estimated cost

$\$K$ is the known cost from a previous project

q1 is the size of the new project

q2 is the size of the old project

p is the cost capacity factor raised to the power of p. The value of "p" is derived from empirical observations.

Consider a project to build a hotel with 1,000 rooms. If a similarly constructed hotel of 500 rooms was built for $10,000,000, what is the estimate for this 1,000 roomed hotel? (Assume p = 0.8)

$$\$E = 10,000,000 \times (1,000/ 500)^{0.8}$$
$$= 17,411,011$$

This indicates that although the number of rooms doubles the estimated cost only increases by 74%.

3.5 Unit Rates

Also called **parameter costs**. Although a project tends to be a unique undertaking, much of the work may be repetitive. Parameter costs are developed from unit rates for common items of work based on previous projects. This technique estimates a project's cost from an empirically developed book of unit rates. For example consider the following parameters (table 6.7):

Per linear metre:	House piping, wiring, welding
Per square metre:	Decorating, painting, house building
Per cubic metre:	Concrete, water supply
Per tonne:	Ship building, cargo freight
Per HP or KW:	Generator power, electrical supply
Per mile or Km:	Car hire, transport
Per hour:	Labour, plant hire

Table 6.7: Unit Rates

Unit rates work well in a controlled work environment. However, many projects by virtue of their location and scope of work may involve other considerations:

- Unit rate estimating is appropriate for a contractor with a record of small jobs within a limited geographical area.

- As the contracts increase in size so the data base samples will tend to decrease in number.
- Costs are influenced by remote locations, logistics, travelling distances and the conditions of the roads.
- Weather conditions can be statistically predicted but what happens in practice may be very different (El Nino).
- Are there utilities available; water supply, power supply, accommodation, public transport, etc? Further considerations will be outlined in the estimating problem section later in this chapter.

Unit rates are probably the most commonly used estimating technique and will form the basis of most estimates. Unit rates are commonly used as they provide a simple contract to measure and budget. Even a fixed price contract usually contains a unit price clause for additional work. When I worked in a ship repair yacht in the Middle East, most of our work was tendered and charged this was from a booklet of tariffs.

4. Day Work

Day work is the term used to quantify the hourly rate or daily rate for labour, materials, plant, preliminary and general (P&G's). The complete project could be financed on day work as a cost plus contract. This type of contract used to be quite common on military projects, but not on commercial projects where fixed prices are preferred by the client.

On a fixed price project the client often requests day work rates to be quoted at the tender stage to provide a framework for costing changes and additional work. The contractor's overheads and profit are included in the rate. The contractor must ensure that the day work sheets are signed by the client at the end of each shift. The client meanwhile needs to monitor performance to ensure good productivity.

5. Estimating Format

The final estimate will be a compilation of figures from many different sources. The challenge here is to present them all in one coherent document (summary). Consider the following estimating formats (tables 6.8, 6.9 and 6.10):

WBS	Description	Budget
1.1		
1.2		
1.3		
1.4		
1.5		
Project Management fee		
Sub-Total		
Profit		
Total		

Table 6.8: Estimating Format

In table 6.8 the WBS work packages form the main structure of the estimate and they can be subdivided further into CPM activities if a higher level of detail and accuracy is required.

WBS	Labour	Material	Machinery	Transport	Total
1.1					
1.2					
1.3					
1.4					
1.5					
Project Office					
P&G's					
Sub-Total					
Profit					
Total					

Table 6.9: Estimating Format

In table 6.9 the columns have been subdivided into the different types of costs (labour, material, machinery and transport) as discussed earlier in the chapter.

WBS	Jobbing	Factoring	Inflation	Economy of Scale	Unit Rates
1.1					
1.2					
1.3					
1.4					
1.5					
Project Office					
P&G's					
Sub-Total					
Profit					
Total					

Table 6.10: Estimating Format

In table 6.10 the costs have been subdivided into the different estimating methods as discussed earlier in the chapter.

It is essential to impose discipline and structure to the estimate so as to ensure that all parties are working to the same system. This can be achieved through company policies and standard procedures. These will obviously evolve and develop from the experience gained on previous projects. Using a standard estimating sheet for your type of work has many advantages:

- All the information can be rolled-up to one summary document or page.
- The structure of the estimating sheet is based on experience (learn from your achievements and mistakes).
- If the estimate is setup on a spreadsheet, you only need to input certain parameters as preset algorithms will calculate the rest and give you a professional looking quotation sheet.
- The estimating sheet's purpose is to calculate the work content - the schedule is developed from the CPM analysis.

6. Contingencies

So far the estimating has assumed that normal working conditions and practices will prevail. Unfortunately the real world does not work that way and allowances need be made for risks and uncertainties. These allowances tend to get lumped together under the contingency heading which includes cover for the following non-recoverable items:

- Under estimating work content due to lack of scope definition.
- Delays in finalising designs due to client, designer and certifying authority.
- Additional work caused by design errors.
- Rework caused by production mistakes.
- Rework and replacement caused by material or component failure.

- Labour and equipment standing idle caused by import delays and inclement weather.
- Lost production caused by industrial action, strikes, work to rule or go slow.
- Limited supply of skilled labour locally.

The size of the contingency will depend on many factors:
- Type of project.
- General efficiency and competency of the company.
- Degree of risk and uncertainty.

The contingency allowance is usually added as a percentage to either, each work package or a blanket cover for the whole project, but not both. A blanket cover is obviously the easiest to apply, but this may unnecessarily increase your quotation. Adding a contingency at the work package level allows you to be more selective. Consider the following format (table 6.11):

WBS	Description	Budget	Contingency	Total
1.1				
1.2				
1.3				
1.4				
1.5				
Project Management fee				
Sub-Total				
Contingency				
Profit				
Total				

Table 6.11: Contingencies (proforma)

You need to establish ground rules for managing the contingency;
- How should it be calculated?
- Who owns it?
- Who will manage it?
- How will it be allocated?
- Who will be advised of its existence?

7. Escalation

During periods of high inflation long term projects must consider the time value of money. The options are for the contractor to include an allowance in their quotation or for the client to escalate a base date tender. The mechanics of an escalation clause are:
- The client and contractor agree on which escalation index to use.
- The contractor quotes at **today's prices** with no contingency for inflation.
- Progress claims are escalated using published indices.

8. Bidders Dilemma

When tendering in a competitive market the contract price is one of the main selection criteria. The pricing dilemma facing management is the trade-off between reducing their profit and improving their chance of winning the contract, or increasing their profit, but reducing their chance of winning the contract.

Reducing the profit margin will improve the chances of your quotation being selected, but if the quotation is significantly lower than your competitors this will unnecessarily erode your profits. Therefore before quoting a low price, first assess the market competition, your competitors' level of work, the client's budget and the state of the economy.

On the other hand if the estimate is too high and the contract is awarded to your company, this will nicely increase your profits in the short term, but reduce the chances of further work if the same estimating data base is used on subsequent tendering.

If the quotation is reduced to secure the work what effect will this have on the original estimate? If the project manager requires 10,000 hours for a job and the quotation is reduced to 8,000 hours, then a project manager still requires 10,000 hours unless productivity is increased, production automated, or scope of work reduced.

9. Estimating Problems

The following list is a collection of points to be considered when estimating. Some of the common pitfalls to be aware of include:

- Keeping new technology under control - consider incrementally increasing technology, phased implementation and proving systems progressively. This is less risky than the big bang approach.
- Misinterpreting the scope of work and omissions.
- Risk and uncertainty are not considered.
- If work is priced out at the department average, regardless of who is doing the work, this simplifies the estimating, but the client may not be happy paying engineers' rates for an apprentice.
- The performance of individuals within a trade can vary considerably depending on their ability and commitment.
- Poorly defined or an overly optimistic schedule.

- Inflation on a long term project not considered.
- Lack of historical data, especially if this is a new type of project for the company.
- The main contractor will be at risk if they have to give a fixed price quotation to their client based on budget estimates from their subcontractors. However, the subcontractors may not be in a position to give a fixed quotation if the detailed drawings are not available.
- Closeout Report: Some managers prefer not to document their problems: *"If my project fails the last thing I want around is hard data to nail me."* In which case the company is doomed to repeat their failures.
- Make sure that costs are debited from the appropriate activity and not off-loaded to the activity with the fattest budget otherwise this will devalue your closeout report, and mislead future estimating.
- Consider your response to this reaction when requesting information, *"My people have no time to collect data, they are too busy doing the work."*
- A NASA astronaut was asked what concerned him most about the flight? He replied, *"It's not sitting on a potential fuel bomb that concerns me most, but the 10,000 components that were made by the lowest bidder."* (See the film Capricorn 1, which takes this problem to extreme possibilities).
- Terms and conditions of contract not quantified.
- Validity of the quotation not stated.
- Expenses often forgotten when estimating include:
  - a) Commissioning and customer acceptance.
  - b) Training of the client's technicians to use the installed equipment.
  - c) Protective painting.
  - d) Writing user manuals.

This concludes the chapter on *Project Estimating*. The following chapter will overview the *Planning and Control Cycle*.

Key Points:

- Estimating techniques and methods enable you to make quick and reasonably accurate quotations.
- Establish your cost structure (labour and materials) to simplify your estimating.
- Use estimating proformas to structure your estimates and quotations.

Further Reading:

Begg, David., *Economics,* McGraw-Hill
Institute of Chemical Engineers, *A Guide to Capital Cost Estimating*

Case Study and Exercises:

Estimating techniques enable you to produce a reasonably accurate estimate quickly and efficiently. Although most companies set out to follow a tender schedule, when '*push comes to shove*', many contracts are decided at the last minute, in which case it is essential to be able to respond quickly with an accurate estimate. Outline a number of estimating techniques you have developed in your line of work which enable you to respond accurately and quickly to a clients enquiry. Your presentation (written or verbal) should consider the following:

1. The range of estimates, noting the accuracy, the time to produce and the cost to produce.
2. Separating direct costs from indirect costs which you need to calculate overtime and crashing.
3. The material procurement costs presented as a percentage.
4. The project office costs.
5. The estimating proforma.

"Fill her up please"

CHAPTER 7

Planning and Control Cycle

This chapter will overview the project planning and control cycle, which is at the heart of project integration. This is where the project manager is responsible for co-ordinating the contributions of all the project participants to meet the stakeholders needs and expectations. The PMBOK defines project integration management as; '... *the process required to ensure that the various elements of the project are properly co-ordinated.'*

This chapter will outline how the various project management planning and control tools and techniques discussed in this book relate to each other and how the core of project management integration involves making trade-offs between competing objectives and alternatives, in order to meet the stakeholders requirements. It is important to appreciate that a change in one parameter may change other parameters, for example, the late delivery of a drawing, or component could delay the start of an activity which could have resource and cash-flow implications.

Planning is an important component of the planning and control cycle, because the planning process not only establishes what is to be done, but also smooths the way to *'make-it-happen'*. The challenge is to select and apply the available planning tools and techniques effectively. Planning asks questions, encourages participation, creates awareness, prompts action, solves problems, and formalises decisions based on consensus.

The planning process communicates planning information to the project team and stakeholders and obliges them to '*sign-on*' and pledge their support. When plans are drawn up by those who are going to implement them, they feel obliged (if not totally committed) to complete as planned. Conversely non-involvement in the planning process may lead to plans being ignored, dragging heels, misinterpretation, and '*not designed here*' attitude - which in turn leads to a time consuming analysis of the behaviour side of project management.

Planning is all about thinking forward in time. What varies is how far ahead the plans stretch and how precise they are. Churchill is reported to have said, "*It's wise to look ahead, but foolish to look further than you can see.'*

1. Project Planning Steps

Although the planning steps are outlined here as a sequence of discrete operations, in practice other factors may influence the sequence and there will almost certainly be a number of iterations, compromises and trade-offs before achieving an optimum plan (see figures 7.1 and 7.2).

Project Charter: The project charter officially acknowledges the start of the project, and should outline the purpose of the project, the beneficial changes and key objectives, together with the means of achieving them. (See *Scope Management* chapter).

Feasibility Study: The feasibility study develops the *project charter* and project brief into a project proposal. It offers a structured approach for identifying the stakeholders and assessing their needs. It reviews closeout reports, together with investigating other options and alternatives to support the project's business viability (see *Feasibility Study* chapter).

Scope Management: The scope of work defines what the project includes and just as importantly, what is not included in order to meet the stated objectives. On an engineering project, for example, the scope of work would be developed into a list of drawings, bill of materials (BOM) and specifications (see *Scope Management* chapter). Scope management also includes a closeout report to document achievements and opportunity to learn from mistakes.

Build Method: The build method outlines how the product will be assembled or implemented, for example, it considers the position of the crane and storage on a high-rise building, or the methods of communication and data storage on an IT project.

Execution Strategy: The execution strategy considers the '*buy or make*' decision. If the product is to be purchased this is a procurement issue, but if the product is to be made in-house this is a resource issue where the execution strategy should identify the equipment and labour pool.

Work Breakdown Structure (WBS): The WBS is one of the key scope management tools used to subdivide the scope of work (as outlined by the build method and the execution strategy), into manageable work packages that can be estimated, planned, assigned and controlled (see *WBS* chapter). pg 115 →

Organisation Breakdown Structure (OBS): The OBS or responsibility matrix is setup to manage the project as outlined in the execution strategy. The OBS links the WBS work packages to the company, department or person who is responsible for performing the work (see *WBS* chapter for diagram). The OBS can be further developed to include delegated responsibility, level of authority and lines of communication. Projects are often managed by a project manager and project team that is specially setup for the project and disbanded on completion. The integration of the project team and company departments is often through a matrix structure where the project team overlays the company's hierarchical structure - achieving '*buy-in*' by all stakeholders is critical for the project to be successful.

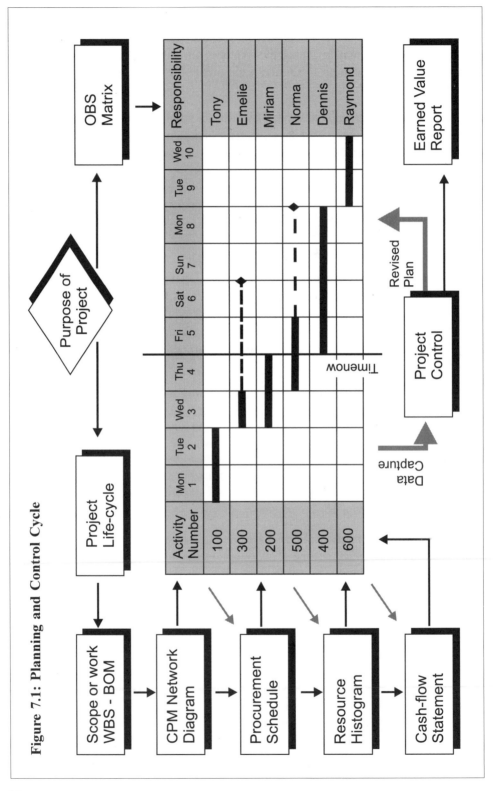

Figure 7.1: Planning and Control Cycle

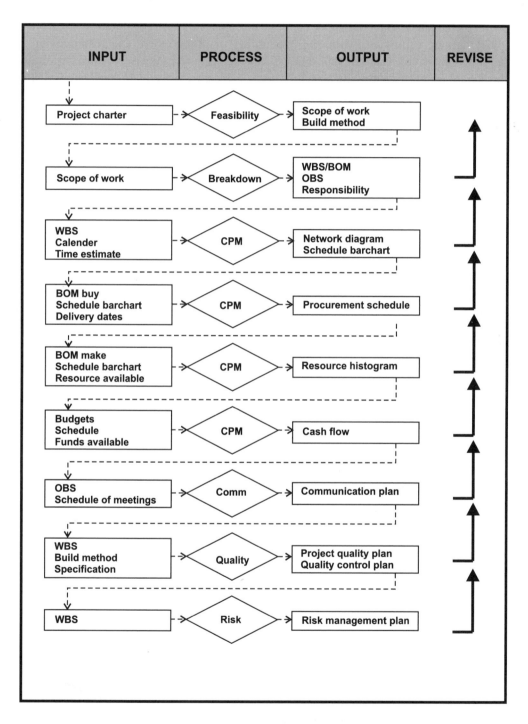

Figure 7.2: Planning and Control Cycle (alternative presentation)

Critical Path Method (CPM): The CPM uses a *network diagram* to present the work packages and activities in a logical sequence of work that is developed from the build method and other constraints (internal and external). Activity duration and work calendars are estimated, while the availability of procurement and resources are assumed not to constrain the time analysis. The CPM time analysis (forward pass and backward pass) calculates the activities early start, early finish, late start, late finish, float and the critical path (see *CPM* chapter). This information is often presented in an activity table and *schedule barchart*.

Schedule Barchart: The barchart is one of the most effective and commonly used means of communicating schedule information. It enables the project participants to easily walk through the sequencing of the project's work. The planning structure can be further simplified by focusing on hammocks, key dates and milestones (see *Schedule Barchart* chapter).

Procurement Schedule: The execution strategy *'buy or make'* decision will determine if the bill of materials is a procurement issue or a resource issue. The procurement function is to supply all the bought-in items at the best price, to meet the project schedule However, long lead items need to be identified early on, so that they can be ordered and/or the schedule barchart revised (see *Procurement Schedule* chapter).

Resource Histogram: The resources required to complete the work outlined in the *schedule barchart* are forecast and compared with their availability. Resource overloads, or resource underloads need to accommodate both project and company requirements. The resource smoothing needs to consider other company projects and outside contractors, before revising the *scheduled barchart* (see *Resource Planning* chapter). The resources can be integrated with time to produce a manpower 'S' curve that forms the baseline plan for *earned value* calculations.

Budgets and Project Cash-Flow: The project accounting process not only establishes and assigns budgets to all the work packages, but also determines the project's cash-flow. There may be cash-flow constraints restricting the supply of funds that will require the *scheduled barchart* to be revised (see *Project Accounts* chapter). The costs can be integrated with time to produce the budgeted cost for work scheduled (BCWS) that forms the baseline plan for the *earned value* calculation.

Communication Plan: The communication plan includes the process required to ensure proper collection and dissemination of project information. It consists of communication planning, information distribution *(lines of communication)*, a schedule of project meetings, progress reporting and administrative closeout (see *Project Communication* chapter).

Project Quality Plan: The project quality plan outlines a quality management system (quality assurance and quality control), designed to guide and enable the project to meet the required condition. This may include pre-qualifying project personnel and suppliers, developing procedures, quality inspections and quality documentation (see *Quality Management* chapter).

Risk Management Plan: The risk management plan includes the process of identifying, analysing, and responding to project risk. It consists of risk identification, risk quantification and impact, response development and risk control. It should also include a disaster recovery plan to accommodate the worst possible scenario. (See the *Project Risk Management* chapter).

Baseline Plan: The baseline plan may be considered as a portfolio of documents which outline how to achieve the project's objectives. The level of detail and accuracy will depend on the project phase and complexity. The *baseline plan* should be a coherent document to guide the project through the execution and project control cycle.

2. Project Control Cycle

The project control cycle is presented as a sequence of steps to guide the project to a successful completion. The *baseline plan* outlines the course to steer, but once the project starts you can be sure things will deviate; be it late deliveries, sickness, absenteeism, or scope creep. The project control cycle monitors project performance and compares it against the *baseline plan* - it also includes a mechanism for incorporating scope changes. Project control also relates to keeping the project team and personnel interested in the project, together with continuing support and commitment from senior management and all the stakeholders.

Work Authorisation: As the *single point of responsibility* the project manager is responsible for delegating and authorising the scope of work. The issuing of instructions to the appointed contractors and other responsible parties signals the start of the execution phase of the project. The methods for authorising work, reporting and applying control should be discussed and agreed at the handover meeting, so that all parties know how the project will be managed. **A record of all decisions and instructions should be kept to provide an audit trail.**

As the project progresses there will be changes to the baseline plan that need to be authorised. These would tend to be authorised by issuing a revised document, typical examples include:

- Issue revised drawing for a scope changes
- Issue revised schedule for schedule changes
- Issue revised budget for cost changes.

Expedite: Once instructions, orders and contracts have been issued, project expediting takes a proactive approach to make the instructions happen. It involves the follow up function to confirm that; orders have been received by the subcontractors, internal planning issued, materials have been procured, skilled labour available, work has started as planned and the schedule completion dates will be achieved. Any variance should be reported through the data capture system.

Tracking and Monitoring Progress: The data capture system records the progress and current status of all the work packages and activities. The accuracy of the data capture has a direct bearing on the accuracy of all the subsequent reports (project status, trends and forecast).

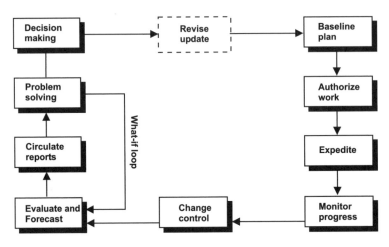

Figure 7.3: Project Control Cycle

Change Control: The change control function ensures that all changes to the scope of work are captured and approved by the designated people before being incorporated in the *baseline plan*. Change control is also concerned with influencing the factors that create changes to ensure that changes are beneficial (see *Scope Management* chapter).

Evaluation and Forecasting: The project's performance is analysed by comparing actual progress against planned progress within the CPM model and extrapolating the trends and use '*what-if*' analysis to forecast the project's position in the future (see *Project Control* and *Earned Value* chapters).

Problem-Solving: The problem-solving function is to generate a list of possible solutions, options and alternatives. This may be achieved through interactive brainstorming sessions and quality circles.

Decision-Making: The decision-making function collates information and decides on an appropriate corrective action. **One of the main management functions is to make decisions**. In-fact it may be argued that the sole purpose of generating information is to make decisions. The following steps outline a typical decision-making process:

- Define project objectives
- Define the problem
- Collect information
- Develop options and alternatives
- Evaluate and decide course of action
- Ensure buy-in of the project team
- Implement the decision.

All these decision-making steps are intrinsically part of the control cycle. The decisions can now be made on what control to apply to keep the project on course.

Revise Baseline Plan: If there are any changes within the project the *baseline plan* must be revised to reflect the current scope of work and incorporate any corrective action. By saving the old *baseline plan* an audit trail of changes can be archived. The control cycle is now complete and the next cycle will authorise the changes and corrective action. If the project slips by more than 10%, it can be argued that the whole project should be rescheduled to introducing a sense of realism and attainability.

3. Reporting Frequency

The **frequency** of the reporting cycle should reflect the needs of the project. Short reporting periods, when there is a high level of change and uncertainty in the project, long periods when there is little or no change. For example, during project start up and during the commissioning phase the reporting cycle may be reduced to daily or even hourly, while under normal conditions the reporting cycle is usually weekly or monthly as outlined in the schedule of meetings (see *Project Communication* chapter).

As a rule of thumb the reporting cycle should leave sufficient time to implement corrective action to bring any project deviation back on course without delaying any critical activities. If the reporting is reasonably accurate the worst that can happen in a week, is you lose a week.

Parting thought from the SAS before they embark on military action; *"... the 6P's of planning are; Proper Planning Prevents Piss Poor Performance".*

Key Points:

- The planning and control cycle integrates and co-ordinates the contributions of all the project participants.
- Although the planning cycle may consist of many separate techniques, collectively a change in one parameter may change another parameter.
- The control cycle guides the project to a successful completion by monitoring performance and applying corrective action where necessary.

Case Study and Exercises:

The planning and control cycle integrates all the planning and control techniques into one document. All the contributions can now be co-ordinated, processed and disseminated. By integrating the techniques the relationship between parameters can be determined and managed (in isolation and together).

You have been appointed project manager to design, build and commission a Wind Farm on the Isle of Lewis. The plan it to line the coast with wind generators that can produce the equivalent power of two nuclear power stations!!! Although the islanders may be willing partners in accepting the project, there could be plenty of other obstacles. Your assignment is to prepare a presentation for a handover / start-up meeting to the project team and stakeholders. Some of the items to be discussed should include:

1. How you intend to develop the planning and control cycle.
2. How you intend to compile the baseline plan, manage it, update it and communicate it to the project team.
3. The role of the expeditor - the project managers' ears and eyes.
4. Reporting cycle, and how it may change during the project.
5. Project integration showing how the various parameters are related.

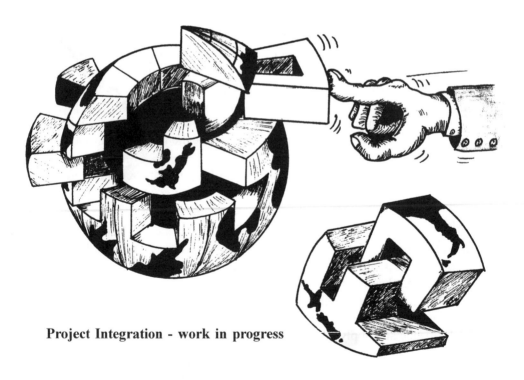

Project Integration - work in progress

Scope Management

Effective scope management is one of the key factors determining project success. Failure to accurately interpret the clients' needs or problems will produce a misleading definition (*scope of work*). If this causes rework and additional effort, there may be project cost and time implications. Therefore project success will be self-limiting if the *scope of work* is not adequately defined.

Scope management is defined by the PMBOK as; *'... the processes required to ensure that the project includes all the work required, and only the work required, to complete the project successfully. It is primarily concerned with defining and controlling what is or is not included in the project.'*

Scope management defines what the project will accomplish, what it will deliver, what it will produce and where the work packages start and finish. Since most projects seem to be riddled with fuzzy definitions, scope management takes on a greater importance to avoid scope creep, and avoid adding features and functionality to the product that were not part of the original project contract without an appropriate increase in time and budget.

1. Project Initiation

The PMBOK defines project initiation as; *'... the process of formally recognising that a new project exists, or that an existing project should continue into its next phase* [of the project life-cycle].*'*

Projects by definition have a start and finish, for a contracting company the start will probably be simple to identify - invitation to tender, or the award of contract. However, for the client organisation, the start of a project may not be so clear-cut. Some projects evolve as the embryo of an idea responding to market changes and new technology. In this environment, formal project recognition should be in the form of a *project charter* (with authority and budgets). It is important to distinguish between whims and ideas (white elephants) and items that could significantly benefit the company.

t Charter: Also called **terms of reference**, or **project mission**, should be a worded document outlining what is to be done and the boundaries of the project. For example the project could be to build an Olympic stadium for 100,000 people, to Olympic standards, to be complete six months before the start of the Olympics, for x million dollars.

Unless the aims of the project can be precisely defined in a few short words it could imply that the client is not clear exactly what they want to achieve. The *project charter* should also include:

- Background to the project
- Key assumptions
- Business needs, and other commercial needs
- Scope of work
- Identify key activities, budgets and dates
- Comment on how the project is to be managed
- Role of the project manager (responsibility and authority) and reporting structure.

The *project charter* essentially formalises the project and should be documented and signed off - if this is not done by senior management, then the onus falls on the project manager, because the *project charter* provides the project manager with the authority to apply company resources to the project.

The *project charter* will help you gain support and commitment from senior management. It may sometimes seem that senior management think that project risks are non-existent; that the project manager does not need any authority and that changes to the scope of work will never occur. Unfortunately, this is not the case; in fact it is just the opposite. Therefore, you need to develop a *project charter* that addresses these issues early on and get it approved. It will make the project managers job much easier later on, if you get sign-off on these issues at the outset.

2. Scope Planning

The PMBOK defines scope planning as; '*... the process of developing a written scope statement as the basis for future project decisions including, in particular, the criteria used to determine if the project or phase has been completed successfully.*' The scope planning outlines the project philosophy that:

- Defines the boundary of the project and confirms common understanding of the project scope amongst the stakeholders.
- Forms the basis of agreement between client and contractor by identifying both the project objectives and major deliverables.
- Is a guide and constraint for the configuration management process influencing change control. During the commissioning phase the scope planning will help to confirm that the project has been implemented to the required condition.

Scope planning develops a written statement that acts as the basis for future decisions and establishes a criteria for the completion of an activity, completion of a project phase, or the completion of the project itself. As the project progresses, the scope statement may need to be revised to reflect changes to the scope of the project.

3. Scope Definition

The PMBOK defines scope definition as; '... *subdividing the major project deliverables into smaller, more manageable components* ...' This will help to improve the accuracy of the estimate and assign single responsibility to the work packages (see the *Work Breakdown Structure* chapter).

The scope definition outlines the content of the project, how the project will be approached and explains how it will solve the client's needs or problems. Scope definition establishes a method to identify all the items of work that are required to complete the project. The **build method** outlines how the product will be built (or implemented) and the WBS can be used to provide a subdivision of the *scope of work* into manageable work packages. Responsibility can then be assigned to the work packages for accomplishment.

4. Scope Verification

The PMBOK defines scope verification as; '... *the process of formalising acceptance of the project scope by the stakeholders.*' Scope verification can be related to the phases of the *project life-cycle.* The *scope of work* should be formally approved at the end of each phase (after the *feasibility study* in the concept phase, and at the end of the design and development phase [before implementation]). All changes during the implementation phase should be formally approved, and again when the implementation is complete, the *scope of work* should be approved during the commissioning phase. These controls are essential to establish the *required condition* before implementation and after implementation, to confirm the *required condition* has been achieved.

5. Scope Change Control

The PMBOK defines scope change control as:
- (a) *Influencing the factors which create scope changes to ensure that changes are beneficial* [to the project].
- (b) *Determining that a scope change has occurred.*
- (c) *Managing the actual changes when and if they occur.*

All projects are subjected to scope changes at some time during their life-cycle. The scope change control system, or *configuration management* is a system designed to effectively manage the change of scope process. *Configuration management* is the process of identifying and managing change to the deliverables and other work products as they evolve through the *project life-cycle*. It helps ensure that the proposed changes are necessary, appropriate and that the integrity of the system is maintained.

The system should establish a framework to monitor, evaluate and approve the changes by the designated people before the change is incorporated into the revised *baseline plan*. This will ensure that the revised *baseline plan* always reflects the current status of the project. Change control is also concerned with influencing the factors that create changes to ensure that changes are beneficial. The scope change approval system should be agreed by all stakeholders at the outset and confirmed at the handover meeting. The *configuration management* system offers:

- A change control system that formally documents a procedure defining the steps by which official project documents may be changed.
- Lists the only people who have the authority to make changes to the scope of work, in both the client and contractor organisations.
- A current and up-to-date description of the product.
- Traceability of previous baseline configurations.
- A record and an audit trail of approved changes.
- A framework to monitor, evaluate and update the scope baseline to accommodate any scope changes. This will ensure that the revised baseline always reflects the current status of the project.
- Automatic approval for emergency situations.

The *project life-cycle* clearly outlines two aspects of the *configuration management* system that have a similar scope change approval system, but different budgetary structures:

- Scope design and development
- Scope changes

Scope Design and Development: During the design and development phase, the project brief and proposal are developed into detailed design drawings and specifications. The *configuration management* process here is to guide the design process and develop the scope baseline. The *configuration management* system formalises the design management process by capturing all the proposed scope developments. Before the scope baseline is revised these developments must be quantified, assessed, verified, integrated and approved by the authorised people. Only then will the scope baseline be updated and work authorised for execution. The financial implications of these scope approvals should be included in the project's budget.

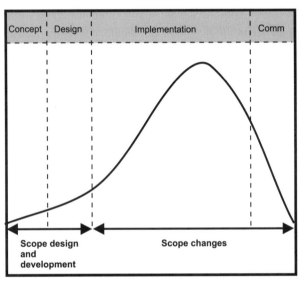

Figure 8.1: Scope Changes

Scope Change Control System: These scope changes would need to go through a similar system of approval against the design philosophy, but now the changes may impact on contractual time and budget agreements. If a change falls within the project proposal, this should be considered as a design development. However, if the change falls outside the proposal framework then the change should be considered as additional to contract and may attract a time extension and additional costs. This is why it is most important to establish a comprehensive proposal (scope planning) as a basis to allocate the cost of these changes.

It is important, particularly on large complex projects, that any scope changes are only approved by the nominated technical experts. This will not only prevent scope changes by do-gooders shooting from the hip, but also ensure that all implications of the proposed changes have been considered. Consider the following (figure 8.2):

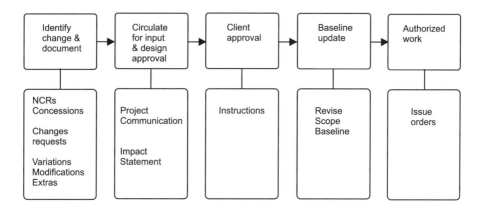

Figure 8.2: Configuration Control Flow Chart

Scope Changes: The control system should allow for scope changes to be motivated by anyone working on the project. Consider the following:

- **Non conformance report** (NCR) usually initiated by quality control when someone has worked outside a procedure, or the product is outside the *required condition*. The non-conformance would either be corrected and fall away or motivate a concession.
- A **concession** requests the client to accept an item that has been built and is functional, but out of specification. If approved this would be shown as a scope change for this project only, it would be shown on the as-built drawings, but not on the master drawings.
- **Change requests** modifications and variations request the client to approve a change to the scope baseline.
- Any **verbal** comments or instructions which change the scope of work should be backed up in writing with a **project communication** document, as verbal agreements are open to dispute.

Change Request: Using a numbered change request form is the preferred method of motivating a scope change. The form should describe the scope change, list associated drawings and documents, together with the reason for the change (see figure 8.3).

Project Communication: The project communication form enables any stakeholder working on the project, to make a formal statement. This could be a question, identifying a problem or making a suggestion. Once the document has entered the system the *configuration management* system will ensure that it is acknowledged and actioned (see figure 8.4).

CHANGE REQUEST			
NUMBER :		DATE RAISED :	
INITIATED BY :			
CHANGE REQUESTED (related drawings / work packages):			
REASON FOR CHANGE :			
APPROVAL:			
NAME	POSITION	APPROVAL	DATE

V

Figure 8.3: Change Request (proforma)

PROJECT COMMUNICATION	
NUMBER: DATE RAISED: INITIATED BY: DESCRIPTION (related drawings / work packages):	
COMMENTS / INSTRUCTIONS:	
WE ACKNOWLEDGE YOUR ENQUIRY / INSTRUCTION: VERBAL FROM: TO: WRITTEN FROM: TO: DATE:	
PLEASE ADVISE HOW WE ARE TO PROCEED: 1. START IMMEDIATELY AND QUOTE WITHIN 7 DAYS 2. START IMMEDIATELY ON UNIT RATES 3. DO NOT START, QUOTE WITHIN 7 DAYS 4. OTHER	
REQUEST FROM: INSTRUCTION FROM: CONTRACTOR CLIENT PROJECT MANAGER PROJECT MANAGER	

Figure 8.4: Project Communication (proforma)

Impact Statement: The impact statement quantifies the implications of making a proposed change. The impact statement generally follows the clients response from the project communication, but in reality it is usually issued at the same time. An information pack is now compiled to collect input, information, comments and approval from the responsible parties.

- Design team (prepare information pack)
- Technical impact (can we make it? What is the impact on the build method)
- Procurement impact (can we buy it?)
- Production impact (do we have the resources?)
- Planning impact (will it delay the project?)
- Cost impact (will it increase the budget?)
- Quality impact (can we achieve the quality requirement?)
- Risk impact (are the risks acceptable?)
- Legal impact (will it change the contract?)
- Project manager approve / reject
- Client approve / reject

All the above documents should be numbered consecutively with a summary sheet showing the present status (see figure 8.5). The client's approval formally authorizes the scope change into the production system - this completes the configuration management control cycle.

IMPACT STATEMENT

NUMBER: DATE RAISED:
INITIATED BY:
DESCRIPTION:(related drawings / work packages)

REFERENCE PROJECT COMMUNICATION:

IMPACT ON PROJECT:		IF YES QUANTIFY
TECHNICAL:	YES/NO	
PROCUREMENT:	YES/NO	
PRODUCTION:	YES/NO	
SCHEDULE:	YES/NO	
COST:	YES/NO	
QUALITY:	YES/NO	
CONTRACT:	YES/NO	
RISK:	YES/NO	

PLEASE ADVISE IF WE ARE TO PROCEED: YES/NO

REQUEST FROM: INSTRUCTION FROM:

CONTRACTOR   CLIENT
PROJECT MANAGER   PROJECT MANAGER

Figure 8.5: Impact Statement (proforma)

Flow Sheet: A flow sheet is used to control the movement of the change requests and impact statements. The flow sheet determines the sequence of circulation, it logs the documents in and out of departments and collects comments, calculations and information, but most importantly it notes the acceptance or rejection of the proposed change (see figure 8.6).

IMPACT STATEMENT FLOW SHEET

IMPACT NUMBER:

DESCRIPTION:

POSITION	DATE IN	DATE OUT	COMMENTS
PROJECT MANAGER			
DRAWING OFFICE			
PROJECT ENGINEER			
PROCUREMENT MANAGER			
PRODUCTION MANAGER			
PROJECT PLANNER			
PROJECT ACCOUNTANT			
QA MANAGER			
COMPANY LAWYER			

Figure 8.6: Flow Sheet (proforma)

There are two possible methods of controlling the movement of the document:
    a) Hub and spoke (see figure 8.7)
    b) Consecutive (see figure 8.8)

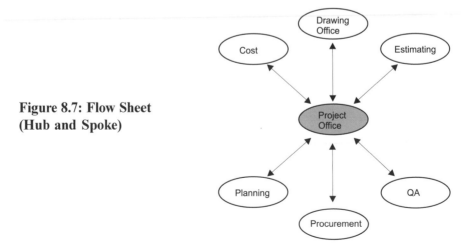

**Figure 8.7: Flow Sheet
(Hub and Spoke)**

Figure 8.8: Flow sheet (Consecutive)

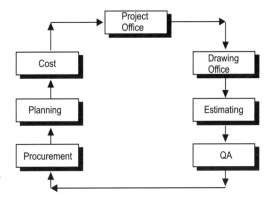

Although the hub and spoke arrangement doubles the movement of the documents, it does enable the project office to know where the documents are at any time. With the consecutive method the lines of communication may be shorter, but if the documents do not reappear timeously, it will require a time consuming witch hunt to find them.

6. Project Closeout

It is important to not only learn from the mistakes and successes of previous projects, but also learn progressively during the present project. The project closeout report can be subdivided into three sections:

- Compile historical data from previous projects to assist conceptual development, *feasibility study* and estimating on future projects.
- Compile historical data from previous projects and the current project to identify trends and potential problem areas on the current project.
- Recommendations on how to manage future projects.

Historical Data: The search for historical data from previous projects will clearly show the benefit of effective closeout reports and filing. Learning from previous experiences is the most basic form of development and it is essentially free. There are, however, limitations with historical data, the correlation between projects may be tenuous. Consider the following:

- The scope of work between projects is unlikely to be exactly the same.
- The cost data will be influenced by inflation
- The manhours will be influenced by automation
- The build methods may be different
- The project manager and leadership style will probably be different
- The client and stakeholders will probably be different.

However, having made certain allowances for any limitations there should be a wealth of similarities. Look closely to see what went right and what went wrong together with any recommendations, because the same mistakes have an uncanny habit of happening again, particularly if the cause has not been addressed.

Project Closeout Report: A closeout report can be generated at the end of each month, project phase, the end of your contract and the end of the project itself. It is advisable to compile the report before the project participants disperse. For best results a structured report format is recommended - consider the following steps:

- Generate a short questionnaire and circulate it to all the key project participants.
- Analyse responses and debrief the key managers.
- Compile draft closeout report for comments. This can also be used as an agenda for a formal closeout meeting.
- Hold a formal closeout meeting attended by all the available participants.
- Compile the final closeout report, circulate it and file it.

An evaluation differs from a status report in that it considers the entire project life-cycle; management systems are evaluated, achievement of objectives are noted, budget comparisons are made, outstanding issues are identified, together with the issues that contribute to the success or failure of the project. The emphasis is on feedback with an open forum. However, resistance may be experienced if closeout reports are new to your company and the benefits not fully appreciated.

Questionnaire: The main benefit of the questionnaire approach is to structure the responses. It must be made quite clear that this exercise is not a **search for the guilty** but an attempt to quantify what actually happened on the project. The net should be cast reasonably wide to include a broad range of opinions. The list of participants should certainly include the following:

- Client
- Project team
- Corporate participants
- Suppliers and subcontractors
- Stakeholders

The questionnaire would typically be structured to include the following questions:

- Identify your position in the project organisation structure and comment on the interfacing with other disciplines.
- Comment on the delegation of responsibility and authority.
- Briefly outline your assigned scope of work.
- Comment on planning schedules, budgets, quality and manpower performance. Where possible quantify performance with statistical data.
- Give a candid assessment of your performance, analysing what went right and what went wrong. Comment on any non conformance reports (NCR) with reasons for any deviations and the level of re-work. If audits were conducted comment on their findings.
- Comment on the lines of communication, the issuing of instructions, the holding of meetings, the availability of information, procedures and reporting.
- Evaluate design and technical changes, as-built drawings and operator manuals.
- Comment on any scope changes and concessions. Evaluate how smoothly the configuration system worked - were the changes approved and implemented timeously.
- Discuss the use of new technology, computerisation and automation.

- Discuss any unexpected problems, how they affected the project and their solutions.
- Comment on the performance of procurement suppliers and subcontractors.
- Comment on manpower performance, their training and any industrial relation problems.
- Evaluate the accuracy of the estimate and list any recommended changes to the company's tariffs.
- Evaluate the contract document and any legal issues.
- Give general recommendations for future projects.

Some participants may be burning to give you their opinion, while others may be reluctant to commit their views on paper. Always be on the lookout for soft data, a simple gesture may speak a thousand words.

Recommendations: Learning from achievements and mistakes and improving productivity are basic economic requirements to fuel sustained commercial competitiveness. These recommendations can provide an invaluable source of direction for future projects. The closeout report should highlight any recommendations simply and clearly, because many years from now this may be the only section that is read.

Besides assisting with the estimating, recommendations from the previous closeout reports should also be tabled at the handover meetings. During the project, take a leaf out of the sports teams book - they watch videos of their games to critique their performance, so they can continually improve their game plan.

Validating the project estimate is essential. Over estimating will generate good profits, but in a competitive market will reduce the chance of winning further tenders. While under pricing will simply reduce company profits. Wherever possible the analysis should indicate perceived trends. These may be in technology, build methods or project management systems. The final statement should comment on the overall success of the project and advise if the company is wise to tender on these types of projects again.

This concludes the chapter on *Scope Management*, the following chapter will discuss the *Work Breakdown Structure* as a methodology for subdividing the *scope of work*.

Key Points:

- It is essential to accurately define the *scope of work* at the outset to limit expensive changes.
- Your project needs an effective change control system to accommodate the changes that invariably happen.
- Produce a closeout report for others to learn from your experiences.

Further Reading:

PMI, PMBOK
Turner, Rodney, *Handbook of Project-Based Management*, McGraw-Hill

Case Study and Exercises:

Scope management defines the purpose of the project by outlining what the project should achieve, together with what should be included in the project, and just as importantly - what should be excluded from the project. For your case study you have been appointed to project manage the refit of a 'super yacht'. Outline how you will manage the scope. Your presentation (written or verbal) should consider the following:

1. Outline how the project charter will establish the boundaries of the project, together with the responsibilities and authority of the project manager.
2. Outline how the scope of work will be defined.
3. There will always be changes to the scope of work. Outline how the proposed system will capture and process any changes.
4. Outline how documents associated with scope management will be communicated and controlled.
5. It is important to learn from the mistakes and successes of your projects. Outline how you will progressively closeout your project.

"It was a good project. It will be missed"

Work Breakdown Structure

The purpose of the *work breakdown structure* (WBS) is to subdivide the scope of work into manageable work packages that can be estimated, planned and assigned to a responsible person or department for completion. The breakdown should group similar work together to improve productive efficiency, built method and executive strategy.

The WBS was originally developed in the 1960's as part of the drive towards improved project definition and it soon became the backbone of the planning and control system. The WBS is an excellent tool for quantifying the *scope of work* as a list of work packages and is an essential tool for ensuring the estimate or quotation includes the complete *scope of work*. The WBS can also be considered as a hierarchical form of mind map that helps to break complexity down into simple manageable components.

Turner defines the WBS as: *'..... a cascade of deliverables, in which the overall product or objective of the project is broken into sub-products, assemblages and components.'*

The main components of the WBS that will be discussed in this chapter are:
- Structure
- Methods of subdivision
- Numbering or coding system
- Level of detail
- Number of WBS levels
- Roll-up
- Integrating the WBS/OBS to assign responsibility.

Work Package: In this chapter the work packages are shown with short description and later with a number. On your projects you may consider also including the following:

- Specifications
- Quality requirements
- Estimate (manhours)
- Budgets

- Duration
- Procurement
- Resources
- Equipment requirements

1. The WBS Structure

There are two methods of presenting the WBS:
- Graphically in boxes
- Text indents.

The WBS is a hierarchical structure which is best presented by a **graphical** subdivision of the *scope of work* in boxes. This logical subdivision of all the work elements is easy to understand and assimilate, thus helping the project participants to quantify their responsibility and gain their commitment and support (see figure 9.1).

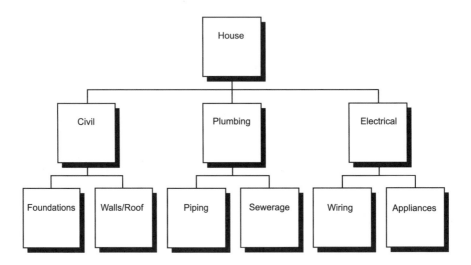

Figure 9.1: House Project WBS Subdivided into Boxes

Although boxes are an excellent means of presentation it is a cumbersome document to develop and edit on the computer. Boxes lend themselves more to graphic software than planning software and the printout for a large project would look best from a commercial printer rather than sticking A4 or A3 sheets together.

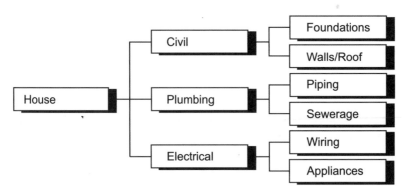

Figure 9.2: WBS Horizontal Presentation (a simple rotation of figure 9.1)

The other method of presentation shows the *scope of work* as **text indents**, where each level is tabbed to represent its level in the hierarchy. If you are using planning software you will have to setup this structure anyway as you input the project data.

1.0.0 House Project
    1.1.0 Civil
        1.1.1 Foundations
        1.1.2 Walls and roof
    1.2.0 Plumbing
        1.2.1 Piping
        1.2.2 Sewerage
    1.3.0 Electrical
        1.3.1 Wiring
        1.3.2 Appliances

Here figures 9.1 and 9.2 are now presented as text indents which is how you would input the information into a planning software package.

2. Method of Sub-Division

Designing the WBS requires a delicate balance to address the different needs of the various disciplines and project locations. There is not necessarily a right or wrong structure because what may be an excellent fit for one discipline may be an awkward burden for another.

As you will see there are many methods of subdividing the *scope of work*, your imagination is the only limiting factor. The best method is the one that works for you and you may use more than one method as the project progresses.

Product Breakdown Structure (PBS): This represents a hierarchical view of the physical assemblies, sub-assemblies, components and parts needed to manufacture the product. Consider the subdivision of an aeroplane (see figure 9.3):

Figure 9.3: Product Breakdown Structure (Aeroplane)

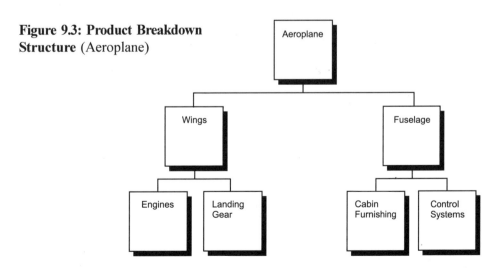

Organisation Breakdown Structure (OBS): This represents a hierarchy of the company managing the project. By linking the OBS with the WBS or PBS this will identify who is responsible for performing the work packages (see figure 9.18 shown later in this chapter). The OBS could contain any of the following subdivisions (see figure 9.4):

- Department or discipline
- Contractor or supplier
- Project team or person.

Figure 9.4: Organisation Breakdown Structure

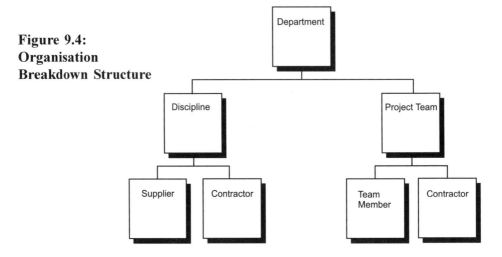

Cost Breakdown Structure (CBS): This represents the financial breakdown of the project into budgets per work package (see figure 9.5). Facilitating top down budgets, and bottom-up estimating.

Figure 9.5: Cost Breakdown Structure (by cost centre and supplier)

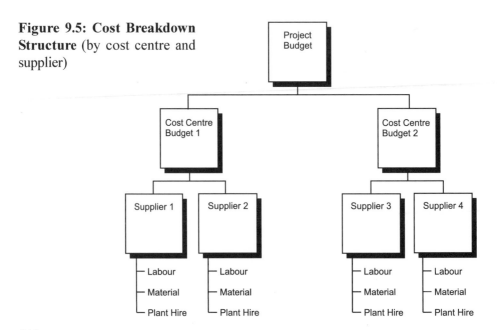

Contract Breakdown Structure also **(CBS):** This represents the relationships between the client with the contractor. At the lowest level this could link the purchase orders with the account invoices (see figure 9.6).

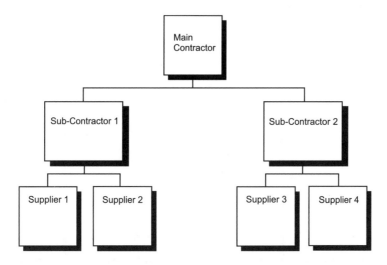

Figure 9.6: Contract Breakdown Structure (by sub-contractor and supplier)

Location Breakdown Structure: This represents the physical location of the work and would be appropriate for a project that has work packages at many sites or locations. Consider a power line project where there may be a number of similar substations along the route (see figure 9.7).

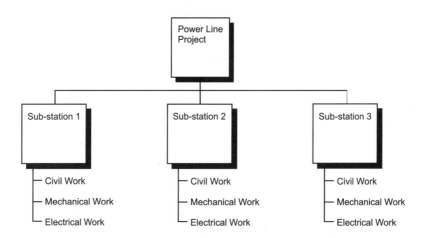

Figure 9.7: Location Breakdown Structure (power line project)

Transport Breakdown Structure: Projects that are characterised by large loads may find that transport and cranage limitations determine their breakdown structure (see figure 9.8).

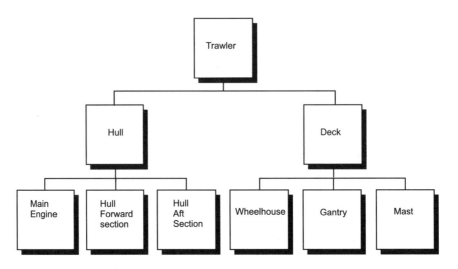

Figure 9.8: Transport Breakdown Structure (with largest units that can be transported by road)

System Breakdown Structure: This represents a systems breakdown that may cut across other breakdown structures, but would be useful when commissioning the project. Consider the following house building project (see figure 9.9).

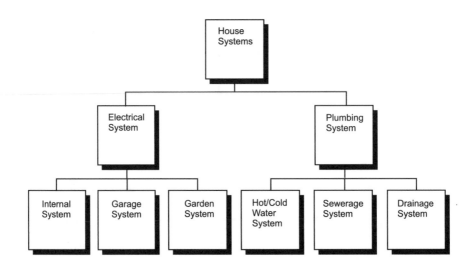

Figure 9.9: System Breakdown Structure (House project)

Project Life-Cycle Structure: This represents a logical subdivision of the sequence of work into project phases (see figure 9.10). This is discussed in the *Project Life-Cycle* chapter.

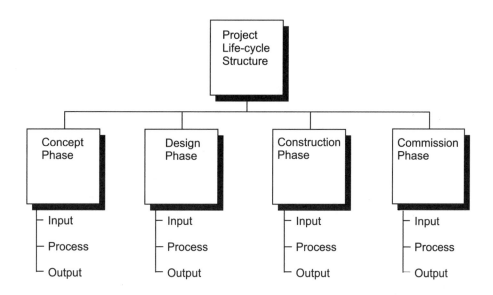

Figure 9.10: Project Life-Cycle Structure

Each element in the WBS needs to be identified by a short description. Although the length of the description may be restricted by the size of the box, the meaning should be clear. As these examples have shown there are many ways of subdividing a project, with some methods being more appropriate than others. The best results are generally gained by using an iterative and heuristic approach that considers a range of subdivisions until an appropriate structure is derived.

3. WBS Templates

Although location and discipline are popular criteria for subdivision, managers sometimes find difficulty thinking of methods to subdivide their projects. In practice companies that use the WBS, often set up a standard WBS proforma or template for their projects. Instead of starting each project with a blank sheet of paper, consider using a WBS from a previous project as a template. A standard WBS ensures consistency and completeness as it becomes a planning checklist with all the components that your particular type of project would contain. Having a structured checklist also reduces the risk of omitting the obvious.

Even if the complete WBS template cannot be used, there may be portions of the template which are similar and can be copied across. Using proven structures will greatly speed up the planning process and help to structure your thinking. Figure 9.11 below outlines a WBS where the first level is subdivided by location, the second level by discipline and the third level by expense. This format could be used as a standard WBS for the company. The only changes per project would be to the description rather than the structure.

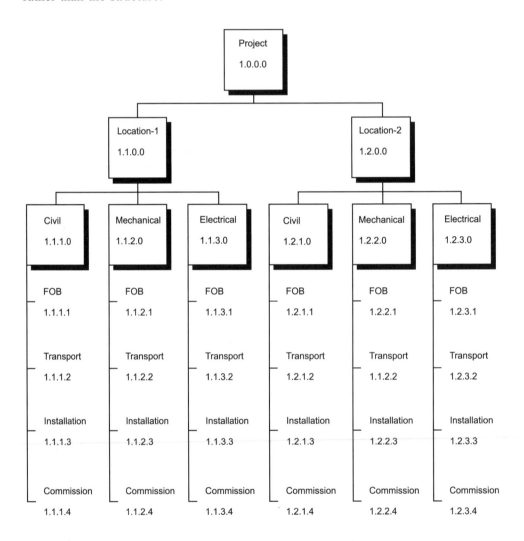

Figure 9.11: WBS Standard Format or Template (this can be used on similar types of projects) Note: FOB = free on board a ship, train or road transport)

4. How Many WBS Levels?

With each level of the WBS the *scope of work* is subdivided into more work packages with a corresponding increase in the level of detail. For practical purposes three or four levels should be sufficient to achieve the desired level of planning and control - any more than that and like a pyramid the base of the WBS would start to become unwieldy. The number of levels is influenced by:

- Level of detail
- Level of risk
- Level of control
- Estimated accuracy
- Work package value
- Work package manhours.

If more than three or four levels are required this can be addressed by using sub-projects, where the lowest level work package of one project constitutes the highest level of another project. This situation is common on projects where a main contractor uses many subcontractors. In this way, the WBS can effectively increase the number of breakdown levels, with each project manager focusing on their own *scope of work* and responsibility.

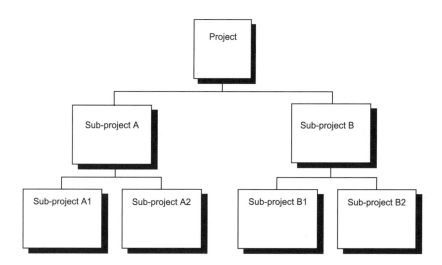

Figure 9.12: WBS Breakdown by Sub-Projects (with each project manager focusing on their own scope of work)

Project Control: The appropriate level of control relates to the complexity and risks embedded in the project. Project control is the ability to steer the project to a successful completion. The *earned value* technique may suggest an appropriate $ value, duration or workhours for the work packages (see figure 9.12).

Risk and Uncertainty: The WBS structure should reflect the level of risk and uncertainty in the project. Where the level of risk is high the WBS can be subdivided further to generate more information and thus (possibly) reduce the risk. Consider the figure 9.13, where selected areas of high risk have been subdivided to a lower level.

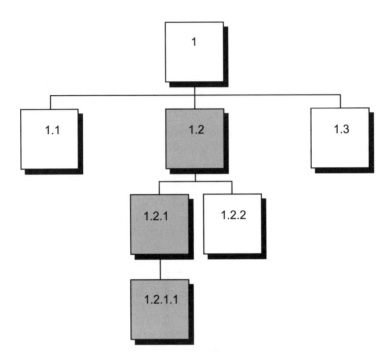

Figure 9.13: WBS (subdivided by level of risk and uncertainty)

5. Estimating

If your company wins contracts by competitive bidding it is important to have a system for generating accurate quotations quickly. The WBS offers a top down subdivision of the work, while estimating at the work package level, offers a bottom up roll-up of project costs. The WBS reduces the possibility of overlaps and underlaps. Overlaps of work cause conflict, while underlaps can be expensive - forgetting an item on a fixed price contract would be to your account. The **accuracy** of the estimate will increase progressively as the work package's level of detail increases. As a rough guide the level of accuracy should be at least the same as, or better than, the project's profit margin.

6. The Numbering System

One of the beneficial features of the WBS is its ability to uniquely identify by a number or code all the elements of work in a numerical and logical manner. With a unique number, all work packages can be linked to the project's schedule, purchase orders, resources, accounts, together with the corporate accounts and the client's accounts. If all your projects use a similar numbering system this will make it easy to retrieve information (actual costs and duration) from past projects' data bases and closeout reports.

The numbering system can be alphabetic, numeric, or alphanumeric (letters and numbers), in most of the examples here the numbering systems will be numeric. Consider the following example:

Level 0: The first number [1.0.0] represents the first work element on the level zero. It is normal practice to have only one item at this level i.e. the total project. The project may have its own unique number, see figures 9.14 and 9.15.

Level 1: At the first level of subdivision the first work element will be numbered [1.1.0] and the second work element numbered [1.2.0]. Thus the other work elements will be numbered sequentially; [1.3.0], [1.4.0], [1.5.0] etc.

Level 2: These numbers are then further subdivided at the second level from the first element at the second level into [1.1.1], [1.1.2], [1.1.3], [1.1.4] etc.

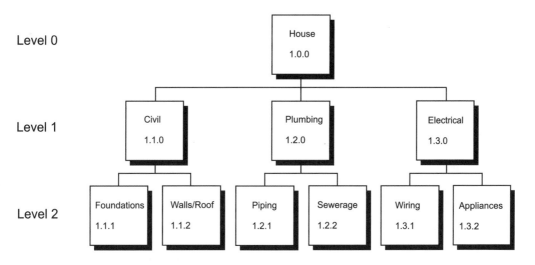

Figure 9.14: WBS Sub-Division by Numbering System

125

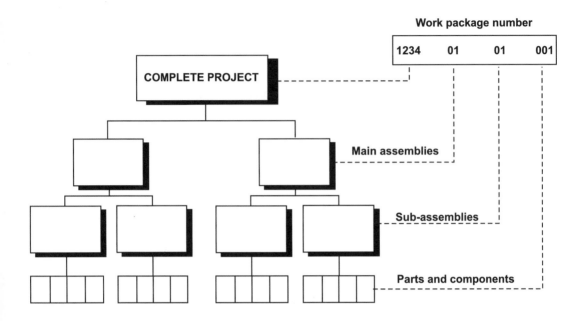

Figure 9.15: WBS Numbering System (this example shows how the numbering system can lead to very long work package numbers)

Project Number: Most projects are given a project number and a description to distinguish them from all the other projects the company may be working on. The project number may come from a number of sources:

- Estimate number
- Quotation number
- Contract number
- Invoice number
- Purchase order number
- Client's order number.

Many projects also have a **name** or humorous nickname to help association. Marine projects would use the ship's name. London's city airport was originally known as the STOL port (short take off and landing). With increased computer graphics a project icon is also a consideration.

7. WBS Roll-up

The roll-up facility is normally used to roll-up project costs for budget planning and control purposes. By suitably structuring the WBS, budgets can be established per department, per location or per subcontractor (see figure 9.16).

Figure 9.16 : Roll-Up House Project

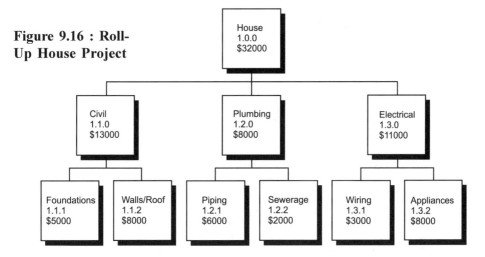

The WBS roll-up technique lends itself to anything that flows in the project, i.e. manhours, lines of software code, cubic meters of concrete, tonnes of steel erected, bricks laid, drawings completed, square meters of paint etc. Any of these could be planned, tracked and controlled using the WBS.

Consider a Drawing Office project where it would be more appropriate to plan and track manhours rather than costs. This is because the chief draughtsman can estimate the time required to complete a drawing from experience, but may not have the data necessary to estimate the costs involved (see figure 9.17).

Figure 9.17: Exercise - Drawing Office Project
(where Mh = manhours)

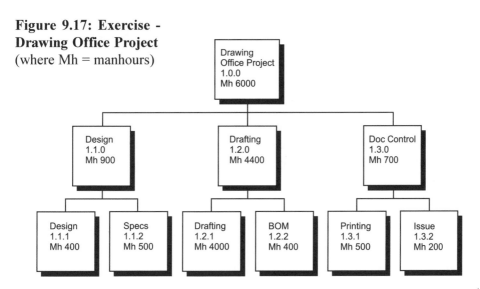

8. Responsibility

Assigning responsibility for performing project work is one of the key project management functions. This can be achieved through the interface between the WBS and the *organisation breakdown structure* (OBS). The WBS / OBS links clearly indicates the work packages and the person responsible for carrying out the work, however it is a rather cumbersome presentation as the level of detail increases. For this reason it is best suited to high level links (see figure 9.18).

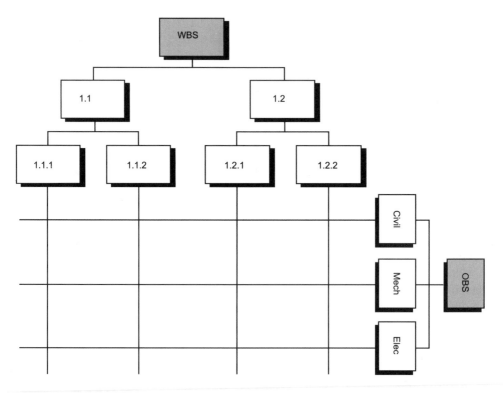

Figure 9.18: WBS / OBS Links

The WBS/OBS links can also be shown simpler and easier on the *schedule barchart*, by either using a responsibility field (also called a responsibility matrix) or printing the persons's name after the activity (See *Schedule Barchart* chapter).

9. Foreign Currency

Some projects are characterised by international procurement from a number of countries. As these exchange rates are prone to fluctuate, then your risk management analysis will need to determine the extent of your exposure to each foreign currency. This can be achieve by structuring the WBS to roll-up a number of foreign currencies and report the total requirement for each (see figure 9.19).

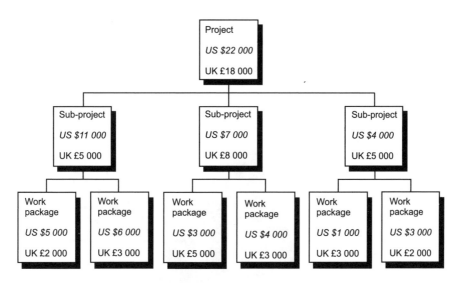

Figure 9.19: WBS by Foreign Currency

The WBS does not indicate when the foreign currency is required, for this you will have to develop the cash-flow statement through the *critical path method* (CPM) which is the topic of the following chapter.

Key Points:

- The WBS subdivides the project into manageable work packages.
- On fixed price contracts the WBS helps to ensure the quotation includes the full *scope of work*.
- The WBS numbering systems uniquely identifies all the work packages.

Further Reading:

Turner, Rodney, *Handbook of Project-Based Management,* McGraw-Hill

Case Study and Exercises:

The WBS subdivides the scope of work into manageable work packages that can be estimated, planned, and assigned to a responsible person or department for completion. You have been appointed project manager (event manager) for a Rolling Stones concert. Outline how you would use the WBS to subdivide the event, considering the following:

1. Methods of subdivision.
2. Develop standard template for future events.
3. Numbering system.
4. Number of levels.
5. What information would you roll-up?

Critical Path Method

For project managers to effectively plan and control a project, they need to be able to process large amounts of data quickly and accurately to enable them to create order in a complex situation. The *critical path method* (CPM) offering a structured approach to project planning, has been designed to meet this need.

This chapter will outline the techniques and practical applications of CPM, taking you step-by-step through the planning stages from developing the logical *network diagram* through to establishing the critical path. Although CPM was originally developed to quantify the **time cost trade-off**, the term is now used interchangeably with PERT. These generic names are understood to mean both time planning on its own, or to incorporate the complete integrated planning and control cycle.

1. Network Diagram (part 1)

The *work breakdown structure* (WBS) provides a structured breakdown of the scope of work into manageable work packages that can be further developed into a list of activities (see *WBS* chapter). The next process is to establish a logical relationship between the activities using a *network diagram.*

The *network diagram* may be defined as a graphical presentation of the project's activities showing the planned sequence of work. In its simplest form only two items of information are required:
- List of activities
- Logic constraints, also called logical links, logical dependency or logical relationships between the activities.

The *network diagram,* also called *precedence diagram method* (PDM) is a development of the *activity-on-node* (AON) (see *History* chapter) concept where each activity is represented as a node or a box.

2. Definition of an Activity (part 1)

An activity may be defined as any task, job or operation that must be performed to complete the work package or project. A WBS work package can be subdivided into one or more activities, with the work packages and activities using different numbering systems. The terms activity, task, work and job are often used interchangeably. In the *network diagram* an activity is always represented by an identity number, which can be alpha and/or numeric and is presented in a box. The activity should be given a description to ensure the project team members understand the work content - this can be expanded later on a job card.

3. Logical Relationships (part 1)

The *network diagram* shows the sequence of the activities where these logical relationships can be either mandatory or discretionary. **Mandatory** or hard dependencies are limitations of the build method, for example, on a construction project the foundations **must** (hard logic) be built before the walls and roof are erected, whereas scheduling the electrical work before the plumbing work is discretionary (soft logic). **Discretionary** logic is the preferred or best practice defined by the body of knowledge. Before we can draw the *network diagram* we must define the logical relationships between all the activities. There are two basic relationships:

- Activities in *series*
- Activities in *parallel*.

Activities in Series: When the activities are in series they are carried out one after the other. When the network is first developed this would probably be the most common type of relationship. An example of activities performed in series on a house project would be the foundation (activity A100), followed by the walls (A200), followed by the roof (A300). Read the *network diagram* as you would a page of writing, the project starts on the (top) left side and moves to the right and downwards (see figure 10.1).

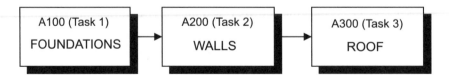

Figure 10.1: Activities in Series

Activities in Parallel: When activities are in parallel they can be performed at the same time, which is a more efficient use of time than activities in series. An example on a house project would be the installation of plumbing (activity A400) and electrical fittings (A500) simultaneously after the roof is fitted (A300), followed by the painting (A600) (see figure 10.2).

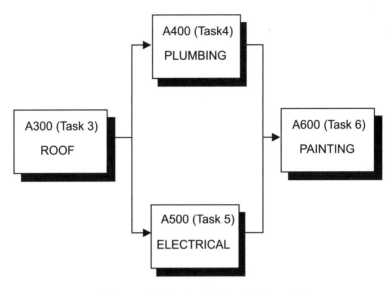

Figure 10.2: Activities in Parallel

4. How to Draw the Logical Relationships (part 1)

The terms logical relationship, constraint, dependency and link are all used interchangeably to represent the lines drawn between the activity boxes. The preferred presentation shows the constraint lines drawn from left to right, starting from the right side of one activity box into the left side of the following box. However, many software packages have the lines drawn from the top and bottom of the boxes. Initially an arrow at the end of the constraint may help you to follow the direction of work flow.

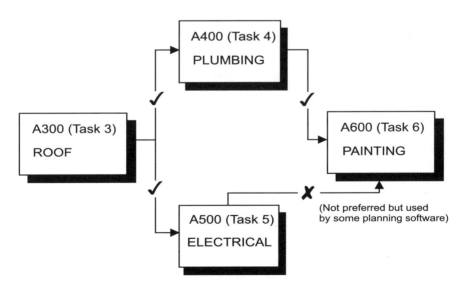

Figure 10.3: How to Draw Activity Constraints

In the past some projects were developed using yellow stickers (as activities) positioned on a large wall. Now with relatively cheap, but powerful planning software it would be rare not to develop a large project on the computer. When viewing the *network diagram* of large projects on the screen or printing them out, most software offers you the facility to control the amount of information in the boxes, reducing the detail right down to only the activity number for a condensed picture. To print out a detailed *network diagram* would be a lengthy task - one client showed me their detailed *network diagram* which would have covered a tennis court!

5. Activity Logic Table (part 1)

For ease of reading, logic information is often compiled in a tabular format, with each record (or line) defining a relationship. Planning software usually names the before and after activities as preceding and succeeding activities as detailed below (see tables 10.1 and 10.2):

Before Activity	Constraint	Following Activity

Table 10.1: Activity Logic Table

Preceding Activity	Constraint	Succeeding Activity

Table 10.2: Activity Logic Table

Using the activity logic in table 10.3, walk through the following worked example (see figure 10.4) where the activities and constraints are labelled.

Preceding Activity	Constraint	Suceeding Activity
Start	C1	A100
A100	C2	A200
A100	C3	A300
A200	C4	A400
A300	C5	A500
A400	C6	A600
A500	C7	A600
A600	C8	Finish

Table 10.3: Activity Logic Table (CPM example)

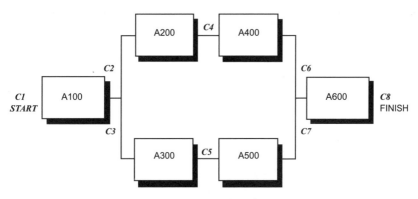

Figure 10.4: Network Diagram
(drawn from table 10.3, C = constraint)

Even if the logic table is not manually generated by the planner, the planning software will compile the logic data in this format. It is therefore useful for the planners to be familiar with this presentation to enable them to validate the network data. A common format for both input and presentation is simply to look at an activity and its preceding activity. Consider the above example (table 10.3 and figure 10.4) and transpose the logic into the table below (see solution on next page):

Activity	Preceding Activity	Duration
A100		2
A200		2
A300		1
A400		4
A500		2
A600		2

Table 10.4a: Activity Logic Table (for solution see table 10.4b)

Some planners prefer to sketch out a rough draft of the *network diagram* using a pencil and plenty of eraser before loading it on the computer. The intention here is to predict what will happen downstream in the project. A common problem when developing the *network diagram* is to introduce activities on the basis of time rather than logic. At this point in the planning process think only of the sequence of the activities - as the constraints of duration, procurement, resources and costs will be introduced later.

Activity	Preceding Activity	Duration
A100	start	2
A200	A100	2
A300	A100	1
A400	A200	4
A500	A300	2
A600	A400, A500	2

Table 10.4b: Solution to Table 10.4a

6. Activity Duration (part 1)

We need two more items of information before we can proceed with the CPM time analysis:
- Activity duration
- Activity calendar or work pattern.

Time units can be expressed as hours, days, weeks, months, or shifts depending on the length of the activities and the project. For simplicity, the time units used in this book will be days (unless otherwise stated), and in part 1 of this chapter we will assume continuous working (seven days a week). An activity's duration will run from the start to the finish of the activity. An activity's duration is linked to resources - increasing the resources will obviously shorten the duration. At this point certain assumptions will have to be made and adjusted later.

7. Calendar / Work Pattern (part 1)

Calendar or **work pattern** are common terms used in the planning software to describe an activity's working profile, in other words, on what days of the week the resources or activity will be working. As a first step we will assume the activity is working seven days a week, this is usually termed **continuous** working.

8. Critical Path Method Steps (part 1)

We are now ready to perform the CPM time analysis to establish the start and finish dates for all the activities. Before we do, let us first recap on the CPM steps we have outlined:
- Draw the logic network diagram
- Assign durations to all the activities
- Impose a work calendar.

In addition to the logic table, an activity table would include the following headings (see table 10.5):

Activity Number	Description	Duration	Calendar

Table 10.5: Activity Logic Table (proforma)

Start Date: We need to give the project a start date (this can always be changed later). The CPM analysis needs a start date from which to schedule the work, if no date is given the planning software would use today's date as the default option. By setting the start date the first iteration will give the planner a feel for the end date of the project using the given logic, activity duration and calendar. If a target completion date is given, the above parameters (logic, duration, calendar and start date), can be adjusted accordingly.

Early Start: The earliest date by which an activity can start assuming all the preceding activities are completed as planned.

Early Finish: The earliest date by which an activity can be completed assuming all the preceding activities are completed as planned.

Late Start: The latest date an activity can start to meet the planned completion date.

Late Finish: The latest date an activity can finish to meet the planned completion date.

Target Start and **Target Finish:** In addition to the calculated dates there may be a number of imposed dates, influenced by the delivery of materials, access to sub-contractors, or other milestones.

Activity Box: The activity box key indicates where to position the values in the activity box. This layout varies with the software package, but the format in figure 10.5 will be used throughout this book.

EARLY START		EARLY FINISH
FLOAT	ACTIVITY NUMBER DESCRIPTION	DURATION
LATE START		LATE FINISH

Figure 10.5: Activity Box (typical layout)

9. Forward Pass (part 1)

We use the term forward pass to define the process of calculating the *early start* date (ES) and *early finish* date (EF) for all the activities. For convenience the *early start* date of the first activity in all the examples will be either day one or the first day of the month (i.e. 1st May).

Consider a simple project with two activities A and B. The relationship between A and B is *finish-to-start*, this means activity A must be completed before B can start.

Activity Number	Preceding Activity	Duration
A	-	3
B	A	4

Table 10.6: Activity Logic Table

Figure 10.6: Forward Pass

The *early finish* date of an activity is calculated by adding the activity duration to the *early start* date, using the following formula.

EF = ES + Duration - 1

In the equation the minus one is required to keep the mathematics correct. The barchart in figure 10.7, will clarify this requirement. Shown as a barchart it can be clearly seen that a three day activity that starts on day 1 will finish on day 3.

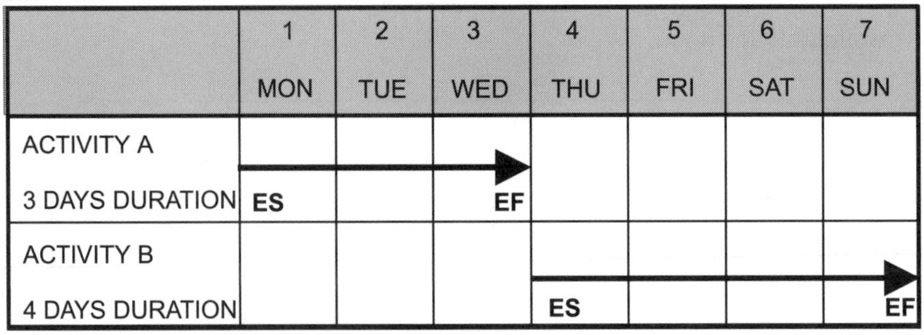

	1	2	3	4	5	6	7
	MON	TUE	WED	THU	FRI	SAT	SUN
ACTIVITY A							
3 DAYS DURATION	ES		EF				
ACTIVITY B							
4 DAYS DURATION				ES			EF

Figure 10.7: Barchart

Using the above equation to find the *early finish* date (EF) of activity A (see figure 10.8),

EF(A) = **ES(A) +Duration (A) - 1**

= 1+3 - 1

= 3

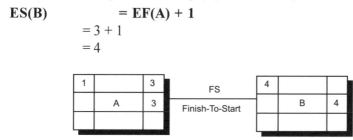

Figure 10.8: Forward Pass

To calculate the *early start* date (ES) of activity B use the following formula (Activity (B) can only start the day after Activity (A) has finished).

ES(B) = **EF(A) + 1**

= 3 + 1

= 4

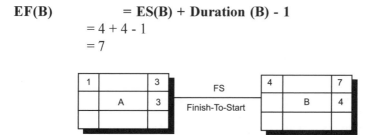

Figure 10.9: Forward Pass

To calculate the *early finish* date (EF) of B use the same formula as we used previously on activity A.

EF(B) = **ES(B) + Duration (B) - 1**

= 4 + 4 - 1

= 7

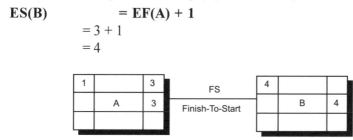

Figure 10.10: Forward Pass

To recap, the *early start* date of any activity is a measure of the time required to complete all preceding activities in the logical order outlined in the *network diagram.*

10. Backward Pass (part 1)

Now that we have completed the forward pass the next step is to perform a backward pass to calculate the *late start* date (LS) and *late finish* date (LF) of each activity. The *late finish* date for the last activity may be assigned, if not, use the *early finish* date of the last activity (see figure 10.11).

LF(B)   **= EF(B)**
            = 7

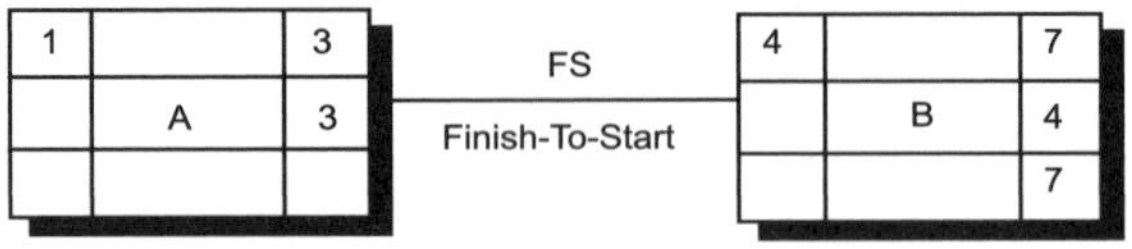

Figure 10.11: Backward Pass

To calculate the *late start* date (LS) of activity B use the following formula:

LS(B)   **= LF(B) - Duration (B) + 1**
            = 7 - 4 + 1
            = 4

Note the plus one in the formula to keep the mathematics correct.

LF(A)   **= LS(B) - 1**
            = 4 - 1
            = 3

LS(A)   **= LF(A) - Duration (A) + 1**
            = 3 - 3 + 1
            = 1

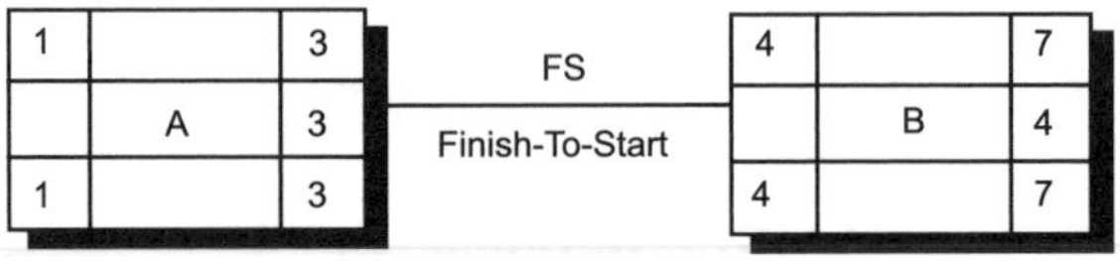

Figure 10.12: Backward Pass

To recap, the *late start* date of any activity is a measure of the time required to complete all succeeding activities, in the logical order outlined in the *network diagram*.

Note: On large networks, when many activities lead into one activity on the forward pass, take the highest *early finish* value to calculate the *early start* date of the succeeding activity. On the backward pass when many activities lead into one activity, take the lowest *late start* value to calculate the *late finish* of the preceding activity.

11. Activity Float (part 1)

Activity **float**, also called **slack**, is a measure of flexibility, or inherent surplus time in an activity's scheduling. This indicates how many working days the activity can be delayed or extended before it will extend the completion date of the project or any target finish dates (milestones). Float is calculated by either of the two equations.

Float = Late Start   - Early Start
Float = Late Finish - Early Finish

Mathematically they are both the same, therefore select the equation you are most comfortable with. Using the previous example:

Float (A)   = **LS(A) - ES(A)**
= 1 - 1
= 0

The float for activity B is also 0. Where an activity has zero float this indicates it is on the **critical path**.

Figure 10.13: Network Diagram Showing Float

This now completes the forward pass and backward pass. You are now in a position to complete the CPM time analysis for the logic table 10.3 and figure 10.4, developed earlier in the chapter.

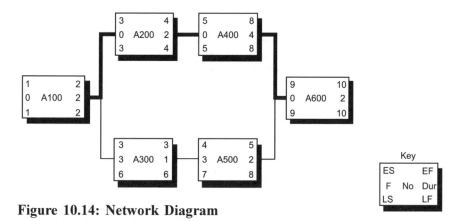

Figure 10.14: Network Diagram
(see table 10.3 and figure 10.4)

This completes the first part of the CPM process - the second part will take the planning and control technique a step further.

12. Network Diagrams (part 2)

To develop the *network diagram* it is advisable that the planner walks through the sequence of work with the managers, supervisors or the people who are going to perform the work, partly to ensure the build method is correct, but mostly to gain their commitment (*buy-in*) and ensure the project achieves its objectives. Note all the assumptions for hard logic, soft logic, duration, calendars, procurement, resource and budget requirements.

Developing the *network diagram* can be a juggling act, particularly if you have a long list of work packages. One way to get started is to select a key activity and work outwards:

- What activities must be done before?
- What activities can be done at the same time?
- What activities can be done next?

Feedback from previous projects is also useful particularly if it provides a template that can be applied in whole or part to your project (see the closeout report in the *Scope Management* chapter). Besides the basic *finish-to-start* there are three other types of constraints between activities. The abbreviation is shown in brackets:

- Finish-to-Start (FS)
- Start-to-Start (SS)
- Finish-to-Finish (FF)
- Start-to-Finish (SF)

Finish-to-Start (FS): The *finish-to-start* (FS) constraint is the most common type of relationship. In the example below activity 200 cannot start until activity 100 is finished. So if activity 100 is completed on Monday then 200 can start on Tuesday (see figure 10.15).

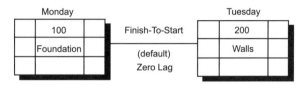

Figure 10.15: Finish-to-Start (FS)

This relationship can be further developed by imposing a delay, or lag, between the activities. For example, if the concrete needs 2 days to cure and the foundations (activity 100) are thrown on Monday, then the building of the walls (activity 200) cannot start before Thursday (see figure 10.16).

Figure 16: Finish-to-Start (with 2 days lag)

Or in barchart form (see figure 10.17):

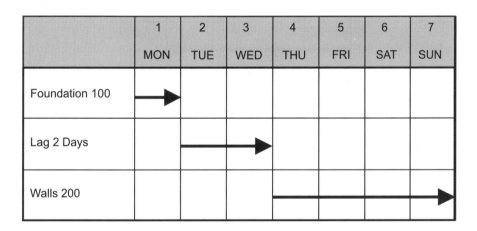

Figure 10.17: Finish-to-Start Barchart (with 2 days lag)

Start-to-Start (SS): The *start-to-start* (SS) constraint represents the relationship between the start dates of the two activities. If activity 600 can start 4 days after 500 has started this would represent a *fast tracking* situation, where the project's duration is compressed by overlapping the activities.

An example of a SS constraint would be the laying of a pipe line. When the first km of the trench has been dug, the pipe laying can start. If the digging starts on a Monday and it takes 4 days to dig the first km, then the pipe laying can start on Friday the 5th day (see figure 10.18).

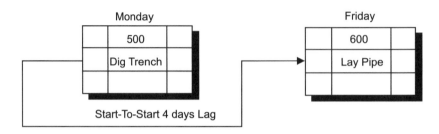

Figure 10.18: Start-to-Start (FS)

Or in barchart form (see figure 10.19):

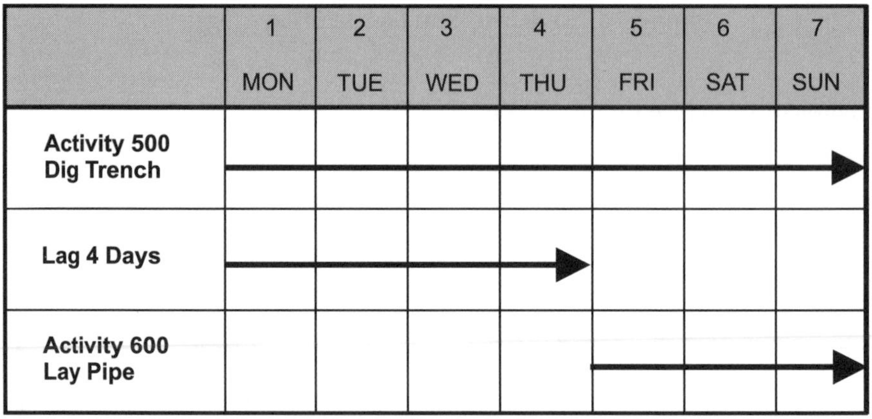

	1	2	3	4	5	6	7
	MON	TUE	WED	THU	FRI	SAT	SUN
Activity 500 Dig Trench							→
Lag 4 Days				→			
Activity 600 Lay Pipe							→

Figure 10.19: Start-to-Start (SS) Barchart

Other SS relationships in this project would be the pipe testing and back-fill of the pipe line. If the start of activity 500 is delayed, then activity 600 will also be delayed. The converse may also be true if resources are available.

Finish-to-Finish (FF): The *finish-to-finish* (FF) constraint represents the relationship between the finish of two activities. For example activity 2000 can finish 3 days after activity 1000 is complete (see figure 10.20). An example here would be the fabrication and painting of a structure. Although there is no constraint mentioned concerning the start of the painting, the painters cannot start painting the last section until the fabrication is finished and then it will take a further 3 days to complete. If the fabrication is completed on a Monday, then the painting can only be completed by Thursday at the earliest.

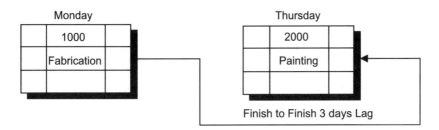

Figure 10.20: Finish-to-Finish (FF)

Or in barchart form (see figure 10.21):

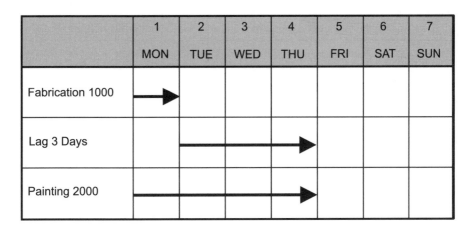

Figure 10.21: Finish-to-Finish (FF) Barchart

Start-to-Finish (SF): The *start-to-finish* (SF) constraint shows the relationship linking the start of an activity with the finish of another activity. This relationship should be avoided like the plague! It is easy to mix-up (SF) and (FS), and then it is virtually impossible to detect. An example of this relationship would be a crane hired for 6 days. The crane has two lifts that must be completed within the 6 days. Therefore 6 days after Activity A100 starts A200 must finish (see figure 10.22).

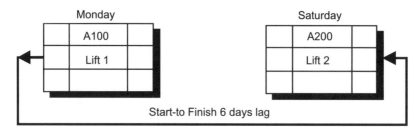

Figure 10.22: Start-to-Finish (SF)

Or in barchart form (see figure 10.23):

	1	2	3	4	5	6	7
	MON	TUE	WED	THU	FRI	SAT	SUN
Lift 1 A100	→						
Lag 6 Days						→	
Lift 2 A200							→

Figure 10.23: Start-to-Finish (SF) Barchart

Note: A discontinuous option is available on some software packages where the activity can be constrained both SS and FF. In this case the resource analysis will schedule the activities discontinuously to match the resources available.

Leads and Lags: A delay may be given to the start or finish of an activity by assigning the constraint a duration (the default is zero). These delays are termed **lead time** before an activity and **lag time** after the activity. An example could be '*waiting for plan approval*' or '*the curing time for concrete*'. The planner may want to keep these durations separate from the activities' duration, because if significant, this could distort the *cash-flow statement* and *resource histogram*.

13. Logical Errors

Before starting the time analysis it is important to validate the network's logic to ensure that there are no logical errors. Some packages perform a **topological sort** to compile the logic relationships into a suitable order, to ensure that no activity is processed before its logical predecessors. There are a number of basic logical errors:

- Logical loop
- Logical dangle
- Redundant precedence relationship.

Logical Loop: Consider the following logical loop that represents an impossible situation. Activity 200 follows 100, 300 follows 200, and 100 follows 300 (see figure 10.24). The figure indicates that one or more relationships need to be reassigned before processing.

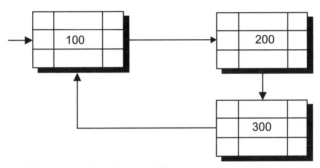

Figure 10.24: Logical Loop

Logical Dangle: As the name suggests a dangling activity is where the activity either comes from nowhere or goes to nowhere. In this example activity 600 follows 500, but what follows 900? Some software packages require the user to define the first and last activities as a start or finish type, as the start does not have a preceding activity and the finish does not have a succeeding activity.

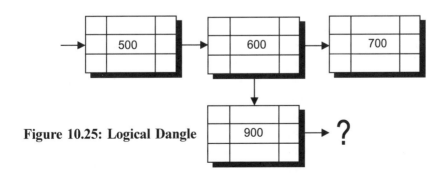

Figure 10.25: Logical Dangle

Redundant Precedence Relationship: When developing the *network diagram* it is only necessary to indicate an activity's immediate predecessors, for example (figure 10.26), 200 is a predecessor of 300 and 100 is a predecessor of 200. Therefore implicitly 100 is a predecessor of 300. It is not necessary to explicitly specify this relationship, if you do, this would be an example of a redundant precedence relationship.

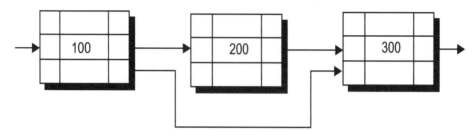

Figure 10.26: Redundant Precedence Relationship

Some project planning software will perform the logical loop, logical dangle and redundant precedence relationship checks as part of the CPM validation. If errors are detected the time analyses (forward and backward pass) will not start and an error message will be sent to the screen. The error messages are usually structured to enable the planner to locate the error quickly. This iterative process may need to be performed a few times before all the bugs are eliminated.

14. Definition of an Activity (part 2)

With the introduction of project planning software, certain terms and norms have been established - these terms will be used wherever possible. The characteristics of an activity include the following:-

- An activity must have a unique activity code or number (A, or 010, or ABC100). The code may be alpha, numeric or alphanumeric. The numbers do not need to be in any sequence because the logical relationships will determine the position of the activity in the *network diagram*. If the numbers are in sequence, however, this may help readability.
- If multi-project resource scheduling is required the activity numbers from the various projects need to be different, otherwise some data will be over written. This can be achieved by either having a unique project code that forms part of the activity number, or assigning a control digit prior to processing.
- An activity must have a description. The description should be as informative and clear as possible. Some computer packages allow the user to define a short description and a long description to suit the report layouts. The description length is usually restricted to fit into the framework of a report. If longer words are used they may be truncated.
- There will be logical relationships between the activities.

- All activities will have a time duration for completing the task, even if it is zero.
- All activities will have a calendar or work pattern to indicate when the work can be scheduled, even if it is seven days a week (continuous working).
- The activity can have target start and finish dates assigned. Certainly a starting date or finishing date for the project is required. Target dates would be influenced by delivery of bought-in items, availability of equipment or access to sub-contractors.
- An activity may need items to be procured, by linking the procurement to the activity a *procurement schedule* can be produced.
- An activity may need resources, by linking the resources to the activity they can be scheduled to produce a *resource histogram*.
- As time and resources are linked to the activities they can be integrated to generate a manpower S curve against time for planning and control purposes.
- An activity will incur expenses. If these costs are linked to the activities the costs can be scheduled and rolled-up to produce a *cash-flow statement* and planned expenditure curves (BCWS). See *Earned Value* chapter.
- If a WBS is used, the activities can be linked to the work packages. This will enable the costs to be entered at the activity level and rolled-up to be reported at a higher level (see *WBS* chapter).

An example of an activity would be:

Identity	A100
Description	Dig the house foundations
Calendar	5 days per week / Mon to Fri
Duration	20 working days
Procurement	Bought in items
Resources	5 men per day
Budget	$20,000
WBS	1.1.1
Logic	List preceeding activities
Target date	Assigned start or finish dates

Table 10.7: Activity Details

Activity Duration: A certain amount of inefficiency should be allowed for within the system. As one activity finishes, the next activity may not start immediately, but take a day or so to get organised.

15. Calendar / Work Pattern (part 2)

Up to now all the calculations have assumed the project is working seven days a week. This is usually not the case, so we use a calendar or work pattern to define when work will take place. Before we can calculate an activity's start and finish date we need to know what days of the week the activity will be working. For example will the activity be working Monday to Friday, or Monday to Saturday or perhaps everyday of the week? We also need to know when the resources will take personal and company holidays together with public holidays.

The planning packages allow the user to define a number of calendars, which can be linked to either the activity or the resource. Listed below are the characteristics associated with a calendar:

- The calendar defines the days on which work can be scheduled.
- A number of calendars can be defined. They can be assigned to any of the trades or even one person if appropriate. Each calendar being a unique combination of rest days and holidays.
- Rest days are the days of the week that are always taken off, i.e. weekends, Saturday and Sunday. Planning software packages generally assume continuous work (a default option is a seven day working week) except for the days the activity is not working (i.e. the rest days and holidays).
- Holidays can be defined as public holidays, works holidays, or your own personal holidays. Essentially days on which the resources will not be available in addition to the rest days.
- Activities and resources can be linked to a calendar number.
- If the activity does not have a calendar, the planning software may flag an error or default to a five day week.

Example: The calendar and start date can change the duration of the activity. Consider this example, if the calendar is to work Monday to Friday, an eight working day activity could take either 10 or 12 calendar days depending on where the weekends fall (see figure 10.27).

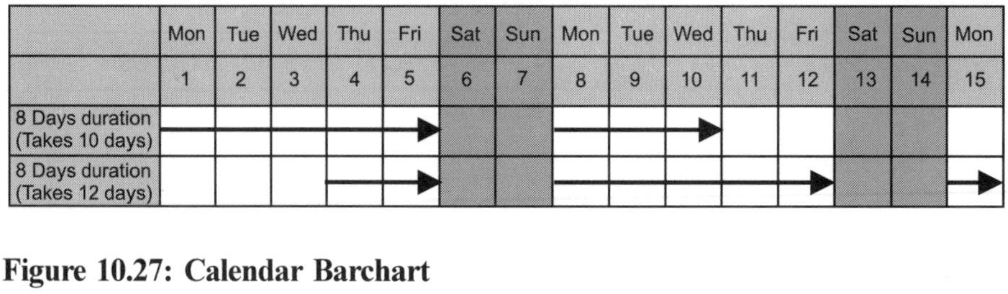

	Mon	Tue	Wed	Thu	Fri	Sat	Sun	Mon	Tue	Wed	Thu	Fri	Sat	Sun	Mon
	1	2	3	4	5	6	7	8	9	10	11	12	13	14	15
8 Days duration (Takes 10 days)					▶					▶					
8 Days duration (Takes 12 days)					▶							▶			▶

Figure 10.27: Calendar Barchart

Consider also activity 200 (figure 10.28) which has a Monday to Friday calendar and is dependant on activity 100 which finishes on Friday 5th, because of the calendar, activity 200 cannot start before Monday 8th.

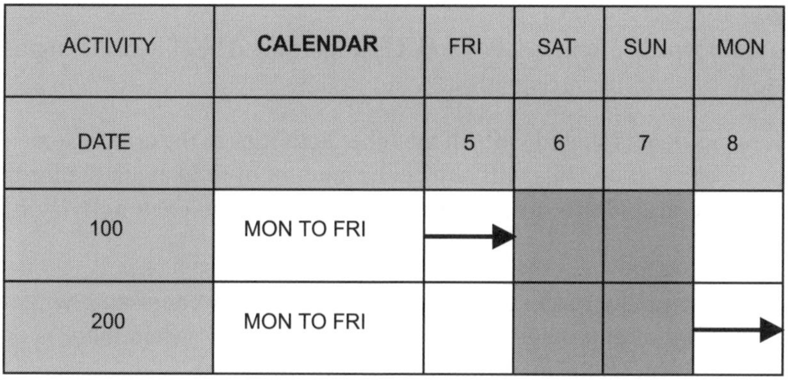

ACTIVITY	CALENDAR	FRI	SAT	SUN	MON
DATE		5	6	7	8
100	MON TO FRI				
200	MON TO FRI				

Figure 10.28: Calendar Barchart

16. Activity Float (part 2)

Float is a measure of an activity's flexibility, quantifying how many working days the activity can be delayed before it will extend the completion date of the project, or any target finish dates.

The critical path is defined as the series of activities that have zero float. The critical path always runs through the project from the first activity, to the last activity. As a project approaches completion a number of network arms may become critical, giving more than one critical path.

If a project has a number of 'finish' activities on different arms of the network then each of these arms will become critical, if each activity takes its own *early finish* date as its *late finish* date. In the example (figure 10.29), activity 300 although indicated as critical could finish up to 7 days later. To prevent activity 300 from becoming critical either link it to the latest activity or assign a target finish date nearer the end of the project.

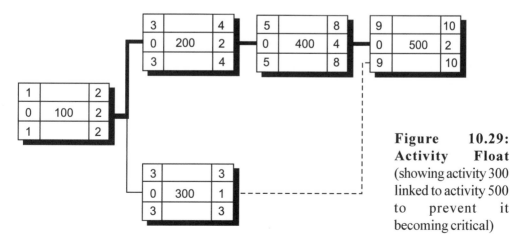

Figure 10.29: Activity Float (showing activity 300 linked to activity 500 to prevent it becoming critical)

The presentation of the critical path is usually highlighted by:
- Heavy print
- Different type of line
- Red line.

There are three main types of float in CPM and it is important to be able to distinguish between them to avoid confusion and errors.

Total Float: Here the float is shared with all the other activities in the arm. If some of the float is used by one activity, this will reduce the amount of float available for the other activities on the arm. **Care must be taken not to assume each activity has all the float to itself** (see appendix 1).

Free Float: This is a measure of the amount of float the activity can use up without effecting the *early start* of any other activity. This only happens when there is one activity in the network arm linked to a critical activity or milestone.

Negative Float: When calculations show that an activity must start before the preceding activities are finished, this is indicated as negative float. It is an unworkable situation that occurs when an activity falls behind planned progress, but the end date remains fixed. The value of the negative float indicates how much the activity's duration or logic must be shortened (or by how much the project is behind schedule).

This concludes the chapter on *Critical Path Method*. The following chapter will show how the output from the CPM analysis can be presented in a *schedule barchart*.

Key Points:

- The *network diagram* outlines the logic or sequence of work.
- The calendar outlines when work can be scheduled.
- Activities with zero float are on the critical path.

Further Reading:

Charoenngam, Chotchai, and **Popescu**, Calin, *Project Planning, Scheduling, and Control in Construction: An Encyclopedia of Terms and Applications*, Wiley
Lewis, James, *Project Planning, Scheduling & Control: A Hands-On Guide to Bringing Projects in on Time and on Budget*, McGraw-Hill
Lockyer, Keith, *Critical Path Analysis*, Pitman

Case Study and Exercise:

The CPM offers a structured approach to planning and controlling project information. The CPM methodology is best learnt by setting up your own network diagram and calculating all the start and finish dates. For this case study you have been appointed project planner for a drawing office project. Using the techniques in this chapter and appendix 1, 2 and 4, consider the following:

1. Network diagram.
2. Forward and backward pass.
3. Identify the critical path.
4. Adjust the calendar.
5. Change end date and recalculate.

"Your move"

Schedule Barcharts

The *scheduled barchart* is one of the most widely used planning and control documents for communicating schedule information. It was originally designed before the first World War by an American, Henry Gantt, who used it as a visual aid for planning and controlling his shipbuilding projects. In recognition, planning barcharts often bear his name - called Gantt charts.

Barcharts are widely used on projects because they provide an effective presentation which is not only easy to understand and assimilate by a wide range of people, but also conveys the planning and scheduling information accurately and precisely. Microsoft conducted a survey recently of their *Microsoft Project* software users - the findings indicated that 90% of the users preferred the Gantt view in preference to the *network diagram*.

The terms *planning* and *scheduling* are often used interchangeably. However, if a distinction is required, *planning* refers to the process of generating a time framework for the project, which becomes a *schedule* when start and finish dates are assigned to the activities. In the past *scheduling* generally referred to *resource scheduling*.

The barchart can either be developed on its own for a simple project, or linked to the *critical path method* to present the schedule of a complex network. Either way the *scheduled barchart* must be developed as a time structure for the *procurement schedule*, *resource histogram* and the *cash-flow statement*.

The barchart should be used in conjunction with your daily diary. The daily diary still provides one of the best tools for noting appointments, key dates, reply-by dates and planning your day's activities.

1. How to Draw a Barchart

The barchart lists the activities *(scope of work)* in the left hand column, against a time scale along the top of the page. The scheduling of each activity is represented by a horizontal line or bar, from the activity's start to finish. The length of the activity line is proportional to its estimated duration. Consider the following list of activity data from a house building project (table 11.1):

Activity Description	Duration	Start Date	Finish Date
Lay foundations	4 days	1 March	4 March
Build walls	8 days	5 March	12 March
Install roof	3 days	13 March	15 March

Table 11.1: Activity Data (house building project)

The calendar time scale is usually presented in days or weeks, but hours, months and years are also possible. The examples here will use days (see figure 11.1).

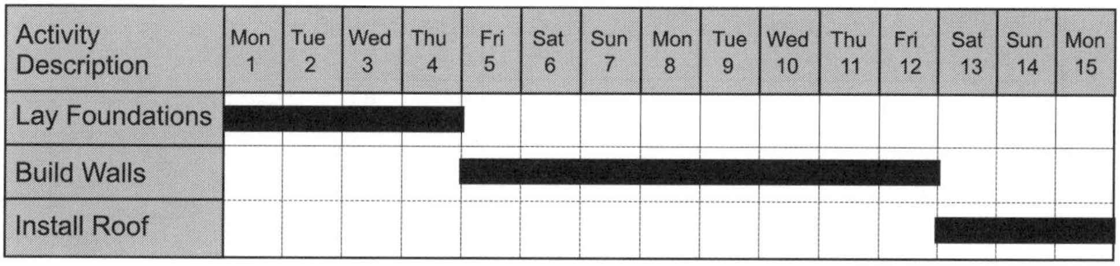

Activity Description	Mon 1	Tue 2	Wed 3	Thu 4	Fri 5	Sat 6	Sun 7	Mon 8	Tue 9	Wed 10	Thu 11	Fri 12	Sat 13	Sun 14	Mon 15
Lay Foundations	████	████	████	████											
Build Walls					████	████	████	████	████	████	████	████			
Install Roof													████	████	████

Figure 11.1: Simple Barchart (house building project)

2. Tabular Reports

Tabular reports provide the link between the CPM time analysis and the *scheduled barchart*. On complex projects it is preferable to develop the WBS and *network diagram* before the *schedule barchart,* as the *network diagram* is the best document to establish the logical sequence of work. Table 11.2 is the output from the CPM example (figure 11.14) in the previous chapter, with its corresponding barchart (see figure 11.2). Note how the bars are drawn from each activity's *early start* to *early finish*. Tabular reports provide an excellent structure to store and present project information and should be used in conjunction with the other planning documents.

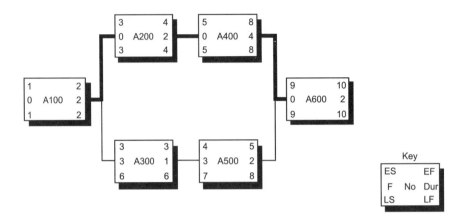

Repeat of Figure 10.14: Network Diagram (*Critical Path Method* Chapter)

Activity Number	Duration	Early Start	Early Finish	Late Start	Late Finish	Float	Responsibility
A100	2	1	2	1	2	0	Sandra
A200	2	3	4	3	4	0	Linda
A300	1	3	3	6	6	3	Linda
A400	4	5	8	5	8	0	Linda
A500	2	4	5	7	8	3	Sandra
A600	2	9	10	9	10	0	Sandra

Table 11.2: Tabular Format (transferred from figure 10.14 CPM chapter)

Activity Number	Mon 1	Tue 2	Wed 3	Thu 4	Fri 5	Sat 6	Sun 7	Mon 8	Tue 9	Wed 10
100	▬	▬								
200			▬							
300			▬							
400					▬	▬	▬	▬		
500				▬	▬					
600									▬	▬

Figure 11.2: Scheduled Barchart (note the A has been removed from the activity number to simplify the activity number)

3. Activity Float

The barchart presentation will now be further enhanced with the introduction of activity float (figures 11.3 and 11.4). The accepted presentation is to show the float at the end of the activity from *early finish* (EF) to *late finish* (LF), and denote it as a dotted line with a symbol at the end, usually a diamond or upturned triangle. Figure 11.3 shows the float both before and after the activity bar.

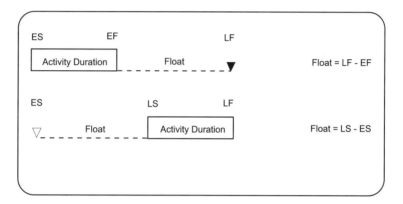

Figure 11.3: Activity Float

By implication it may be assumed that any activity without float is on the critical path. However, in practice planners are reluctant to show float as it is only human nature for people to work to their late finish, thus making all activities critical.

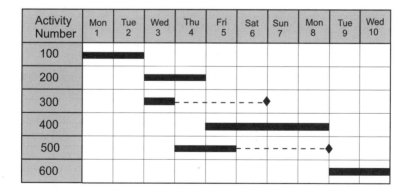

Figure 11.4: Barchart (showing activities 300 and 500 with float)

4. Select and Sort Functions

The **'select'** or **'filter'** and **'sort'** or **'order'** functions that are available on software packages, enable the planner to select which activities are included in the barchart and determine the order they are presented. This facility will ensure schedule information is presented to the right person in the appropriate format.

Select: The select function indicates where the schedule information can be found in the project's data base, consider the following:
- 'Select' where activity data is present, this may sound obvious, but if an activity has no schedule information you may not want to show it on the barchart.
- 'Select' where float = 0 (this will select all the activities on the critical path).
- 'Select' where float < (less than) 7 days (this will select all the activities that should be working next week otherwise they will become critical).
- 'Select' where responsibility = 'Sandra' (this will only select Sandra's scope of work).
- 'Select' where early start > (greater than) 1st Jan and < (less than) 1st March (this will select all the activities planned to start in January and February).

These are just a few examples of the select techniques available to extract information from your data base.

Sort: Once the data has been selected the next step is to arrange the data into a suitable order for presentation:
- **Numerical:** Ascending or descending. This could be the WBS or activity numbers, activity duration or float. Also consider ordering by least cost for activity crashing (acceleration) purposes.
- **Alphabetical:** This could separate out schedule information by responsibility - name, department, company or location (this is how company telephone directories are sorted).
- **Date:** Barcharts are usually sorted by *early start* (see figure 11.5) to present the activities in the order they are starting. This will arrange the activity bars top left (first) and bottom right (last), giving the characteristic cascade effect.

Activity Number	Mon 1	Tue 2	Wed 3	Thu 4	Fri 5	Sat 6	Sun 7	Mon 8	Tue 9	Wed 10
100	▬	▬								
300			▬	-	-	- ◆				
200			▬	▬						
500				▬	▬	-	-	- ◆		
400					▬	▬	▬			
600									▬	▬

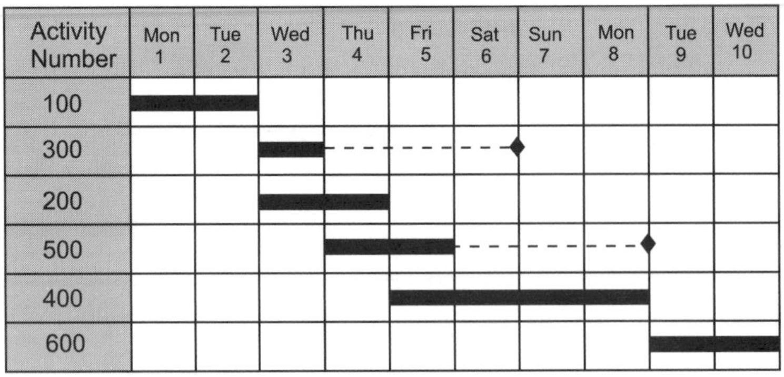

Figure 11.5: Barchart Sorted by Early Start (giving characteristic cascade effect)

By skilfully using the above commands the data can be arranged in the format required for calculation or presentation. Sorting is an iterative process, with each sort the data becomes more structured. Using the previous example again (figure 11.2), select information where activity data is present and sort by *early start* (see figure 11.5). Note the activity numbers are not in sequence any more. Consider now sorting by responsibility and *early start* (see figure 11.6).

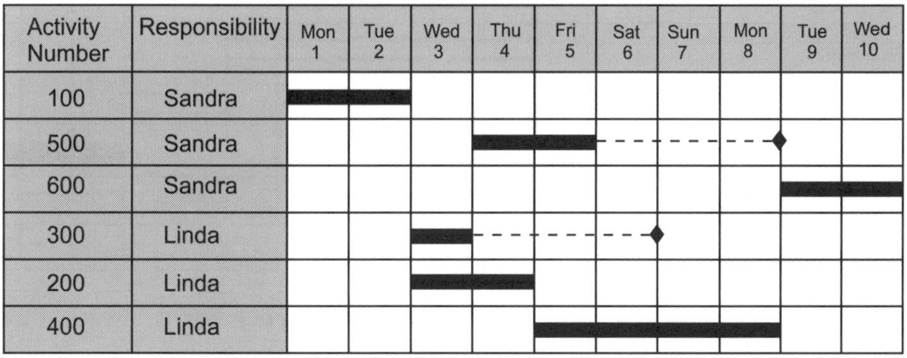

Activity Number	Responsibility	Mon 1	Tue 2	Wed 3	Thu 4	Fri 5	Sat 6	Sun 7	Mon 8	Tue 9	Wed 10
100	Sandra	▬▬									
500	Sandra			▬▬	- - - - - - - ◆						
600	Sandra								▬▬▬		
300	Linda			▬ - - - - - - ◆							
200	Linda			▬▬							
400	Linda				▬▬▬▬						

Figure 11.6: Barchart Sorted by Responsibility and Early Start (this groups Sandra's and Linda's work separately. This can now be printed out and sent to the responsible person)

5. Hammocks

A hammock or **summary activity** is used to gather together a number of sub-activities into one master activity. This is useful for layering or rolling-up the planning presentation and could link in with the WBS structure. Consider the house building project from the beginning of this chapter (see figure 11.1, and table 11.1), with each of the three main activities subdivided into a number of tasks (see table 11.3, and figure 11.7).

Activity Description	Duration	Start Date	Finish Date
Lay Foundations	4 days	1 March	4 March
Dig Footings			
Throw concrete			
Build walls	8 days	5 March	12 March
Brickwork			
Fit windows			
Fit roof	3 days	13 March	15 March
Fit roof trusses			
Fit tiles			

Table 11.3: Hammock Activities (with associated tasks)

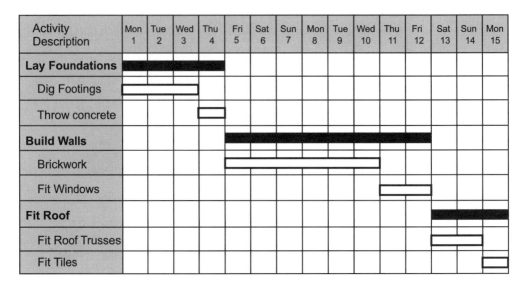

Figure 11.7: Hammocked Barchart (where the hammock bar is always drawn from the start of the earliest activity to the end of the latest activity)

With hammocks the barchart can now be presented at the appropriate level of detail - less details for the senior managers - more detail for the people carrying out the activity at the coalface. This ability to vary the level of detail is fundamental to project planning and control.

6. Events, Keydates and Milestones

The principle difference between an **activity** and an **event** is that an event has zero duration - it is a point in time. An event, also called **keydate** or **milestone** represents a happening on a particular day, this could be when the order is placed, the plans are approved, goods are received or even the start and finish dates of an activity. Consider the following characteristics:

- An event has no duration, it is a point in time. In *Microsoft Project*, for example an event is an activity with zero duration and would appear on the screen as a diamond symbol.
- An event may be the start or finish of an activity, WBS work package, project phase or the project itself.
- An event focuses the project on a checkpoint, a major accomplishment, a deliverable result, a stage payment or an approval to proceed.
- An event could be the interface between trades or contractors as one hands over to another.
- Data capture will be more accurate if the *scope of work* is subdivided into milestones.

An example of an event would be the award of contract (see table 11.4).

Identity	100
Description	Award of contract
Budget	Nil
Duration	0 Days
Resources	Nil

Table 11.4: Characteristics of an Event (Award of contract)

Managing events gives a clear focus on when work must be completed and hence a clear measure of progress. Using plenty of milestones pushes the planning down to an appropriate level. Consider figure 11.2 with the start and finish of each activity as an event shown in figure 11.8. This would empower the supervisor to manage their resources to meet these keydates.

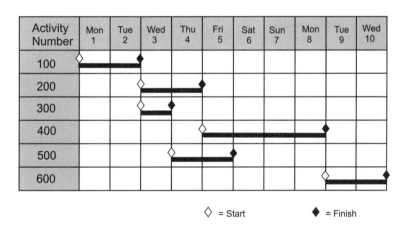

Figure 11.8: Event Barchart (house project showing events at the start and finish of all the activities)

The keydate schedule offers another type of planning presentation which can be used on its own or in conjunction with a *scheduled barchart*.

7. Revised Barchart

The Gantt chart was originally designed as a planning and control tool where the actual progress is marked up against the original plan. This progress bar can be drawn above, inside or underneath the original bar. This way the project manager can see at a glance how each activity is progressing and where control may be required to guide the project to completion. There are two ways of drawing the Gantt chart:

- Draw progress bar relative to timenow
- Draw progress bar to timenow and show the knock-on effect.

Consider the following set of two activities at timenow 2 (figures 11.9 and 11.10):

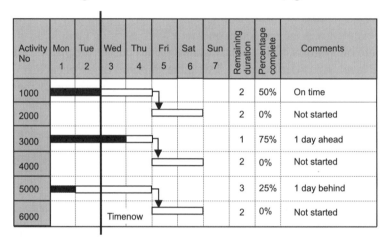

Figure 11. 9: Revised Barchart (draw progress bar relative to timenow 2)

Activity No	Mon 1	Tue 2	Wed 3	Thu 4	Fri 5	Sat 6	Sun 7	Remaining duration	Percentage complete	Comments
100								2	50%	On time
200								2	0%	Not started
300								1	75%	1 day ahead
400								2	0%	Not started
500								3	25%	1 day behind
600			Timenow					2	0%	Not started

Figure 11.10: Revised Barchart (draw progress bar to timenow 2 and show the knock-on effect)

Drawing the progress relative to timenow (figure 11.9) is easy to mark-up by hand and clearly indicates where control is required. If the progress over successive weeks is marked up on the same document progress trends can also be established (see figure 11.12).

If you are intending to apply control to bring the project back on track the knock-on effect to the end date of the project is of little interest, however if any keydates are delayed this could disrupt the project. The disruption on the keydates in the short term can be identified by using a three week rolling horizon barchart (see figure 11.11).

The other barchart showing the knock-on effect (figure 11.10) will show the effect on keydates and also identify where activities may have become critical. The computer will produce this revised barchart at the touch of a button, but to revise this document by hand would be a laborious task.

Baseline Plan: For effective control the project's *baseline plan* must be frozen - accepting only approved changes. Without a *baseline plan* it would be difficult to calculate progress variances and control would be lost.

Data Capture: To draw the revised barchart the planner needs to capture progress information. This can be achieved by setting-up a progress reporting sheet - consider the following (table 11.5):

WBS	Activity	Start Date	Finish Date	Percentage Complete	Remaining Duration

Table 11.5: Data Capture Format (proforma)

The progress report should start with the reporting date or timenow. The progress should be reported against a WBS number or an activity number. The start and finish dates are important milestones which clearly state if the activity has started and if it has finished.

To draw the revised barchart the planner needs to know the remaining duration as the barchart scale is a time scale not a percentage complete scale. Percentage complete and remaining duration are often directly linked, but this can be misleading or inaccurate - consider the following:

When you state that a 10 day activity will take another 4 days to complete, you have implicitly stated that the material, resources and funds are available to complete the work. However by stating that the progress is 60% complete, you have said nothing about when you intend to complete the activity.

On a long duration activity - as the work nears completion the supervisor will have a more accurate feel for the remaining duration as opposed to the percentage complete. Any changes to the activity logic should also be considered when reporting progress.

8. Rolling Horizon Barchart

The rolling horizon barchart, or rolling wave barchart is a simplified barchart which focuses on a short period ahead - maybe two weeks ahead for activities being worked on, and four weeks ahead for pre-planning (make sure all the drawings, procedures, job cards, equipment, materials etc. are going to be in place). This type of barchart lends itself to a manual presentation as the *scope of work* is limited to just the activities that are working.

The rolling horizon barchart can be partly computerised by preparing a planning proforma, as shown below (figure 11.11), which includes the scope of work, but no scheduling. The manager or foreman can then draw up the scheduling data by hand.

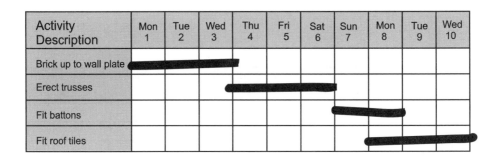

Activity Description	Mon 1	Tue 2	Wed 3	Thu 4	Fri 5	Sat 6	Sun 7	Mon 8	Tue 9	Wed 10
Brick up to wall plate	▬	▬	▬							
Erect trusses				▬	▬	▬				
Fit battons							▬	▬		
Fit roof tiles								▬	▬	▬

Figure 11.11: Rolling Horizon Barchart (marked by hand)

Drip-feeding the job cards limits the opportunity for the shop-floor to change the logic and conveniently forget some activities.

The rolling horizon barchart can also be marked-up on the original barchart - this will give a clear indication of progress, but could become cluttered and confusing. The main purpose is to focus on what can be done, rather than what the original barchart says should be done - this is particularly important when the project is significantly behind as unachievable targets can adversely affect morale.

The rolling horizon barcharts are generally best produced by the team leader or site manager who is at the work face. The planner should then incorporate the information into a master schedule to check the keydates will still be met - and if they have changed, communicate this to the interested parties.

This type of barchart should be very accurate as it is based on the latest data and drawn up by someone working close to the action. It is quick to draw and only includes relevant information on the activities that are working. Care should be taken, however, not to solely use the rolling horizon barchart on its own, as planned activities which are not being worked on may be conveniently forgotten.

9. Trend Barchart

The progress trend barchart enables the project manager to judge the direction and trend of the project at a glance. This is achieved by marking on the original barchart the successive weekly or monthly progress. The points of interest are:
- Activities which are behind schedule - are they catching up?
- Activities which are ahead - are they maintaining their position?

The progress trend barchart shows a number of possible situations (figure 11.12):

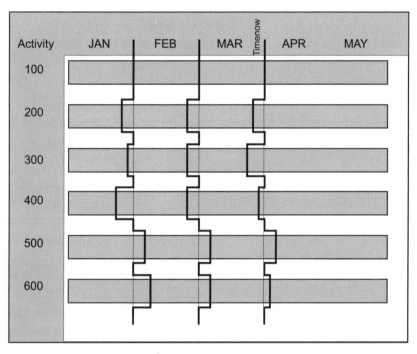

Figure: 11.12. Progress Trend Barchart
(progress reported relative to timenow)

Analysis of the trend barchart (figure 11.12):
   Activity 100 progress as planned.
   Activity 200 progress behind and steady.
   Activity 300 progress behind and getting worse (would be an area of concern).
   Activity 400 progress behind but catching up.
   Activity 500 progress ahead and steady.
   Activity 600 ahead but losing ground (keep an eye on this one).

This simple but effective presentation can be drawn by hand on the original barchart and photocopied for circulation. To limit the number of activities, the trend barchart can be drawn at a hammock level. To quantify the overall performance use this progress trend barchart in conjunction with the *earned value* presentation.

10. Gantt Chart

The positive features of the Gantt chart may be summarised as follows:
- The barchart presentation is easy to assimilate and understand.
- The barchart displays activity progress very clearly and simply.
- Activity float is easier to comprehend when shown on a barchart.
- A *scheduled barchart* is a prerequisite for forecasting the *procurement schedule*, the *resource histogram* and the *cash-flow statement*.
- The revised barchart is an excellent management tool for planning and control.
- A barchart can be used to communicate and disseminate schedule information.
- A barchart is a key document for the management decision-making function.

But the Gantt chart (in its original form) also has two main shortcomings:
- Showing interrelationships.
- Multiple decision-making.

Inter-Relationships: The Gantt chart does not explicitly indicate the sequences and interrelationships between the activities. If an activity is accelerated or delayed it is not always possible on a complex project to see the effect this will have on the other activities.

Multiple Decision-Making: Before an activity can be placed on the Gantt chart a number of factors have to be considered and decided on simultaneously:
- The logical sequence of the activities.
- The activity's duration which depends on procurement delivery, availability of resources and funds available.

An effective plan must address equally these factors of logic, time, procurement, resources and costs. Unfortunately with larger and more complex projects, the Gantt chart is found to be lacking as a planning and control tool if used on its own. The Gantt chart's problems and shortcomings can, however, be overcome by using it in conjunction with the CPM and its *network diagram*.

Project Budget   vs   Project Schedule

11. Logic Barchart

The logic barchart or linked barchart shows the activity's logical relationships explicitly on a barchart format. This technique is certainly appropriate for modest sized projects, but as the number of activities increase on large projects so the presentation will become increasingly cluttered. The logic barchart uses the same techniques used to develop the *network diagram* (see the *CPM* chapter).

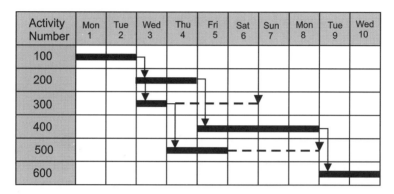

Figure: 11.13. Logical Barchart (showing logical links)

This concludes the chapter on *schedule barcharts,* which is the key document for issuing planning and control information. General Patton is reported as saying; *"A good plan today is better than a better plan tomorrow"*.

Key Points:

- The *schedule barchart* is the most widely used document to convey planning information.
- The selection and sort functions help to structure the barchart presentation.
- The revised barchart assists project control.

Further Reading:

Charoenngam, Chotchai, and **Popescu**, Calin, *Project Planning, Scheduling, and Control in Construction: An Encyclopedia of Terms and Applications,* Wiley
Lewis, James, *Project Planning, Scheduling & Control: A Hands-On Guide to Bringing Projects in on Time and on Budget,* McGraw-Hill
Lockyer, Keith, *Critical Path Analysis,* Pitman

Case Study and Exercises:

The *scheduled barchart* is one of the most widely used planning and control documents for communicating schedule information. You have been appointed project manager or expedition leader of a Royal Geographical Society (RGS) safari in search for the source of the River Nile. You are required to present a barchart which includes the following;

1. Activities sorted and ordered to give the best presentation.
2. Hammocks.
3. Milestones and events
4. Revised barchart.
5. Rolling horizon barchart.

The Project Team marching into action

Procurement Schedule

Project procurement management deals with the acquiring of goods and services required to perform the project's *scope of work*. This could be drawings, materials, equipment or professional services from a number of vendors and suppliers, or company departments outside of the project team.

The PMBOK defines procurement management as; '... *the processes required to acquire goods and services* ...' And the APM bok defines procurement as; '... *the process of acquiring new services or products.*'

The *procurement schedule* should be considered after the *network diagram* and *schedule barchart* have been established, but before the *resource histograms* and *cash-flow statements*. It is important to identify the items which have a long lead time (particularly those items on the critical path), and identify any special handling and storage requirements. The procuring of long lead items may delay the start of its associated activities. These need to be identified and managed by either:

- Accelerating the procurement cycle, or
- Adjusting the schedule barchart.

The trade-off here is between buying the materials early or *just-in-time* (JIT). Using the JIT approach will reduce the pressure on the cash-flow and storage, but will increase the risk of schedule delays.

1. Procurement Cycle

The procurement process can be effectively presented as a cycle outlining a series of discrete steps. In practice there may be some iteration between certain steps and indeed the steps may be carried out in a different order.

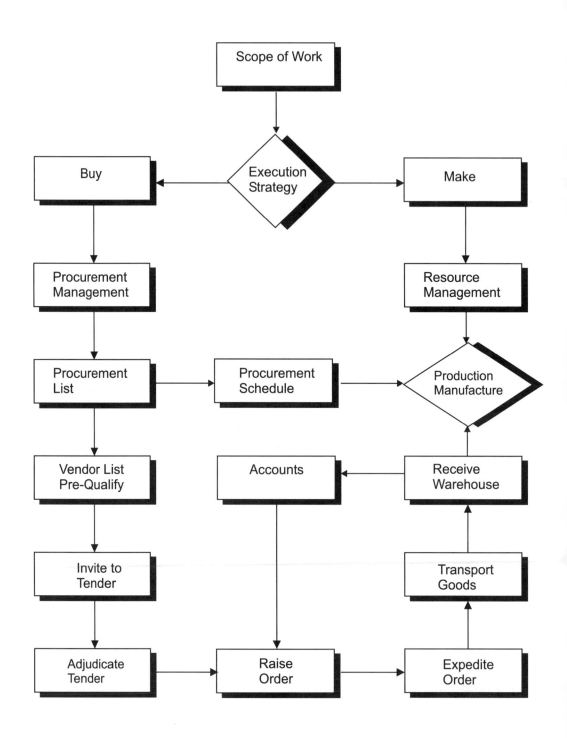

Figure 12.1: Procurement Cycle
(giving an overview and suggested sequence of the discrete steps)

Procurement Planning: The procurement planning will be viewed from the buyers perspective, as the process of identifying what products and services are best procured outside the project organisation. This is the **buy or make** decision which is a key component of the execution strategy:

- What to procure?
- How much to procure?
- When it is required?
- When to procure?
- How to procure (contract)?

Procurement List: The procurement list is developed from the project's *scope of work*. On a construction project the drawing office would generate a *bill of materials* (BOM). This material list should give all the product details; manufacturer, model number, specification, type, colour, rating, level of inspection, etc. From this material list the project manager must decide his execution strategy to **buy-or-make**. This decision may require input from other company departments and outside vendors to assess market conditions and the company's expertise and resource loading.

- **Buy:** When your company resources lack the expertise and machinery, or when your resources are overloaded, or when an outside sub-contractor makes you an offer you cannot refuse.
- **Make:** When your company resources, expertise and machinery are available and under utilised, and the costs are less than using outside sub-contractors.

Procurement Schedule: The *procurement schedule* is developed after the CPM *network diagram* and *schedule barcharts* have been produced, but before the *resource histograms* and *cash-flow statements* have been considered. By working back from the activities *early start* dates, subtracting the purchase order lead time and the *just-in-time* (JIT) margin, this will give the order by date.

Order Date = ES - Lead Time - JIT (see table 12.1)

Supplier and Vendor List: All potential suppliers and vendors need to be identified and pre-qualified according to the *project quality plan*. You need to be satisfied that the supplier has the production and quality management systems to deliver the product to the required specification, quality standards and schedule. The reputation and financial stability of the company should also be considered.

Invite to Tender: Compile a bid package (enquiry document) for the suppliers to quote against. As the initial enquiry document is the basis for the contract, it should be progressively adjusted and marked up as more information becomes available.

Tender Adjudication: Scrutinise the quotations (tenders), and compile a technical and commercial bid tabulation to ensure you are comparing '*apples with apples*'. Consider suppliers suggestions and negotiate to achieve the best price and conditions, while striving for a win-win arrangement. This process should take advantage of market conditions, but should also be governed by your company's ethics policy.

Raise the Order: Comply with corporate standard terms and conditions of contract (see types of contracts in the *Risk Management* chapter). The purchase order should be a stand alone document, superseding all previous documentation and correspondence, and must be formally accepted by the supplier. Where possible pass on any contractual requirements from your client with a back-to-back agreement with your suppliers. You do not want to be held liable for, a schedule penalty for instance, which you cannot pass on to your supplier who may be the cause of the delay in the first place. For this reason it is risky to finalise your contracts with your sub-contractors before signing a contract with your client.

Expedite: Follow-up the order to ensure and encourage the suppliers to meet their contractual requirements (particularly quality and time). Expediting makes the order happen.

Transport: Consider the different methods of transport (see *Project Estimating* chapter). Where possible the product's quality should be checked and confirmed before leaving the factory, this particularly applies to items being exported.

Insurance: Consider placing the order for the transport and insuring yourself so that if there is a problem or claim, you can deal with the transport and insurance companies directly - you will be more motivated to push for a speedy settlement than any middle man.

Receiving: Check the goods against delivery note, check the delivery note against the order and check the quality of the products against the required condition. A project I was working on received two counter rotating gearboxes for an Offshore Supply Vessel, but on inspection they were found to both rotate the same way! Fortunately this was picked up by the receiving inspection which gave the shipyard time to have the correct type shipped over.

Warehousing: Store the delivered items for safe keeping and retrieval. Check if warehousing requires any special handling equipment and storage facilities. Issue the stock against the required internal requisition order.

Accounts: The accounts should check the budget, purchase order, invoice and delivery note for variances before making payments.

2. Procurement Schedule

The *procurement schedule* integrates the procurement list, the project schedule, the procurement lead time and warehousing *just-in-time* (JIT) stock control. Consider the following house building example (see figure 12.2):

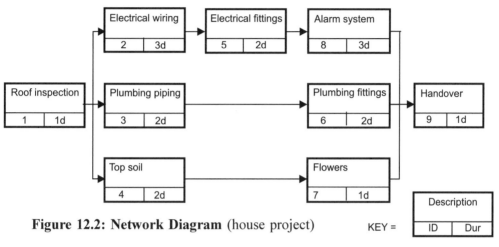

Figure 12.2: Network Diagram (house project)   KEY =

ID = Activity Number
Dur = Activity Duration

House Procurement: The shell of the house has been completed and activity 1 (in this case) is the roof inspection. The *network diagram* (figure 12.2), and *scheduled barchart* (figure 12.3) have been calculated as shown. On **day 1** you decide to procure all the required materials for the next phase of the project. The lead time, which includes **day 1**, is given by the supplier for their scope of supply. The items are required to be on site the day before the activity is scheduled to start (JIT). The required dates have been transferred from the *early start barchart* to the table of procurement details (table 12.1).

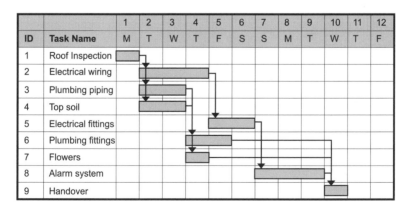

Figure 12.3: Schedule Barchart
(house project)

Activity No	Description	Lead Time (days)	Delivery Date	Required Date	Variance (days)
1	Roof inspection	-	-	-	-
2	Electrical wiring	1	1	1	0
3	Plumbing pipes	3	3	1	-2
4	Top soil	3	3	1	-2
5	Electrical fittings	3	3	4	1
6	Plumbing fittings	4	4	3	-1
7	Flowers	6	6	3	-3
8	Alarm system	8	8	6	-2
9	Handover	-	-	-	-

Table 12.1: Procurement Details (house project)

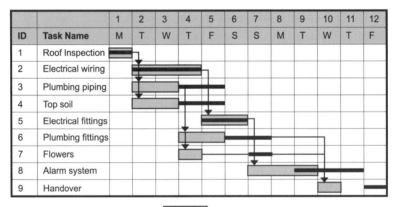

Figure 12.4: Revised Schedule Barchart (house project)

   ☐ = Original plan

   ▬ = Re-scheduled (for procurement)

Procurement Analysis:

Activity 1 - Can start and finish as planned, no procurement required.

Activity 2 - The material should arrive on the **1st day**, therefore it can start and finish as planned.

Activity 3 - The material will not arrive until the **3rd day**, therefore it cannot start until the **4th day** and finish 2 days late.

Activity 4 - The material will not arrive until the **3rd day**, therefore it cannot start until the **4th day**.

Activity 5 - The material arrives on the **3rd day**, but it cannot start until activity 2 has finished.

Activity 6 - Although the material arrives a day late this activity cannot start until activity 3 is complete (logic constraint).

Activity 7 - Although this activity is delayed 2 days by activity 4. It is delayed a further day by the late delivery of materials.

Activity 8 - The material will not arrive until the **8th day**, therefore this activity cannot start before the **9th day**.

Activity 9 - Is delayed by activity 8 and therefore the handover is delayed to the **12th day**.

If any activities are delayed due to late procurement look at the *network diagram* to see if the knock-on effect delays any other activities. The *schedule barchart* indicates when the procurement is required, working back, the lead time will indicate when the procurement item must be ordered. If any of the items are going to be late, then the barchart must be re-scheduled.

3. Expediting

The progress expeditor (progress chaser) follows-up on all the purchase orders and instructions encouraging them to happen by continually monitoring the suppliers. On a large project the expeditor becomes the project manager's eyes and ears as he takes on a criminal investigating approach. Consider asking the following questions:

- Have you received the order?
- Is the order understood?
- What is your job number?
- Who is your project manager or foreman?
- Has the job been planned into your production system? (Show me)
- Do you have all the construction drawings, specifications and planning information?
- Have the materials and components been ordered / received / inspected / passed / and are they available? (Show me)
- Have the instructions been received by the foreman?
- Are there suitably qualified resources available? (Name them and show qualifications)
- Is the work progressing as planned?
- Are there any problems?
- Will you meet the contracted delivery date?

By asking all these questions the expeditor becomes an invaluable source of progress information giving early warning of any supply problems so that the project manager has time to respond.

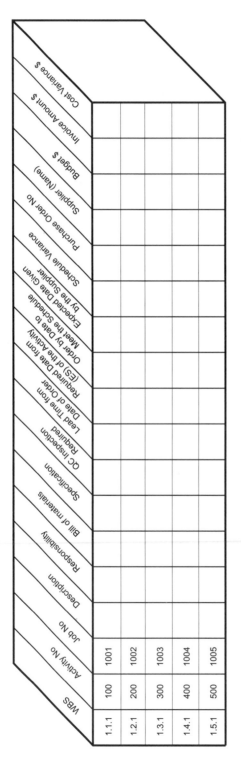

Figure 12.5: Procurement Control Cube

4. Procurement Control

Once the *procurement schedule* has been developed, the procurement control function is the project management process to **'make-it-happen'**. This can be effectively achieved by expediting the plan through a procurement control document. The purpose of the procurement control document is to gather all the information together (on one sheet if possible) and summarise all the related functions. These fields may include the following (see figure 12.5):

5. B2B Procurement

B2B (business-to-business) procurement platforms are a new type of business facility offered by the Internet. At their simplest, B2B market places are just on-line catalogues. Sellers list their products with prices, specifications and delivery terms. Buyers scan the catalogues, place their orders electronically, and can even make payment on-line. Using this method we have bought books from <www.amazon.com> and a computer from <www.dell.com> to write this text.

The potential benefits for buyers include dramatically reducing procurement administration costs and times, lower material prices, faster supply chains, and reduced inventory requirements. The benefit for the sellers include increased sales volume, lower cost of making a sale, and reduced inventory requirements.

Procurement bureaucracy can make orders cost more than the item being bought. Examples in the US military are rife - $600 for hammers, $2400 for a toilet seat, and a staggering $14,000 for a coffee maker for their bombers. On average, e-procurement can reduce the cost of raising an order from $100 to $10 - a significant saving. Procurement cycles can also be reduced - Shell estimates within the oil industry procurement can be reduced from 3 weeks to 30 seconds. Oil supplier's administration costs are also reduced - typically from $5 for processing a telephone order to 20 cents for on-line orders.

The B2B procurement systems are being successfully driven by large companies who are collaborating on a market sector basis, for example, Boeing, Lockheed Martin, BAE Systems, and Raytheon have combined to form <Exostar> a global B2B website for their industry.

B2B procurement, therefore, offers the project manager (project office) the opportunity to;

- reduce transaction costs.
- generate less paperwork.
- provide an economy of scale through consolidated purchasing
- reduce the level of unapproved *'rough'* purchases.

But the project manager also needs to be aware of the associated risks of accessing this global market. Although web browsing will identify a wider range of products, if these are procured from overseas there will be more links in the supply chain and longer lead times. One of our military clients told us about an administration building they were planning. They recognised that the lift had a long lead time, so they ordered it from a Dutch manufacturer - six months later the project was shelved, six months after that the lift arrived!!! Fortunately they were able to on-sell the lift without a penalty, but it does highlight a problem with procuring long lead items from overseas.

6. Just-In-Time

Just-in-time is a procurement management system that provides the production line with components as they need them. This will reduce stock levels and stock investment, but will also increase the risk of production disruption.

Toyota cars developed the *kanban* system, which is known in the West as *just-in-time* (JIT). This was one of the most spectacular features of the Toyota car production system. To avoid the build-up of huge stocks from suppliers they devised a revolutionary system which would order parts only when they were needed, by simply sending back the empty container for the supplier to fill up. It eliminated huge inventories and waste which cluttered up the car factories. It was a ruthless discipline that squeezed the supplier for even cheaper and faster parts production.

The Toyota system created a greater attention to both the customer who could order their special car without extra cost, and the worker who was much more involved in maintaining quality, much more aware (industry wise) and better educated than their Western contemporaries. However, the downside of JIT is that it makes companies far more sensitive to interruptions - the Kobe earth quake for example, immediately caused supply failures to companies that were not carrying stock!

Another feature of the Toyota production system is continuous improvement. They operate an open system that they are prepared to show foreigners, because they are confident they are five years ahead of the West. *"If we lose confidence we will become closed. If we think there can be no more improvement, the system will perish."*

As the value of the procured goods and services increases, particularity with the trend to out-sourcing work, so the procurement function which could be over 50% of the budget, will have a greater influence on project success. This concludes the chapter on *Procurement Scheduling*. The following chapter will discuss *Resource Planning,* the next technique in the planning and control cycle.

Key Points:

- Subdivide the *bill of materials* (BOM) into **buy or make**.
- Identify long lead items. Order early to meet the schedule, or reschedule to accommodate any delays.
- Expedite all important orders to ensure they happen as planned.

Further Reading:

Turner, Rodney., *Handbook of Project-Based Management,* McGraw-Hill
Rowlinson, Steve (editor), *Procurement Systems: A Guide to Best Practice in Construction*

Case Study and Exercises:

The procurement function supplies the goods and services required to perform the project's scope of work. You have been appointed the procurement manager or chief chef for a wedding. Your case study is to outline how you will address the following issues;

1. Outline how you determine the '*buy or make*' decision?
2. Outline your procurement cycle.
3. Outline a typical procurement schedule for the wedding, and give examples of how long lead items affect your JIT scheduling.
4. Outline how expediting makes your projects happen.
5. As the power of the Internet grows, so B2B procurement will become more common. Outline how B2B is being used (or could be used) on your project.

Resource Planning

Project managers face a challenge with every project, trying to execute the tasks to meet the required quality standards, while expending minimum possible time, cost and resources. The discussions so far have assumed an unlimited supply of resources, however, in reality this is obviously not the case, so here the text will outline methods and techniques for integrating resource planning with time planning.

A resource may be defined as the machine or person who will perform the scope of work. Resource planning is therefore forecasting the resources required to perform the scope of work within the time plan. The resource constraint should be considered after the *network diagram, schedule barchart* and *procurement schedule* have been developed, but before the *cash-flow statement*.

1. Resource Estimating

The resource estimate is linked directly to the *scope of work* and bill of materials (BOM). The *scope of work* may be expressed as so many tonnes of steel, or so many square metres of wall to be painted. From this description the estimator can convert the *scope of work* into manhours per unit "X".

The next step is to consider the direct trade-off between the resource requirement and the activity's duration. Consider the following, if the *scope of work* is to erect 12 tonnes of steel and the estimator knows from past experience that the work can be done in 150 manhours per tonne and the men work 10 hour shifts, then the equation is:

$$\frac{(12 \text{ tonnes} \times 150 \text{ man-hrs per tonne})}{10 \text{ hrs per day}} = 180 \text{ man days}$$

The resource / duration trade-off would then be as follows:-

Mandays	Resource Available	Duration (days)
180	10	18
180	11	16.4
180	12	15
180	13	13.8
180	14	12.9

Table 13.1: Resource Duration Trade-Off

By varying the resource availability, the duration of the activity will change. As the time and budget parameters are the first to be planned, the room for resource planning may have already been constrained. In this case the resource analysis function is to forecast the manpower resources required to meet the time and budget (these may already have been agreed in the tender).

In the above example (table 13.1), the duration was expressed as a fraction of a day. In reality you may find that the smallest reasonable time unit is half a day or even a whole day. This will obviously depend on the type of work and the flexibility of your workforce.

In practice the figures are not always so simple - certain industries work in multi-trade gangs, for example, a bricklayer, plasterer, electrician, carpenter and labourer may work together and the estimated total hours may include a contribution from each trade.

2. Resource Forecasting

The next step is to forecast the total resource requirement by discipline or interchangeable resource. An interchangeable resource is when you have a pool of workers and any one of them could perform the work. This is done by compiling all the resource estimates and presenting them in a structured resource table. The following headings for the resource table are typical of those used by the project management software (see table 13.2 and figure 13.1).

Activity Number	Resource Type	Quantity per day	Resource Duration	Lead Time
100	Builder	2	2	0
200	Builder	4	4	2
300	Builder	3	2	6

Table 13.2: Resource Table

Activity Number	Mon 1	Tue 2	Wed 3	Thu 4	Fri 5	Sat 6	Sun 7	Mon 8	Tue 9	Wed 10
100	2	2								
200	0	0	4	4	4	4				
300	0	0	0	0	0	0	3	3		

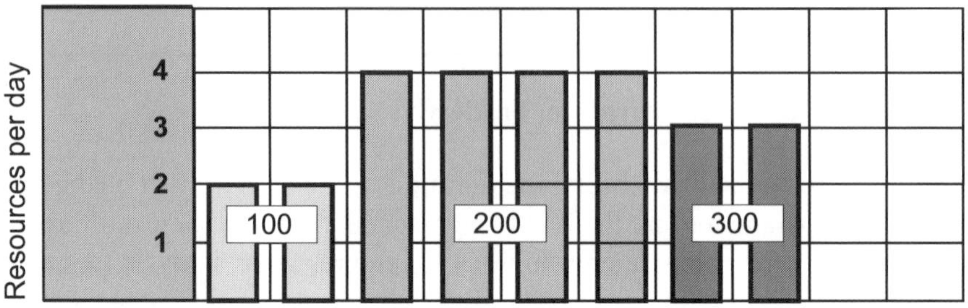

Figure 13.1: Resource Forecast - Barchart and Histogram (the barchart shows the number of resources per activity per day, and the histogram shows the total resource required per day)

Activity Number: (from table 13.2) The resource information is addressed through an activity number. Therefore the timing of the resource can be linked directly with the schedule of that activity. This is why it is necessary to perform the CPM analysis, activity scheduling and procurement scheduling before the resource analysis. This way you ensure the logic and sequencing of work is achievable and the materials and equipment are available.

Resource Type: This field is used to distinguish the different types of resource, for example, it could be Mr. Smith, an engineer, a welder or in this case a builder.

Quantity per Day: Use this field to enter the quantity of resource required per day, in this case activity 100 requires 2 builders per day.

Duration: Use this field to indicate how many days the resource will be working on the activity. This number can be less than the duration of the activity, but obviously not more.

Lead Time: The lead time is the difference between the activity's scheduled start and the resource's start. For activity 200 the builder starts two days after the *early start* of the activity.

If there is more than one resource working on an activity, use additional lines of information. If the resource quantity per unit time varies, a number of entries are required to define the profile mathematically. The resource table can be developed by taking horizontal or vertical slices through the resource profile.

3. Resource Availability

The next step is to quantify the resources available inside and outside the company. The following points should be considered:

- Other resource commitments - if your company is involved in a number of projects which all draw from a common labour pool, the other projects' requirements must also be considered (also called multi-project resource scheduling).
- The anticipated sickness and absenteeism rate - a planner from a UK shipyard advised me that they have to allow for a 25% absentee rate based on their past time sheets (see figure 13.2).

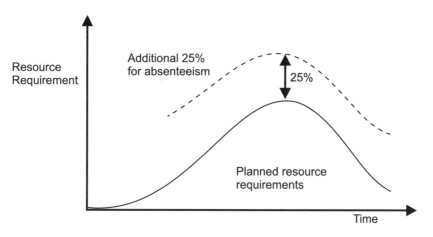

Figure 13.2: Planning for 25% Absenteeism

Keeping the above points in mind, the resource availability table will be developed. Consider the following example (table 13.3 and figure 13.3):

Resource Type	Quantity Per Day	Available From	Available To
Engineer	3	1 December	15 December
Engineer	3	2 January	31 January

Table 13.3: Resource Availability

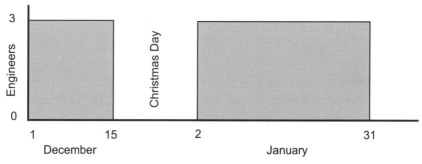

Figure 13.3: Resource Availability Histogram

This resource profile indicates the extent of the Christmas break when no engineers will be available. The resource availability table differs from the resource forecast table in that it is linked to the resource, or resources and not to an activity. It simply identifies the resource and the quantity available between certain dates.

Company holidays, public holidays, religious holidays and maintenance shutdowns can be programmed in. This step ensures that no work can be scheduled when the workforce is not available. A new line will be required in the resource table to define each non-working period.

4. Resource Histogram

The *resource histogram* is a popular planning tool because it gives a good visual presentation which is easy to assimilate and understand. The prerequisites for drawing the *resource histogram* are:

- *Early start barchart* (after considering the procurement requirements which ensures the materials and equipment are available)
- Resource forecast per activity.

By using the *early start barchart* it is assumed that the planner wishes to start all activities as soon as possible and keep the activity float for flexibility. Once the resource requirements have been added to the *early start barchart*, the daily requirements are summed by moving forward through the barchart one day at a time to give the total resource required per day.

The total daily resource requirements are then plotted vertically to give the *resource histogram*. It is important to note that separate *resource histograms* are required for each resource type. Consider the following example (table 13.4):

Activity No	Start Date	Finish Date	Resource Per Day
100	1	2	2
200	3	4	2
300	3	4	6
400	5	6	3
500	7	10	1
600	11	11	2

Table 13.4: Resource Table

Step 1.   Draw the barchart (see figure 13.4).
Step 2.   Transfer the resource per day from the table 13.4, to the barchart.
Step 3.   Add the resource per day vertically to give a total daily requirement.
Step 4.   Plot the *resource histogram* (see figure 13.4).

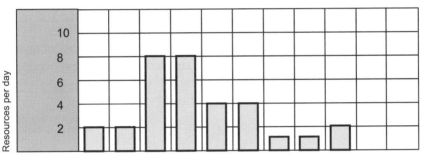

Activity Number	Mon 1	Tue 2	Wed 3	Thu 4	Fri 5	Sat 6	Sun 7	Mon 8	Tue 9	Wed 10	Thu 11
100	2	2									
200			2	2							
300			6	6							
400					3	3					
500					1	1	1	1			
600									2		
Total	2	2	8	8	4	4	1	1	2		

Figure: 13.4. Barchart and Resource Histogram

5. Resource Loading

The resource forecast is now compared with the resources available. The ideal situation is when the resource requirement equals the resources available. Unfortunately, in the real world this seldom happens, because it is not always possible to adjust supply with demand, so some form of rescheduling is required.

A resource overload is when the resource forecast requirement exceeds the available resources, while a resource underload is when resource forecast is lower than the available resource. A resource overload will lead to some activities being delayed, which could delay the completion of the project. While a resource underload will under utilise the company's resources, which could have a detrimental effect on the company's profitability.

Consider the example in figure 13.4, when there are only 6 resources available, the resource loading will be as displayed in figure 13.5.

The resource histogram now shows the forecast and available resources both as a histogram and numerically. The overloads and underloads can now be identified and addressed as follows:

- **Resource Smoothing:** Assign resources to critical activities first, then try moving the other activities to ease any overload and under-utilisation.
- **Time-Limited Resource Scheduling:** The end date of the project is fixed, so resources must be increased to address any overloads.

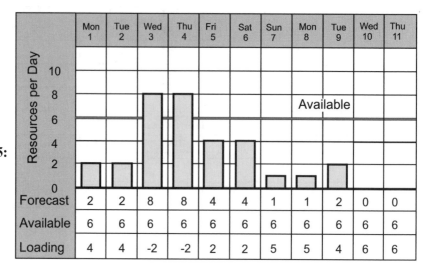

	Mon 1	Tue 2	Wed 3	Thu 4	Fri 5	Sat 6	Sun 7	Mon 8	Tue 9	Wed 10	Thu 11
Forecast	2	2	8	8	4	4	1	1	2	0	0
Available	6	6	6	6	6	6	6	6	6	6	6
Loading	4	4	-2	-2	2	2	5	5	4	6	6

Figure 13.5: Resource Loading

- **Resource-Limited Resource Scheduling:** The maximum number of resources is fixed, so the end date may need to be extended to address any overload.
- **Increase Resources:** To address an overload.
- **Reduce Resources:** To address an underload (under utilised).

6. Resource Smoothing

Resource smoothing is the process of moving activities to improve the resource loading profile. The first step is to select the resource to be smoothed, because it is not possible to smooth for more than one resource at a time. To decide which resource to smooth consider:
- The resource that is most overloaded.
- The resource that is most used on the project.
- The least flexible resource - this could be the resource that comes from overseas, is difficult to get hold of, or is least available.
- The most expensive resource to hire.

After you have smoothed for the chosen resource, the other resources must follow the revised schedule. Unfortunately, you will have to accept this compromise with the other resources, because to smooth for another resource may put the first resource back into overload. Resource smoothing levels the resource overload to meet the resource available. The *resource histogram* can be levelled by moving activities away from the overloaded area by either:
- Changing the logic of the network.
- Moving non-critical activities within their float so that the end date of the project is not affected, while making sure the network logic is maintained. This is similar to assigning resources to critical activities first.

Continuing with the example (figures 13.4 and 13.5), the resource overload can be addressed by simply moving activity (task) 200 by two days. However as the *network diagram* shows (see figure 13.6), activity 200 has a *finish-to-start* relationship with activity 400, therefore activity 400 will also have to move forward by two days. The resulting barchart and smoothed resource histogram are shown in figure 13.7.

**Figure 13.6:
Network
Diagram**

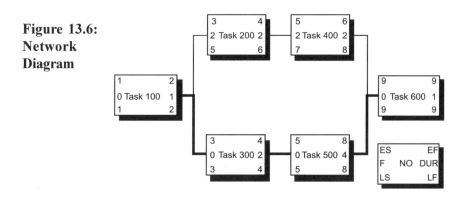

Activity Number	Mon 1	Tue 2	Wed 3	Thu 4	Fri 5	Sat 6	Sun 7	Mon 8	Tue 9	Wed 10	Thu 11
100	2	2									
200					2	2					
300			6	6							
400							3	3			
500					1	1	1	1			
600									2		
Total	2	2	6	6	3	3	4	4	2		
Running Total	2	4	10	16	19	22	26	30	32		

Move >>>> (row 200)
Move >>>> (row 400)

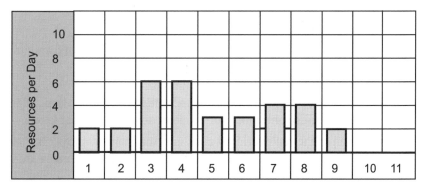

Figure 13.7: Barchart and Smoothed Histogram

7. Time-Limited Resource Scheduling

Time-limited resource smoothing is used when the end date of the project cannot be exceeded. In which case any resource overloads will have to be addressed by increasing the resources when they are required (see figure 13.8). This situation could occur when:

- The project has heavy time penalties.
- The project is part of another project with critical access dates, for example, an accommodation module for an offshore platform.
- Building a new hotel to meet the summer season.
- Opening an event, i.e. the Olympic Games.

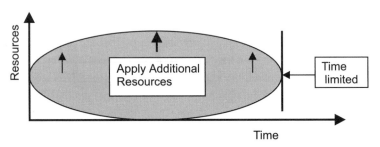

Figure 13.8: Time-Limited Resource Scheduling

Once the end date of the project and milestones have been contractually agreed, time-limited scheduling will become a powerful tool to assist the planner to achieve these commitments.

8. Resource-Limited Resource Scheduling

Resource-limited resource scheduling is when there is a resource limit which cannot be exceeded. If there are any resource overloads then some planned activities will have to be delayed. If this process delays any critical activities, then the end date of the project will be extended (see figure 13.9). This situation could occur in any of the following situations:

- A confined space will limit the number of people able to work there.
- Where there are limited facilities, for example the number of bunks available on an offshore platform.
- Where there are equipment limitations, e.g. the number of computers, machines, drawing boards, lifts or scaffolding.
- Health & safety requirements may limit the number of workers in a certain area.
- Restricted access might limit the movement of materials and equipment, e.g. building a house on a mountain slope or downtown office block.

The frustration of the real world, of course, is that your employer will always expect you to achieve the contractual end date even though the resources are not available (see figure 13.10).

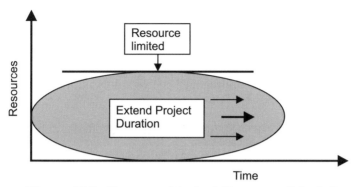

Figure 13.9: Resource-Limited Resource Scheduling

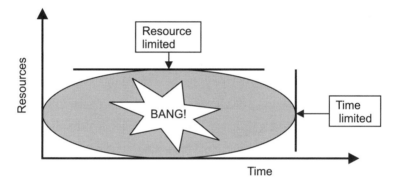

Figure 13.10: Time-limited and Resource-Limited Scheduling
(stress - something must give!!)

9. How to Increase Resources

When the resources are overloaded there are a number of options to increase the resources available:

- **Working Overtime:** This will increase the number of workhours available without having to employ more staff. This can be achieved by working more hours per day and more days per week, however working overtime will increase the labour rate and may reduce productivity.
- **Working Shifts:** This will increase the utilisation of machines, equipment and also increase the number of manhours worked in confined spaces.
- **Increase Productivity:** Education and training should improve productivity especially if it incorporates automation. However, this is really a long term strategy, which may not be able to address your short term needs.
- **Job and Knock:** When the workers have finished a job, they can leave the factory, although they will be paid for the full day or shift. Hopefully this will motivate them to increase their productivity and not drag out the job.

- **Learning Curve:** If the project involves a certain amount of repetitive work, the planner could expect to see the number of manhours reducing on subsequent units. Consider the following example (table 13.5, figure 13.11) from a boatyard manufacturing a series of similar yachts. This example shows a learning curve where the manhours per unit reduce exponentially until it reaches an optimum efficiency.

Scope	Manhours
Hull 1	15000
Hull 2	13000
Hull 3	10000
Hull 4	9000
Hull 5	9000

Table 13.5: Manhours per Hull

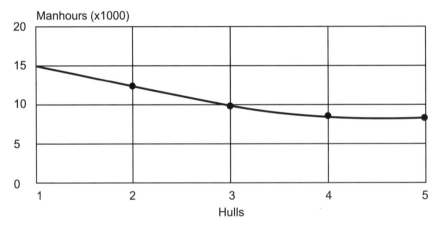

Figure 13.11: Learning Curve (showing reducing manhours per hull)

- **Sub-Contractors:** Using sub-contractors will increase the workforce in the short term. The benefit here is that there are no long term commitments, but the labour costs will be higher. You may need to allow for a learning curve, quality control and supervision issues. Using sub-contractors can also be useful to compare the performance of your in-house workforce.
- **Scope of Work:** If it is not possible to increase resource availability, as a last resort you may consider reducing the *scope of work* to meet a fixed end date.

10. Reduce Resources

When the resources are under loaded, or under utilised there are a number of options for reducing the available resources:

- Move unemployed resources to other activities, particularly critical activities.

- Move unemployed resources to R&D jobs, or fill-in jobs which either have a resale value or can be used by the company, e.g. building a spec house.
- Hire out resources internally or externally - the hire rate can be competitively reduced to at least make a contribution to their salary.
- Pre-manufacture components before they are needed. However, check the trade-off between resource utilisation and the additional cost of the trial assembly, disassembly and handling.
- Maintenance of equipment during slack periods.
- Train your workforce during slack periods to gain new skills which will make them more productive and flexible in the future.
- Send the under utilised workforce on leave.

The profit of a company in the long term may well depend directly on the efficient utilisation of its resources.

11. Resource Planning and Control

The initial CPM analysis was performed without considering the resource constraint. Now that the resource analysis is complete, certain activities may have been moved during the resource smoothing, the *baseline plan* will therefore need to be re-scheduled.

The *earned value* technique often uses resources to gauge a project's performance. Using the example in figure 13.7 the *baseline plan* is expressed as the running total to give the characteristic S curve (see figure 13.12). *Earned value* calls this curve the *budgeted cost for work scheduled* (BCWS). (In this case we are using manhours instead of costs, see *Earned Value* chapter for more details).

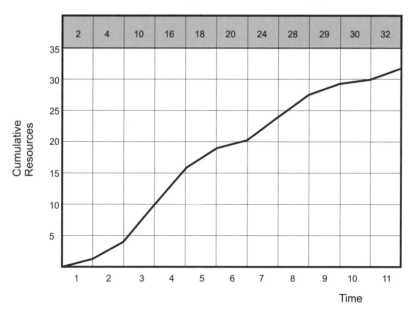

Figure 13.12: Cumulative Resource S Curve (developed from figure 13.7)

The resource calculations outlined above indicate the optimum resource utilisation to meet project objectives, but they do not address the human element. The project manager must bridge the gap, in terms of communicating explanation and persuasion, between what should be done mathematically and what can be done practically. It is generally accepted that a workforce will tend to be more adaptable and committed when given the opportunity to participate in the planning process. Some planning and control considerations are:

- When a project is running late, bringing in more resources may well delay the project even further.
- It may be possible to split activities which have float. In this situation workers would be moving between unfinished jobs. Concern here would be for the lost production time while moving, setting up and reorganisation. However, in reality this is quite common.
- Clients often require a manpower plan to check that the contractors have sufficient resources to meet project objectives.

12. Multi-Project Resource Scheduling

Up to now the manpower resources have only been considered for a single project. Consider what happens when the company is running many projects at the same time, each calling on the same pool of resources.

Multi-project resource scheduling addresses this problem by joining all the projects together to form one large company project. This allows the total requirement of the projects to be compared with the total company pool of resources. Any smoothing will now consider all the projects at the same time.

In the CPM chapter it was recommended that all the activities, even of other projects, should have different numbers. The reason becomes evident when performing multi-project resource smoothing. If two activities have the same number the last activity entered will overwrite to the previous one - with disastrous results. It is, however, a problem which can be simply addressed by assigning a prefix or suffix to the activity number or adding the project number.

Multi-project scheduling adds a further dimension to resource management enabling senior management to prioritise the projects, this will assign resources to the high priority projects first.

13. Planning Software

Resource analysis requires a tremendous amount of mathematical calculation. It is therefore desirable to use computer software for this type of analysis. Planning software generally use the following steps:

- Select where the data is located.
- Order the data for the calculation.
- Calculate the resource information using pre-defined algorithms.

Select: Selection of data tells the computer where to look for information in the data base. Typically select where resource information is present.

Order: The ordering of the activities is the first step in building a priority list for the assigning of resources. Although there is no '*right*' or '*optimum*' priority list it is generally accepted that a set of decision rules will produce a better schedule than an *ad-hoc* approach. On a large project it may not be physically possible to manually test all the resource conflicts so some routine must be set up. A typical priority order would be:

1st priority: *Early start*

2nd priority: Total float (critical activities first)

3rd priority: Duration (least duration first)

4th priority: Record number

The priority would be established by first looking at the activity's *early start*. If more than one activity has the same *early start*, it then looks for the activity with the least amount of float. If there is more than one activity with the same float, it then looks for the activity with the longest duration and if that is not sufficient it then orders the activities by record number. It is not always possible to justify your priority decision rules on logical grounds and the results cannot be assumed to be an optimum solution. The following points should, however, help to establish a framework for your priority.

- On a long project it may not be realistic to schedule in any great detail many months from timenow, because as the project rolls forward the situation and trade-offs may well change. With this line of thinking, *early start* should have a high priority.
- The size of the float is a measure of the amount of flexibility or movement an activity has before it affects the critical path. Resources should be assigned first to the activity with the least amount of flexibility, i.e. critical activities.
- The duration and cost would be a measure of the size of the activity, therefore, assign resources to the larger and more expensive activities first.
- If no clear priority can be established using the above conditions, simply order by activity number or record number.

During the life of the project it is often found that the priority list might change to accommodate internal and external pressures. This can be easily incorporated during the regular progress revisions. This concludes the chapter on *Resource Planning*, the following chapter will discuss the financial side of project management, particularly the *cash-flow statement*.

Key Points:

- Compile *resource histograms* to compare resource forecast and resource availability and report loading.
- Allocate resources to the critical activities first.
- The cumulative resource manpower S curve is used for the *earned value* calculation.

Further Reading:

Gido, J., and **Clements**, J., *Successful Project Management*, South Western College Pub, part of ITP (International Thomson)

Turner, R., *Handbook of Project-Based Management*, McGraw-Hill

Case Study and Exercises:

The executive strategy *'buy or make'* decision will determine if project production is a procurement or resource issue. A *'make'* decision will therefore require resource planning. For this case study you have been appointed project manager for a Water Utility's repair and maintenance project office. Outline how you would address the following:

1. Consider the *'buy or make'* decision?
2. Estimate the resource requirements, allowing for a learning curve?
3. Forecast the resource loading and draw the resource histogram?
4. Smooth the resources.
5. Increase or decrease the resources.

"Have you chaps met?"

Project Accounts

The financial success of a project depends not only on the project making a profit, but also financing the project through the *project life-cycle*. Statistics clearly indicate that more companies go into liquidation because of cash-flow problems than for any other reason. The PMBOK defines cost management as; *'... the processes required to ensure that the project is completed within the approved budget.'* And the APM bok as; *'... estimating the proper cost that should reasonably be expected to be incurred against a clear baseline, understanding how and why actual costs occur, and ensuring that the necessary response is taken promptly to ensure actual costs come under budget.'* It is therefore essential for the project manager to plan and control the project's cash-flow.

Project accounting should not be confused with financial accounting or management accounting which are used within the corporate environment. From the definitions, however, you will see there is some common ground and overlaps.

Financial Accounting: Keeps a record of all the financial transactions, payments in and payments out, together with a list of creditors and debtors. This information gives the financial status of a company using the generally accepted accounting principles. The three main reports are; the balance sheet, the income statement and the *cash-flow statement*.

Management Accounting: Also called **cost accounting**, uses the above financial information particularly from the profit and loss account to analyse company performance. This analysis will assist management decision-making with respect to estimating, planning, budgeting, implementation and control.

Project Accounting: Uses a combination of both financial accounting and management accounting together with some special project management tools (*WBS, CPM* and *earned value*) to integrate the project accounts with the other project parameters.

1. Cash-Flow Statement

The *cash-flow statement* is a document which models the flow of money in and out of the project. The time frame is usually monthly, to coincide with the normal business accounting cycle. The *cash-flow statement* is based on the same information used in a typical bank statement, except that here the income (cash inflow) and expenditure (cash outflow) are grouped together and totalled. In a project the sub-contractors' income would come from the monthly progress payments, and the expenses would be wages, materials, overheads, interest and bought-in services. The client's income would come from the operation of the facility (after the project has been completed) and the expenses would be the invoices from the sub-contractors and suppliers. Consider the following example where:

* **Brought forward** amount for January is $5,000
* **Income:** January $10,000, February $15,000, March $20,000
* **Expense:** January $8,000, February $12,000, March $16,000

Use the following steps as a guideline to solve the exercise.

Step 1: Set up the *cash-flow statement* headings (see table 14.1). Use monthly headings (fields or columns) to cover the duration of the project.

	January	February	March
Bought Forward			
Income			
Total Available			
Expenses:			
Total Expenses			
Closing Balance			

Table 14.1: Cash-Flow Statement (proforma)

Step 2: The brought forward (B / F) for January is given at $5,000 (see table 14.2).
Step 3: List the inflow of cash items from the income statement for January, February and March, $10,000, $15,000 and $20,000 respectively.
Step 4: Calculate the total funds available for January by adding the total income to the brought forward amount.
Step 5: List the outflow of cash items from the expense statement for January, February and March, $8,000, $12,000 and $16,000 respectively.
Step 6: Calculate the total outflow of funds for January.
Step 7: Calculate the closing statement for January, funds available minus expenditure.
Step 8: The closing statement for January now becomes the B/F, or opening statement for the next month, February.

Repeat this procedure every month for the rest of the project. Follow the calculations through the worked example, note that a mistake in January will have a knock-on effect.

	January	February	March
Bought Forward	$5,000	$7,000	$10,000
Income	$10,000	$15,000	$20,000
Total Available	**$15,000**	**$22,000**	**$30,000**
Expenses:	$8,000	$12,000	$16,000
Total Expenses	**$8,000**	**$12,000**	**$16,000**
Closing Balance	$7,000	$10,000	$14,000

Table 14.2: Cash-Flow Statement (solution)

2. Cash-Flow Timing

There is a catch unfortunately. The *cash-flow statement* as the name suggests is a measure of the cash in and cash out of the project's account. The catch is that this may not be the same as the sales figures or expenses for the month, because of the timing of the payments. Listed below are some typical examples of cash-flow timings:
- Part payment with placement of order - this is often used to cover the manufacture's cost of materials and ensure purchaser's commitment particularly on imported goods.
- Stage payments, or progress payments for items which may take many months to complete.
- Payment on purchase - this is normal practice with retailers.
- Monthly payments for labour, rent, telephone and other office expenses.
- 30 or 60 days credit; normal terms for bought-in items.
- 90 days credit - large hypermarkets will pay their suppliers 90 days after delivery, even though they may have an average stock rotation of 20 days or less. This means that even if they sell at cost they can still make a profit on the return from their positive cash-flow.

It may help your understanding to look at the data presented the other way round.
- Labour costs are usually paid in the month they are used.
- Material costs can vary from an up-front payment, cash on delivery (COD), to 1 to 3 months credit.
- Bought-in services and plant hire costs can be paid within 1 to 3 months after delivery.
- Income from client - up-front payment, stage payments or progress payment one month after invoice.

These figures are usually compiled monthly on a creditors and debtors schedule. It is the project accountant's responsibility to chase up late payments.

Non Cash-Flow Items: Company assets should not appear on a *cash-flow statement* as they do not represent a movement of cash. Although appreciation and depreciation may represent a flow of value, it does not represent an inflow or outflow of cash physically. This also applies to the revaluation of property, good will and the value of the company's shares.

3. Cost Distribution

The *cash-flow statement* is an integral part of the *critical path method* (CPM) - it combines the WBS, the estimate, project schedule, *procurement schedule* and *resource histogram*. At this point we need to make some assumptions about the distribution and profile of the cost and cash-flow with respect to the schedule of the activities. For ease of calculation it is usually assumed to be linear unless otherwise stated (see figure 14.1).

Labour costs are generally uniform over the duration of the activity. Whereas the cost of materials and other bought-in items may need to be qualified, as stated in the previous section, they can vary from up-front payments to 1, 2 or 3 months later depending on the supplier.

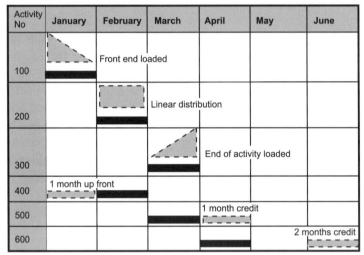

Figure 14.1: Cost Distribution

   = Cash flow

     = Activity schedule

Projects with many activities will tend to smooth out any distortions caused by non-linear cash-flows. However, if there are activities with disproportionately large material or equipment payments, these can be separated out to form new activities with appropriate duration to match the expense profile.

Worked Example: Before going any further let us consolidate the above information by trying another worked example. Using the following information, produce a *cash-flow statement* for the months January to June.

* Brought forward for January is $5,000.
* Sales forecast @ $10 each unit. The client takes two months to pay the account.

Nov:	1,000	Mar:	500
Dec:	1,500	Apr:	1,200
Jan:	1,600	May:	1,300
Feb:	900	Jun:	1,400 (units)

* Cost of sales:
[1] Overheads are $300 per month.
[2] Material $2 each unit. Supplier gives one month credit.
[3] Labour $1 each unit. Paid in month used.
[4] Loan repayment:

	February:	$14,000
	April:	$16,000
	May:	$15,000
	June:	$2,000

Before looking at the solution on the following page, try the exercise yourself. Build up the *cash-flow statement* one step at a time.

Step 1: Using a *cash-flow statement* proforma (table 14.3) check all column and row headings.

	January	February	March	April	May	June
Bought Forward						
Income						
Total Available						
Expenses: (1)						
(2)						
(3)						
(4)						
Total Expenses						
Closing Balance						

Table 14.3: Cash-Flow Statement (proforma)

Step 2: The brought forward value for January is given, insert this into the opening balance cell.

Step 3: The income in January will come from sales in November because the client takes 2 months to pay their invoices. The sales for November, being 1,000 units @ $10 each, gives $10,000. Enter this value in the income cell. The sales figures for the remaining months will have the same stagger.

Step 4: The overhead costs are $300 per month running throughout the project. Enter this in the overhead expense row.

Step 5: The material expense for January will come from the purchases made in December since the supplier gives 1 month credit. 1,500 units @ $2 each is $3000. Place $3,000 in the material expense row for January. The other months will once more follow the same stagger.

Step 6: The labour expense occurs in the month of use, so for January 1,600 units @ $1 each gives $1,600. Enter $1,600 in the labour expense row for January and so on for the other months.

Step 7: The loan repayments in this example have been preset by the bank, enter $14,000 in the loan expense row for February and so on for the other repayments.

Step 8: All the data should now be positioned in the *cash-flow statement*. The next step is to run the calculation through the months from January to June. The total funds available for January are the brought forward $5,000 plus the income $10,000 giving $15,000.

Step 9: The total expenses for January are overheads $300, materials $3,000, labour $1,600 and zero for loan payment, giving $4,900.

Step 10: Subtract the total expenses $4,900 from the total funds available $15,000 [step (8) - step (9)], giving $10,100. This is the closing amount for January.

Step 11: The opening amount for February is the same as the closing amount for January, $10,100.

These calculations are repeated for every month of the project (see table 14.4). A negative amount can be printed as -10 or (10). Accountants prefer to use brackets like this (100) to indicate negative cash-flow. Any negative cash-flow will either need to be avoided or financed by borrowing (overdraft). Unless up-front payments have been organised, the initial stages of a project usually experience negative cash-flow due to all the setting up costs and material procurement.

	January	February	March	April	May	June
Bought Forward	$5,000	$10,100	$6,700	$20,100	$10,600	($3,400)
Income	$10,000	$15,000	$16,000	$9,000	$5,000	$12,000
Total Available	$15,000	$25,100	$22,700	$29,100	$15,600	$8,600
Expenses: (1)	$300	$300	$300.00	$300	$300	$300
(2)	$3,000	$3,200	$1,800	$1,000	$2,400	$2,600
(3)	$1,600	$900	$500	$1,200	$1,300	$1,400
(4)	$0	$14,000	$0	$16,000	$15,000	$2,000
Total Expenses	$4,900	$18,400	$2,600	$18,500	$19,000	$6,300
Closing Balance	$10,100	$6,700	$20,100	$10,600	($3,400)	$2,300

Table 14.4: Cash-Flow Statement (solution)

4. Cash-Flow (example figure 14.2 and table 14.5)

Consider the following project comprising of only three activities; material, labour and transport. The costs are committed when the work is performed, however, the cash-flow depends on the timing of the income and expenses. The timing of the expenses are shown in the barchart, where the material supplier gives a one month credit, the labour is paid in the month used and the transport company requires payment one month before the work is performed. The income from the client is a **20%** mark up of expenses and paid one month after the work is performed (see figure 14.2 and table 14.5).

	May	June	July	Cash flow information
Material (delivered to workshop)	4000	5000		1 month credit
Labour		3000	6000	Pay in month of use
Transport to site			2000	Pay 1 month up front

Figure 14.2: Barchart (example figure 14.2 and table 14.5)

	May	June	July	August
Bought Forward	$0	$0	($4,200)	($5,600)
Income	$0	$4,800	$9,600	$9,600
Total Available		$4,800	$5,400	$4,000
Expenses: Material	$0	$4,000	$5,000	
Labour	$0	$3,000	$6,000	
Transport	$0	$2,000	$0	
Total Expenses	$0	$9,000	$11,000	
Closing Balance	$0	($4,200)	($5,600)	

Table 14.5: Cash-Flow Statement (example figure 14.2 and table 14.5)

5. Cash-Flow Statement (example figure 14.3, 14.4 and table 14.6)

Consider another example developed from the weekly barchart (figure 14.3). Given the *schedule barchart* and cash-flow, calculate the *cash-flow statement* from April to July. Figure 14.3 outlines the work schedule while figure 14.4 outlines the associated cash-flow. The brought forward for April is $10,000 and the forecast rate of invoicing (FRI) for this period of the project has been agreed at $15,000 per month. Calculate the cash flow from figure 14.3 and 14.4 before looking at the solution in table 14.6.

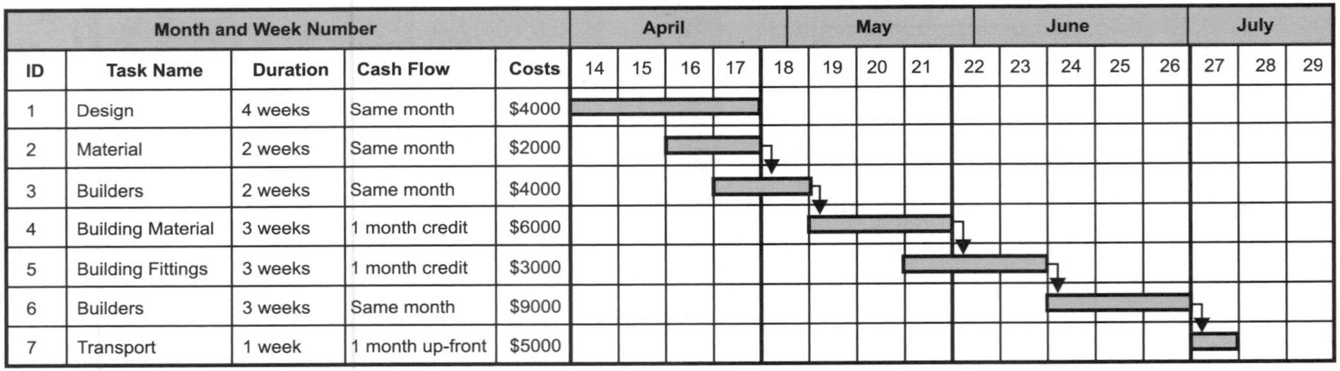
Month and Week Number
April
May
June
July
ID
Task Name
Duration
Cash Flow
Costs
14 15 16 17 18 19 20 21 22 23 24 25 26 27 28 29
1 Design 4 weeks Same month $4000
2 Material 2 weeks Same month $2000
3 Builders 2 weeks Same month $4000
4 Building Material 3 weeks 1 month credit $6000
5 Building Fittings 3 weeks 1 month credit $3000
6 Builders 3 weeks Same month $9000
7 Transport 1 week 1 month up-front $5000

Figure 14.3: Schedule of Work

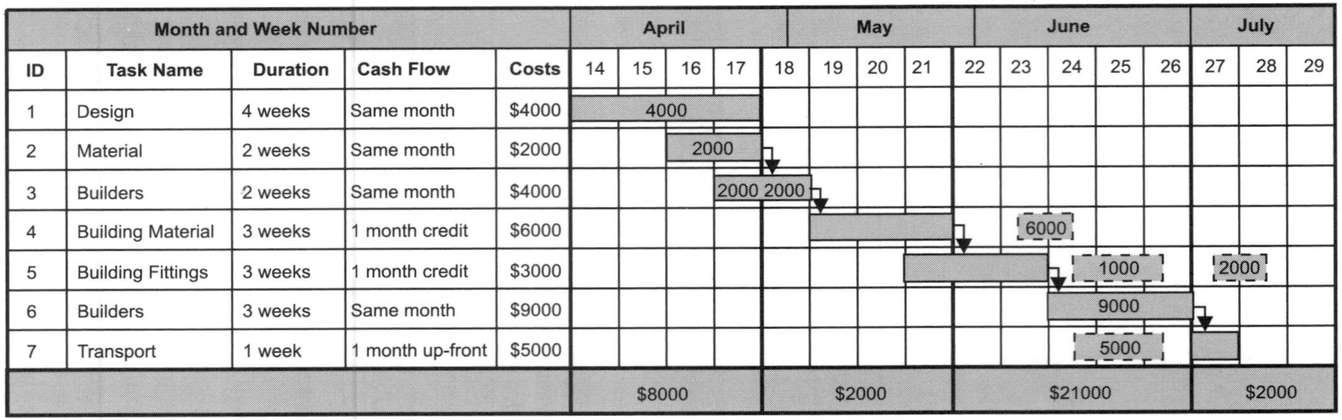
Month and Week Number
April
May
June
July
ID
Task Name
Duration
Cash Flow
Costs
14 15 16 17 18 19 20 21 22 23 24 25 26 27 28 29
1 Design 4 weeks Same month $4000
4000
2 Material 2 weeks Same month $2000
2000
3 Builders 2 weeks Same month $4000
2000 2000
4 Building Material 3 weeks 1 month credit $6000
6000
5 Building Fittings 3 weeks 1 month credit $3000
1000
2000
6 Builders 3 weeks Same month $9000
9000
7 Transport 1 week 1 month up-front $5000
5000
$8000
$2000
$21000
$2000

Figure 14.4: Cash-Flow Imposed on Barchart

	April	May	June	July
Bought Forward	$10,000	$17,000	$30,000	$24,000
Income	$15,000	$15,000	$15,000	$15,000
Total Available	**$25,000**	**$32,000**	**$45,000**	**$39,000**
Expenses:	$8,000	$2,000	$21,000	$2,000
Total Expenses	**$8,000**	**$2,000**	**$21,000**	**$2,000**
Closing Balance	**$17,000**	**$30,000**	**$24,000**	**$37,000**

Table 14.6: Cash-Flow Statement
(solution to figures 14.3 and 14.4)

6. Invoicing

Invoices are documents used to request payment. The project office often sits in the middle of the cash-flow (between the client and the sub-contractors). An invoice control sheet (figure 14.5) can be setup to summarise all the related documents:

- Scope changes
- Progress report
- Invoice ledger
- Payments ledger

Consider the following invoice control sheet (table 14.7). The scope of work is subdivided by WBS along the top and by expense / income

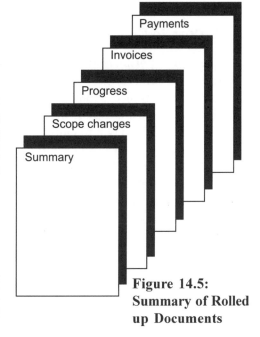

Figure 14.5: Summary of Rolled up Documents

WBS	1.1	1.2	1.3	1.4
Contract value	$100,000	$20,000	$30,000	$25,000
Sum of Scope changes	$25,000	$5,000	$20,000	($5,000)
Total contract value	**$125,000**	**$25,000**	**$50,000**	**$20,000**
Progress report				
Percentage complete	**15%**	**20%**	**80%**	**60%**
Milestone payments				
Total payable	**$18,750**			
Invoice paid todate	$15,000	$4,000	$35,000	$10,000
Retention or performance bond				
Balance ( ) if over paid	$3,750			
Pay latest invoice?	$3,750 (yes)	$1,000	$7,000	$1,500

Table 14.7: Invoice Control Sheet

along the left hand side. The sum of agreed changes are added to the contract value to give the total contract value. The progress payments can be based on milestones or percentage complete. The percentage complete times the contract value gives the total the client should pay to date. Deduct the total invoices to date plus any retention from the total payable to give the maximum amount the client would be prepared to pay. If the invoice is less than this amount - you can pay the invoice.

Question: From table 14.7 would you pay the invoices for work packages 1.2, 1.3 and 1.4? (Solution at end of chapter)

7. Cost-To-Complete

The *cost-to-complete* should be reported and compared with the expected financial return for the project. If the *cost-to-complete* were to exceed the return, then the future of the project should be reviewed. It may be an option to suspend or abort the project. Consider the following:

- The British Nimrod airborne warning system was scrapped after ten years of development and £800 million sterling, was this the right decision?
- The Channel Tunnel operations are running at a profit, but the return on the investment is not sufficient to pay the interest on the loans. Should the project have been scrapped half way through?
- When the oil price slumped from $35 a barrel to $15 in 1985, what affect did this have on oil field development?
- Why was the cost of the Sydney Opera House allowed to become 16 times the original budget.
- Should **sunk costs** be considered when considering a project's continuing viability?
- Committed costs are those costs which **will** have to be paid in the near future, either because the work has been performed or the order has been placed.
- The *cost-to-complete* and project return should be rolled-up to give a total picture of the project. At the work package level the project may win some and lose some.

Project number	Project Budget	Payments todate	Committed costs	Cost to complete	Project return on investment
1000	$50,000	$20,000	$0	$20,000	$55,000
1001	$100,000	$30,000	$20,000	$50,000	$80,000
1002	$40,000	$20,000	$10,000	$30,000	$75,000
1003	$120,000	$10,000	$5,000	$90,000	$80,000

Table 14.8: Cost-to-Complete

Question: Consider the progress report (table 14.8) and identify which projects could cause concern (see end of chapter for solutions).

8. Cash-Flow Envelope

In the text so far we have not considered the timing of the cash-flow within the monthly time frame itself. The worst condition would be for the accounts department to be paying all the expenses to your creditors at the beginning of the month, whilst the income from your client arrives at the end of the month. Although the balance at the end of the month may be positive, during the month the account would have been overdrawn. To represent this situation graphically see figure 14.6 (Fellows).

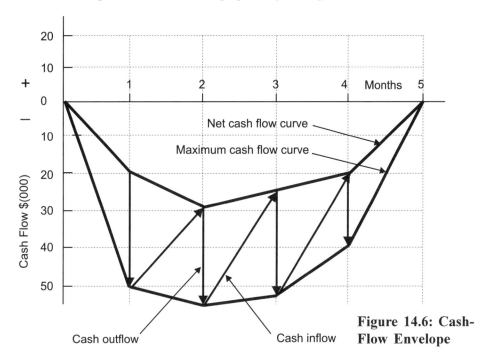

Figure 14.6: Cash-Flow Envelope

From the graph (figure 14.6) the following points can be deduced:

- The area between the net cash-flow curve and the x-axis shows the long term finance requirement.
- The area between the maximum cash-flow curve when negative and the lower of either the x-axis or the net cash-flow curve, will show the short term finance requirement.
- The project is completely self financing when both the net and maximum cash-flow curves are above the x-axis.

9. How to Draw an Expense S Curve (BCWS)

Another method for modelling the cash-flow is to use **S curve** analysis, which provides the link between the CPM and the budget. Experience has shown that a project's accumulated costs tend to follow the **S curve** shape. To draw the **S curve** use the procedure in the *Resource Planning* chapter and appendix 3.

Step 1: Draw an *early start* barchart for the project (see figure 14.7).

Activity list	MAY		DAYS													
	1	2	3	4	5	6	7	8	9	10	11	12	13	14	15	16
100	50	50														
200			50	50	50	-	-	-	-	- ◆						
300			10	10	10	10	10	10								
400			50	50	-	-	-	-	-	-	-	- ◆				
500					10	10	10	10	10	-	-	-	-	- ◆		
600								30	30	30	30	30	30	30		
700					30	30	30	-	-	-	-	-	-	- ◆		
800																50
Expenses per day	50	50	110	110	90	50	50	20	40	40	30	30	30	30	30	50
Accumulated expenses	50	100	210	320	410	460	510	530	570	610	640	670	700	730	760	810

Figure 14.7: Barchart (showing expenses per day)

Step 2: Assign values linearly per day. Activity 100, for example, is $100 over two days, giving $50 per day.

Step 3: Add the cost values vertically to get daily totals. For the 3rd May add the daily amount for activities 200, 300 and 400, which are $50, $10 and $50 respectively, giving a daily total of $110.

Step 4: Plot the daily total costs on a graph of costs against time, to obtain the daily rate of expenditure curve (see figure 14.8).

Step 5: Accumulate the daily values from left to right to give the total to timenow. Thus the accumulated total for the 3rd May is the sum of the daily totals; $50, $50 and $110, giving $210.

Step 6: Plot accumulated figures on a graph of cost against time (figure 14.8). This will produce the distinctive **S curve**.

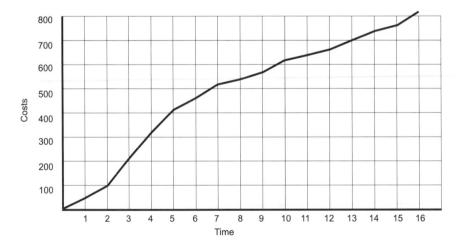

Figure 14.8: S Curve (accumulated expenses)

Banana Curve: If the **S curve** for the *early start* and *late start* are drawn on the same graph they produce a distinctive banana type curve (see figure 14.9). The banana curve indicates the different timing of the cash-flows of activities beginning *early start* as opposed to activities beginning *late start*. Project planners normally schedule activities at the *early start* to ensure all the float time is available. However, the accountant may see things differently and feel that activities should begin at the *late start*. The advantage with activities beginning *late start* is that the payments will be delayed and finance charges reduced. This approach, however, could backfire on the accountant in the later stages of the project if there are delays, because now there is no float available to accommodate these delays, so the activities must be crashed if the project is to finish on time. This means the float that was freely given away in the early stages of the project may now be expensive to buy back.

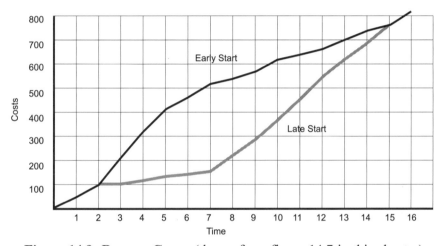

Figure 14.9: Banana Curve (drawn from figure 14.7 in this chapter)

10. Project Cash-Flow Response

How can the project manager respond to the project *cash-flow statement*, if the closing amount is **negative**, try:

- Delaying expenditure payment or arrange longer credit periods.
- Bring forward the income payments. If your project is financed by stage payments, make sure these are completed as soon as possible.
- If the negative cash-flow is being caused by the purchase of materials, ask the client to pay the suppliers directly. (Note: You may lose your mark up and discount).
- Arrange finance well in advance. Bank managers do not like to receive calls on a Friday afternoon to arrange finance for your company salaries. The bank managers also have to plan their cash-flow.
- Delay working on activities with float.

If the closing amount is **positive**, try:
- Looking into ways of investing the money at a good rate of return.
- Start activities earlier than planned, thereby finishing the project sooner.
- Make sure the cash flow stays positive.

Having worked through a few examples, you should now appreciate that when there are changes to the income or expenses, all the following values will change.

11. Performance Bonds and Retention

Retention may be defined as holding back payment of a certain amount of a contractor's income for a period of time to ensure they comply with the contract. The normal practice is to withhold 10% per month until 5% of the contract value is reached. This sum will then be held by the client, or arbitrator against agreed defects for a period of up to one year after commissioning. For retention to work effectively, checks must be made to ensure that the contractor is not over claiming. Why use retention ?
- To encourage the contractor to finish the project within the agreed conditions.
- To have something tangible to hold against the contractor in the event of substandard work or default.
- Provide funds to pay another contractor to complete the activity.
- *"Money speaks louder than words"*.

Performance bonds can be used instead of retention. Here a legal document is drawn up by a bank guaranteeing the client the same conditions as a retention. The advantage to the contractor is that they are paid in full (no retention), which should improve their cash-flow.

12. Benefits of Using a Cash-Flow Statement

Although statistics clearly indicate that more companies go into liquidation because of cash-flow problems than for any other reason, the full benefits of cash-flow management are not always appreciated. Listed below are some of the many benefits associated with using cash-flow modelling techniques.
- The manager can plan ahead knowing what funds are required, when they are required and how much is required.
- It gives timely warning of negative cash-flow which needs to be financed and positive cash-flow which should be invested.
- It gives a forecast *rate of invoicing* (FRI) to your client so that they can produce their own *cash-flow statement*. This is often a contractual requirement with some of the larger corporations.
- The *cash-flow statement* is the main item of a business plan, as it will show the bank manager or lender how much you need, when you need it and most importantly when you will pay it back. It will also show that you have done your homework.
- A cash-flow loan reduces the amount of paperwork compared with secured lending.

- Cash-flow will establish the lending and repayment dates, which usually makes the loan cheaper than an overdraft. With an overdraft the bank has no idea when the company is going to borrow or payback, so the bank has to build up an extra margin to cover its own funding costs.
- 'Secured' lending, even if it is based on the borrower's assets, still depends on the borrower's cash-flow to pay for the loan. Assets are only worth as much as an outsider is prepared to pay for them and that valuation is likely to be based on the asset's ability to produce cash.
- The *cash-flow statement* can be developed into expenditure curves, rates of expenditure and accumulated expenditure, all of which are required for *earned value* project control.
- The *cash-flow statement* can be used to perform a **'what-if'** simulation which will indicate where the project's sensitivity lies. This forms the basis of the sensitivity analysis.
- It can be used as a data source to calculate an investments payback period.
- The *discounted cash-flow* (DCF) introduces a time value to the money.
- The *cash-flow statement* can be the data source for the company's asset register, asset depreciation and company taxes.

These benefits clearly indicate why the *cash-flow statement* is axiomatic to effective project cost planning and control. This concludes the chapter on *Project Accounts* and all the planning techniques outlined in the *planning and control cycle*. The following chapter will discuss *Project Control*.

Solutions: To questions in this chapter.

Invoicing: 6 (1.2) yes
Invoicing: 6 (1.3) no
Invoicing: 6 (1.4) yes

Cost-to-Complete: 7 (1000) okay
Cost-to-Complete: 7 (1001) okay
Cost-to-Complete: 7 (1002) okay
Cost-to-Complete: 7 (1003) investigate

Key Points:

- Statistics clearly indicate that more companies go into liquidation because of cash-flow problems than for any other reason.
- Negative cash-flows need to financed well in advance.
- The cost S curve forms the basis of the *earned value* calculation.

Further Reading:

Fellows, R., **Langford,** D., and **Newcombe,** R., *Construction Management in Practice,* Construction Press
Turner, Rodney, *Handbook of Project Based Management*

Case Study and Exercises:

The financial success of a project depends not only on the project making a profit, but also financing the project through the *project life-cycle*. As project manager you are responsible for the project accounts. Outline how you would address the following:

1. Develop the cash-flow statement. Identify the expenses that could cause negative cash-flow.
2. Adjust the timing of the activities to improve the cash-flow without unduly increasing the critical path risk.
3. Invoicing work-in-progress.
4. Cost-to-complete.
5. Retention and performance bonds.

Project Control

Murphy's Law: *If everything seems to be going well, you obviously do not know what's going on!*

The development of a project plan or *baseline plan* discussed in the previous chapters, completes the first phase of the *planning and control cycle*. The next phase is project execution and control using the *baseline plan* as the means to achieving the project objectives and an outline of the required condition. Needless to say planning is a pointless exercise unless the execution of the plans are tracked and controlled through accurate reporting on performance.

A structured approach to planning and control is recommended by experienced practitioners, because through a well disciplined system all parties will know: what is expected of them, their required performance, and the reports they must generate. The *baseline plan* may be seen as a number of documents which indicate the path the project should follow. Consider the comparison with the course a yacht steers - by taking bearings, the navigator can plot the yacht's position. If the yacht has gone off course they can apply steering control to bring the yacht back on course.

Similarly the project's *baseline plan* is the course to steer, with the tracking and monitoring functions ascertaining the project's position with respect to time, procurement, resources and costs. **If the project is off course, then control in the form of corrective action must be applied.**

It is essential for effective project control that performance is measured while there is still time to take corrective action. This chapter will show that not only is it cheaper to take effective action early on in the project, but as the project approaches completion, the project manager may in fact be powerless to take any effective corrective action at all.

1. The Need for Project Control

As projects increase in size and complexity, so the progress reporting needs to move from a subjective assessment of progress to a more structured approach. The unsuspecting project manager should beware of the over optimistic reporting trap (the Venus Fly trap!).

Consider this situation - if the progress is consistently over reported during the early stages of the project, the managers are only fooling themselves, because the lack of progress will become obvious during the final stages of the project when the over optimistic reporting catches up with itself (see figure 15.1).

This phenomenon is shown in the over optimistic reporting graph (figure 15.1), where the three lines represent planned work, reported progress and earned progress. In this case the reported progress was over stated throughout the project until, at about 80% complete it became obvious that they were only 60% complete and for the next few weeks the reported progress remained static as the earned progress caught up.

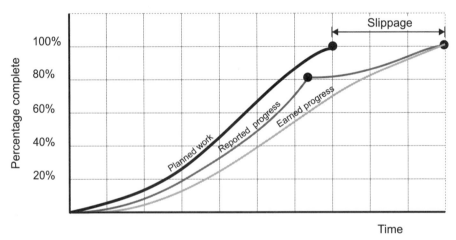

Figure 15.1: Over Optimistic Reporting

If the reported progress had been accurate at the outset, the under performance trend would have prompted corrective action during the early stages of the project. But now at 80% complete the project manager could be powerless to bring the project in on time. Because increasing the workforce will not only increase costs, but could delay the project even more! The US Navy experienced this problem on one of their frigate building projects, which was reported to be 99% complete for over one year!

If the optimistic reporting curve is overlaid on the influence vs cost of changes curves (see figure 15.2) discussed in the *Project Life-Cycle* chapter, then this would further support the argument for accurate reporting at the outset of the project. Not only has the project manager the highest level of influence at the outset, but also the cost of changes are more economical.

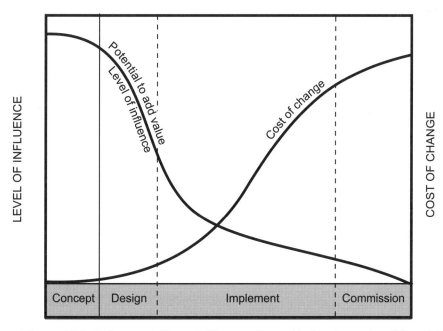

Figure 15.2: Influence / Cost of Change Curve (during the project life-cycle)

2. Scope of Control

It may be argued that as the project manager is the *single point of responsibility*, then he is responsible for everything that happens on the project. Consider the following knowledge areas:

Scope Management: The *scope of work* (SOW) defines what the project is producing or delivering. The control of the *scope of work* is also called **configuration management.**

Planning documents:	Project charter
	Work Breakdown Structure (WBS)
	Activity list / *bill of materials* (BOM)
	Drawing register
	Specification register
	Parts list
	Contract
Control documents:	Project communications
	Impact statements
	Variations and Modifications
	Change requests
	Concessions
	Closeout report

213

Technical Support: Technical support from the design office and drawing office extends from interpreting the client's brief to addressing day to day problems within statutory regulations and good building practice.

Planning documents:	Client's brief
	Statutory regulations
	Specifications
	Design calculations
	Build-method
Control documents:	Configuration control
	Impact statements
	Commissioning
	As-built drawings

Time Management: Outlines the sequence and timing of the *scope of work*.

Planning documents:	Network diagram
	Scheduled barchart
	Keydate / milestone schedule
	Rolling horizon barchart
Control documents:	Progress report (actual vs planned)
	Gantt chart
	Revised barchart
	Earned value
	Trend documents

Procurement Management: The procurement function identifies all the bought-in items. These must be procured to specification, time schedule and budget.

Planning documents:	BOM and parts list
	Procurement schedule
	Material requirement planning (MRP)
	Procurement budget
Control documents:	Purchase order
	Expediting status report
	Revised procurement schedule and budget

Resource Management: Resource management integrates the *scope of work*, resource estimate with the schedule to produce the resource forecast. This is usually related to manpower requirements.

Planning documents:	Resource forecast
	Resource availability
	Resource levelled manpower histogram
Control documents:	Time sheets
	Revised manpower histogram

Cost Management: Cost management allocates budgets and cash-flows to the work packages.

Planning documents: Cost breakdown structure
                       Activity budgets
                       Department budgets
                       Cash-flow statement

Control documents: Expenditure reports (actual vs planned)
                       Committed costs and cost-to-complete
                       Revised budgets
                       Earned value

Change Control: As the project progresses the *scope of work* is revised and controlled through the following documents:

Project communications
Impact statements
Non Conformance Reports (NCR)
Change Requests and Concessions
Modifications and Variation Orders (VO)
Extras to contract
Drawing revisions
Specification and Configuration revisions.

Quality Management: Outlines how the company will assure the product will achieve the required condition.

Planning documents: Project quality plan (ISO 9000)
                       Quality control plan
                       Parts lists and specifications / standards

Control documents: Inspection reports
                       Non conformance reports (NCR's)
                       Concessions
                       Change requests
                       Commissioning
                       As-built drawings
                       Data books and operation manuals

Communication Management: The communication function is to disseminate information and instructions to the responsible parties.

Planning documents: Lines of communication
                       List of controlled documents
                       Distribution list
                       Schedule of meetings and agendas

Control documents: Transmittals
                       Minutes of meetings

Human Resource Management: This function sets the framework for the human factors.

Planning documents:	Project organisation structure
	Responsibility matrix
	Job descriptions
	Work procedures
Control documents:	Time sheets
	Performance evaluations

Environmental Management: This function considers all the external issues that may impact on the project.

Planning documents:	Laws and regulations
	Environmental issues
	Stakeholders analysis
Control documents:	Environmental report

3. Data Capture

Data capture is part of the progress reporting cycle where information is regularly reported back to the project manager on the project's progress and status. The data capture function may be assumed to be at the start of the information cycle and so the accuracy of the subsequent calculations are based directly on the accuracy of the data capture. It is therefore extremely important for the data capture to be at an appropriate level of accuracy. Consider the following points:

- The data capture feedback proforma should be structured in line with the original estimate. This will help to make the data capture less subjective.
- The person responsible for the quality of the data capture needs to be clearly identified by the project manager. One method of improving data capture, is to make the department that uses the information responsible for updating it. This should encourage the users to ensure that the data input is accurate.
- A common integration problem with data capture and the subsequent analysis, occurs when the tracking categories are set up within one structure, while data is collected through another structure. For example the planning department being structured by work package or activity, while the procurement department is structured by supplier. In this case the *baseline plan* is no longer suitable for tracking the project's progress because there is no basis for comparison.
- The accuracy of the data capture will directly influence the accuracy of any reports generated. Data capture with an accuracy of +/- 20% will give subsequent reports an accuracy of +/- 20%. As a guide the accuracy of the report should be the same or better than the profit margin of the project and in line with the level of risk and level of control required.
- A higher level of accuracy is required on critical activities, because any delays to these activities will extend the project's duration.

- Negotiate the design of your reports with the people who will use them. Try to make the reports simple and easy to use, this will help to ensure accuracy and commitment.
- The use of written communication should be encouraged because it addresses the human failing of misinterpretation and forgetfulness.
- Managers should have a propensity for one page reporting, giving quality not quantity. People are more likely to read a one page document than a 50 page report.
- The data capture should be pertinent and relevant. Managers are busy people, so only ask questions where the feedback will be used.
- If information is received after the decision has been made, the value of the information is reduced to being historical.
- A project manager at NASA advised me to "... *use plenty of milestones to report against - people do not tend to lie, however they may be economical with the truth, but they won't lie."*
- The accuracy of data capture can be improved by reporting percentage complete against mini milestones, (see table 15.1).

If these points are used as a guideline for data capture the quality and accuracy of the information should match the appropriate level of control.

Data Capture Example: Consider a drawing office which may need to produce 500 drawings for a project within a short time frame (table 15.1). By setting-up a suitable data capture proforma the project manager will be able to quantify their performance to date and get a feel for *'how they are doing'.*

Data Capture Proforma: The drawing numbers are listed in the left hand column. The *scope of work* is subdivided into five headings (design, draw, check, correct, re-check) and weighted. As each drawing may require different hours, this is accommodated in the planned hours column. The progress is reported as a percentage of each section, so if on drawing 500 the design is 100% complete, this means they have earned 100% of 25%, which equals 25%. And if the sketching of the drawing is 50% complete, this means they have earned 50% of a 50% weighting, which equals 25%, so overall drawing 500 is 50% complete.

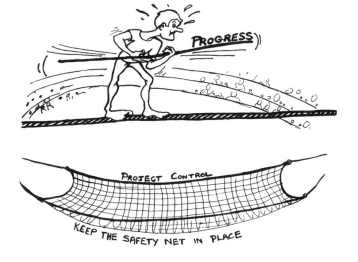

Drawing Number	Design 25%	Draw 50%	Check 10%	Correct 10%	Check 5%	Percentage Complete	Planned Hours	Earned Hours	Actual Hours
100	100%	100%	100%	100%	100%	(Progress)			
	25%	50%	10%	10%	5%	100% (earned)	50	50	50
200	100%	90%	50%						
	25%	45%	5%			75% (earned)	40	30	40
300	100%								
	25%					25% (earned)	60	15	10
400	40%								
	10%					10% (earned)	50	5	5
500	100%	50%							
	25%	25%				50% (earned)	60	30	25
Total						50%	260 hours	130 hours	130 hours

Table 15.1: Data Capture Proforma (Drawing Office)

Analysis of table 15.1: This type of format lends itself to spreadsheet calculations. This project is 50% complete - compare this with the planned progress to see if the rate of work is sufficient to complete the project on time (for this example the data is not given). To measure productivity compare the earned hours with the actual hours. Overall in this case they are the same or a ratio of one. This means the work is being completed at the same rate as the estimate (see *Earned Value* chapter).

Data Capture Formats: The format for a number of other work situations are included for the readers benefit (see tables 15.2, 15.3 and 15.4). Consider designing one for your work environment.

Drawing Number	Sling	Fit and Tack	Weld	Test	Mark-up Butt List	Handover	Percentage Complete
100	20%	20%	35%	15%	5%	5%	100%
200							
300							
400							

Table 15.2: Data Capture Proforma for Pipe Erection

Draw No	Column	Beams	Gratings Ladders Handrails	Final Alignment	Punch List and Fix	Handover	Percentage Complete
1000	20%	20%	40%	5%	10%	5%	100%
2000							
3000							
4000							

Table 15.3: Data Capture Proforma for Steel Structures

Location	Removal	Inspection	Repair	Test	Install	Percentage Complete
Port 1	10%	15%	50%	15%	10%	100%
Port 2						
Port 3						

Table 15.4: Data Capture for Ship Repair Valve Maintenance

With all the managers using the same system the accuracy and consistency of the data capture should improve.

Size of Activity: As the size of the work packages, activity and subsections are reduced so the accuracy of the data capture should increase, but so will the effort to capture the data - you will need to strike a balance. As a guide relate the subsections to the reporting period, so that a subsection is completed within each reporting period. Therefore for weekly reporting the subsection should not be greater than 30/40 hours per person.

Barchart Data Capture: The *schedule barchart* itself can be a useful format for data capture. Ask the foreman or supervisor to mark-up their progress on the *schedule barchart*. The barchart will now contain the plan (last week), progress to date and planned work for next week. This information should be accurate as the foreman is at the operational end of the project. The report is also quick and easy for them to complete in a format they are familiar with.

4. How to Apply Project Control

There are many ways of applying project control, this section has gathered together a number of pointers as a general guide:

- An effective way to achieve commitment is to make the person aware of the cost of any delay to the project.
- When the project involves the repetitive manufacture of components it may be appropriate to change the management style to production management. Production management applies effective control not through activity based planning but through earned manhours. Progress is then monitored and controlled using the production line earned manhours S curve (see *Earned Value* chapter).
- Any changes to the plan should be discussed with the foreman first:
  - To see if they are possible
  - To get their input for the planning
  - To gain their commitment.
- If your resources are being under utilised remember that assigning more men to the job may actually slow down production. This is because those already working effectively will have to spend time explaining the job to the newcomers.
- An excuse often used for not feeding progress back to the planner is, *"We don't have the time"*, or *"We are too busy doing the work"*. It is the project manager's responsibility to ensure that all the project members appreciate that data capture is an important aspect of their management function.
- Short training programmes should be developed to ensure that all the managers appreciate and understand how the information is flowing in the project.
- The process of project tracking and analysis should be seen as a tool for the project manager and not a means of removing responsibility. In fact, by identifying future problems, CPM enforces the project manager's authority to apply timely control to keep the project on course.
- Avoid persecution of the responsible parties if there are overruns, otherwise in future the managers will be reluctant to give you any information for fear that it will be held against them. **Project control should be seen as a tool to assist managers reach their objectives, not as a weapon of attack.**
- Failure to coordinate and communicate information between departments may lead to a dissipation of company resources and duplication of effort. It will also limit the amount of cross checking, which is a useful method for identifying discrepancies and future problems.

- It is the project manager's responsibility to establish priorities and differentiate between what is urgent and what is important. If you allow the workforce to set their own priorities they may leave low paying jobs and jobs they dislike until last. This could adversely affect the scheduling of the project.
- Research has shown that workers tend to have a preference for a regular income, which, if not controlled can influence their progress reporting. For example, if workers are paid **piece-rate** and they have just had a good month, but know the work load for the following month will be less, they may be tempted to under claim in the first month to give them a balanced income in the following month. If project progress is based on worker production claims, this may distort the reported status of the project.
- Respond early to any variation, before small problems become disasters.
- Encourage the team members to inform you of deviations.
- As the schedule is only an estimate, you must expect activities not to be exactly as per the schedule - introduce a degree of flexibility.
- Although plans should be revised to reflect the current progress, it is important not to forget the original baseline plan to guide the project to completion.
- Contractors may be tempted to over claim to improve their cash-flow (in the short term).
- If the project is in serious jeopardy, the client and stakeholders should be involved.

5. Controlling the Project Participants

The effective control of the project participants is essential for project success. Projects are executed by people, who must be managed. This section will outline a simple method to control the numerous transactions between the project manager and project participants.

- Set up a file for each identity on the project, this could be per person, per department, per supplier or per contractor.
- When any of these people are contacted, log the conversation and confirm in writing any agreements. Try to set performance targets which can be monitored and reported back at the next meeting.
- File the minutes of any discussions, memos and emails, and mark actions required.
- As a memory prompt, mark in your work diary all future meetings, items to be expedited and reply by dates.

This procedure can be supplemented by developing an action list.

Action List: The action list is a control sheet which logs all the actions numerically and groups them per responsibility. An action may be any item of work, or re-work that needs planning and controlling by the project manager. The process is as follows:

- Open an action file per work item. This could be a person, department, location or item of work.
- Link to the WBS and activity number.
- Sort the action list per work item, which will usually relate to a person.

- Initiate control.
- Regularly update the list increasing the revision number each time.

The action list lends itself to be set up on a spreadsheet, which will enable you to sort the work by item or action number. Therefore when talking to a manager all their associated work can be sorted and discussed at the same time. How many times have you been talking to someone only to remember an important item after putting the telephone down!! A typical action list structure would be table 15.5:

Work Item	Action Number	Description
Russell	2	Write progress report
Painting	24	Repair damage areas
Procurement	10	Bolt order status
Site	15	Erect scaffold

Table 15.5: Action List

Comments are usually written on the action list and incorporated in the next update. Keep the old lists as they may carry valuable information and telephone numbers you scribbled down. The action list provides an excellent prompt list, the only thing you have to remember is look at your list.

Wordsworth is reported to have said; *"It takes less time to do a job right than to explain why you did the job wrong in the first place".* This concludes the chapter on *Project Control* techniques. The following chapter will take project control a step further outlining the *Earned Value* technique.

Key Points:

- Project control guides the project plan to completion.
- Over optimistic reporting may lull you into a false sense of achievement.
- Develop data capture proformas to accurately capture your earned progress.

Further Reading:

Gido, J., and **Clements**, J., *Successful Project Management,* South Western College Pub, part of ITP (International Thomson)
Turner, R., *Handbook of Project-Based Management*, McGraw-Hill

Case Study and Exercises:

Project planning is a pointless exercise unless the execution of the plans are tracked and controlled through accurate reporting on performance. As project manager of a marketing project to launch a new Hollywood film discuss how you would address the following;

1. Limit over optimistic reporting.
2. List key planning and control documents.
3. Discuss methods of data capture.
4. Set up a data capture proforma which subdivides the work by percentage.
5. Discuss how you would apply control for schedule delays.

PROJECT MANAGER   SUB-CONTRACTOR

Earned Value

This chapter continues the project control theme by introducing *earned value* as an integrated planning and control tool. The *earned value* approach is a development of the **PERT/COST** and the **Cost Schedule Control System** criteria (CSCS) introduced in 1967 circa by the US DoD (Dept of Defence), to fully integrate cost and time.

When this approach is combined with forecasting, the project manager has the best of both worlds. For the project manager to answer the basic question, "*How are we doing?*", the performance measuring mechanism should periodically (usually weekly) assess progress and costs in comparable units (compare apples with apples) against a *baseline plan*. **It is essential for effective project control that performance is measured while there is still time to take corrective action.**

Although the *earned value* technique was initially set up to track the progress of cost and time, in practice it is often more appropriate to track progress measured as **earned manhours** and time. In fact any parameter that flows through the project can be used; software lines of code, tonnes of steel, cubic meters of concrete, metres of pipe, or pages of a document.

1. The Need for Earned Value

The *Project Control* chapter mentioned a situation where a US Navy shipbuilding project was 99% complete for a year - how could this happen? The likely answer is that they were unable to distinguish between planned manhours, actual manhours and earned manhours. Where:

- The planned manhours are an estimate of how you intend to perform the work.
- The earned manhours are a measure of work done.
- The actual manhours are recorded on the clock cards.

The problem occurs when the actual manhours are assumed to be the same as the earned manhours. In this case if the actual manhours are 99% of the planned manhours, then it is assumed that the project is 99% complete, but when they look out the window and see the ship is not finished - obviously something is wrong with their reporting.

Separate Reporting: A similar problem arises when expenses and progress are reported separately - consider the following example (figures 16.1 and 16.2):

Figure 16.1: Project Expenses Against Time

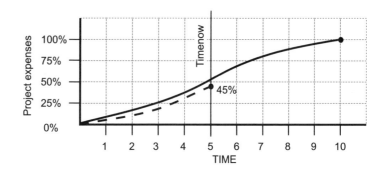

From the expense graph (figure 16.1) the accountant would report that the project is under spent, with planned expenditure 50% and actual expenditure 45%. Here the forecast looks good for the project to be completed under budget.

Figure 16.2: Project Progress Against Time

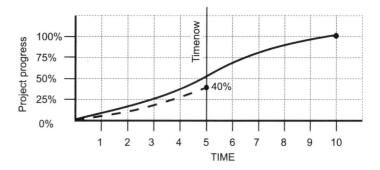

From the progress graph (figure 16.2) the planner on the other hand would not be so optimistic with planned progress 50% and actual progress only 40% complete - the prognosis would predict a project time overrun. But now consider what happens when the two graphs are integrated, the project is 45% spent but has only achieved 40% of the work. The analysis now indicates that not only is the project behind schedule, but is overspent as well, thus giving a strong signal that the project manager needs to apply control to bring the project back on track.

This example clearly shows the **need to integrate** the project's cost and time information. Based on the expense information alone the project manager would have been mislead, believing that the project would meet its objectives without the need for corrective control. As projects grow in size and complexity, so the need for an *earned* *value* measuring system quantifying project performance increases. The project manager needs to know if control is required, where and by how much. *Earned value* provides visibility to the critical areas and identifies the need for further attention.

2. Earned Value Structure

The *earned value* calculations can be presented as either an *earned value* table (see table 16.2) or rolled-up to an *earned value* graph (see figure 16.3). The graph provides an excellent presentation that is easy to assimilate, while the table provides further detail for the project manager to investigate any variances.

Earned *value* more than any other planning and control technique covered in this book is shrouded in **esoteric terminology**. The key to mastering *earned value* is to understand and not be intimidated by these terms. It may be argued that if you wish to enter the field of project management, then you must speak the language of project management.

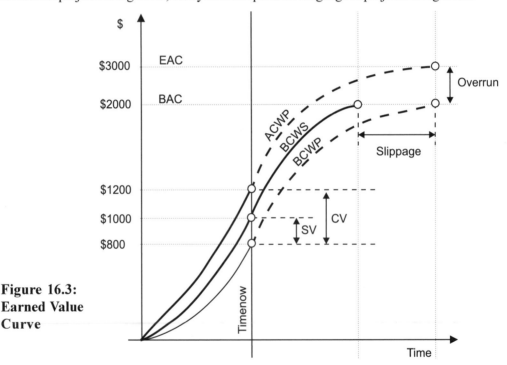

**Figure 16.3:
Earned Value
Curve**

2.1 Earned Value Plan

The *earned value* graph (figure 16.3) is built-up by first outlining the plan.

Budget at Completion (BAC): This is the original cost estimate, budget or quotation, indicating the funds required to complete the work, in this case $2000 (see figure 16.3). Calling this parameter simply *'the budget'* may have been less confusing. At the project management level the BAC does not include profit. The reason for this will become clear later when the actual costs are compared with the planned costs. The BAC becomes a generic term when manhours or another parameter are used.

Budgeted Cost for Work Scheduled (BCWS): This is the integration of cost and time or more commonly manhours and time to give the characteristic S curve, which forms the baseline plan (see the *Project Accounts and Resource Planning* chapters which explain how to draw an S curve).

2.2 Earned Value Status

Once the project starts the progress needs to be captured on a regular basis.

Timenow: Also called **data date**, or **progress date** or **progress at weekending** are the terms used to indicate up to what date the progress has been recorded.

Percentage Complete (PC): The PC is a measure of the activities performance and progress up to timenow and is required for the *earned value* calculation. For this example the PC is 40% at timenow.

Budgeted Cost for Work Performed (BCWP): Also called *earned value*, is a measure of achievement or value of the work done to timenow. The BCWP is calculated by the equation:

BCWP = PC (earned progress at timenow) x BAC
        = 40% x $2000
        = $800

Actual Cost for Work Performed (ACWP): This is the amount payable for the work done to timenow. It is the **real** cost incurred executing the work to achieve the reported progress. Take care to ensure that both **PC** and **ACWP** are based on the same data. A possible mistake is to report progress as the work is performed, but only report costs on receipt of the invoice. This differential cash-flow will make the project accounts look deceptively good in the short term. Another mistake is to compare actual work hours with the planned work hours. As mentioned before in the shipbuilding project this is a meaningless comparison as it says nothing about what work has been performed. For this example the ACWP is $1200 at timenow (see figure 16.3).

2.3 Earned Value Forecast

When the integration of cost and time are combined with forecasting the project manager has the best of both worlds.

Estimate at Completion (EAC): The EAC is a revised budget for the activity, work package or project, based on current productivity. The EAC is calculated by extrapolating the performance trend from timenow to the end of the project. This value assumes that the productivity to-date will continue at the same rate to the end of the project. The productivity is defined by the ratio of costs (ACWP) to *earned value*

(BCWP). If the costs (ACWP) are less than the *earned value* (BCWP), then the EAC will be less than the BAC and vice versa.

$$EAC = \frac{ACWP \times BAC}{BCWP}$$

But $BCWP = PC \times BAC$

Therefore $EAC = \frac{ACWP}{PC \times BAC} \times BAC$

$$EAC = \frac{ACWP}{PC}$$

For this example at timenow (see figure 16.3)

$$EAC = \frac{\$1200 \times 100}{40\%}$$

$$= \$3000$$

The **budget variance** is therefore BAC - EAC, $2000 - $3000 = - $1000. The project is forecast to be $1000 over budget.

Estimate-to-Complete (ETC): is defined as;

$$ETC = EAC - ACWP$$
$$= \$3000 - \$1200$$
$$= \$1800$$

The *estimate-to-complete* is a useful figure for the project manager to compare the funds available (outstanding invoices must also be included) with the *cost-to-complete*. A significant difference should trigger a review of estimates and build methods to search for a corrective solution.

2.4 Earned Value Variances

A variance is simply the difference between planned and actual values. In the *earned value* context there are a number of important flags to attract the project manager's attention, consider the following:
- Schedule variance (SV)
- Cost variance (CV)
- Threshold variance

Schedule Variance (SV): The *schedule variance* calculation is a measure of the time deviation between the planned progress (BCWS) and the earned progress (BCWP). The interesting feature about this time variance is that it is measured in money units.

$$SV = BCWP - BCWS$$
$$= \$800 - \$1000$$
$$= - \$200$$

The sign of the variance will indicate if the project is ahead or behind the planned progress:

Negative variance: The project is behind the planned progress.

Positive variance: The project is ahead of planned progress.

Schedule Variance Percentage (SV%): Converting the *schedule variance* to a percentage will address any distortion caused by the size of the activity. For example an SV of $1,000 is 10% of a $10,000 activity, but only 1% of a $100,000 activity.

$$SV\% = SV \ / \ BCWS$$
$$= -\$200 \ / \ \$1000$$
$$= -20\%$$

Cost Variance (CV): The *cost variance* is a measure of the deviation between the *earned value* (BCWP) and the actual cost of doing the work (ACWP) (see figure 16.3).

$$CV = BCWP \ - \ ACWP$$
$$= \$800 - \$1200$$
$$= -\$400$$

The sign of the variance will indicate if the costs are under or over the estimate.

Negative variance: The cost is higher than the original estimate (BAC).

Positive variance: The cost is lower than the original estimate (BAC).

Cost Variance Percentage (CV%): Converting the CV to a CV% will reduce the distortion caused by the size of the activity.

$$CV\% = CV \ / \ BCWP$$
$$= -\$400 \ / \ \$800$$
$$= -50\%$$

Threshold Variance: The *threshold variances* can be used to flag problem areas and attract the project manager's attention. The threshold limits may be set as a percentage (for example +/- 5%) to give an early indication of an undesirable trend. Tight variance thresholds allow true *management-by-exception*, as negative variances should trigger an immediate response helping supervisors to assign priorities and additional resources. Positive variances identify praiseworthy employee productivity which could have an input into productivity bonuses.

Terminology: The terms outlined here have gained acceptance in the body of knowledge, management press and business schools. They are commonly used in technical articles and management texts. Unfortunately many of the planning software packages have invented new terminology for some of the above items. This new software terminology serves only to confuse, particularly for those users who are struggling to get to grips with a new concept in the first place.

Performance Indices: Performance indices are ratios used to determine the status of the project.

Cost Performance Index CPI: is defined as:

$$CPI = BCWP/ACWP$$
$$= \$800/\$1200$$
$$= 0.66$$

The CPI compares the work earned with the actual cost, if the CPI < 1 then the project is spending more than it is earning and will make a loss if corrective action is not taken.

Schedule Performance Index SPI: is defined as:

$$SPI = BCWP/BCWS$$
$$= \$800/\$1000$$
$$= 0.8$$

The SPI compares the work earned with the work schedule, if the SPI < 1 then the project is behind schedule and if corrective action is not taken it will finish late. The two indices may give results which seem contradictory, for example, CPI>1 and SPI<1. This indicates that the project is under budget, but behind schedule. The question is can the project be brought back on schedule by expending more resources?

Project Control: During the project the activities are usually at various stages of completion; some on target, some ahead of plan, some behind plan, some on budget, some overspent and some under spent. In this situation it is extremely difficult to quantify the project's overall status visually and it may be argued that a subjective assessment of a complex project is bound to be inaccurate. This problem can be addressed by using the *earned value* model to roll-up all the activity data and report a bottom line for the project giving an overall position. Consider the following example (see table 16.1):

Activity	BAC	BCWS	PC	BCWP	Status
100	$100	$100	100%	$100	On time
200	$400	$400	75%	$300	Behind
300	$1,200	$800	90%	$1,080	Ahead
Totals		$1,300		$1,480	

Table 16.1: Earned Value Progress Report

The status report indicates that overall the *earned value* BCWP $1480 is ahead of the planned progress BCWS $1300 and if this continues the project should finish early. If the project manager required further information they would look at the variance at the activity level and in this case would have a closer look at activity 200, which is behind. This technique can be further refined by sorting out the critical activities.

3. Earned Value Table

The *earned value* data can be presented in both a tabular format and a graph. Consider the following steps:

Step 1: Set up an *earned value* table using the following abbreviated field headings:

WBS	BAC	BCWS	PC	BCWP	ACWP	SV	CV	EAC
1.1	$2,000	$1,000	40%	$800	$1,200	($200)	($400)	$3,000
1.2								
Total								

Table 16.2: Earned Value Table

Step 2: List the full scope of work in the WBS column.
Step 3: Input BAC values for all work packages.
Step 4: Calculate BCWS to timenow.
Step 5: From the data capture sheet transfer the values for PC and ACWP.
Step 6: Calculate BCWP = BAC x PC
Step 7: Calculate SV, CV and EAC
Step 8: Sum the following columns: BAC, BCWS, BCWP, ACWP and EAC.
Step 9: Calculate the total PC, SV and CV.

4. Earned Value Graph

The *earned value* graph (see figure 16.3) is produced using the following steps:
Step 1: Draw the BCWS curve (see how to draw an S curve in the *Project Accounts* chapter).
Step 2: Draw the BCWP curve to timenow and extrapolate until the line intersects with BAC (see notes on extrapolating - figure 16.4). This intersection will give a forecast completion date. This completion date however, should not be looked at in isolation because it does not consider the network logic, critical path and timing of the activities.
Step 3: Draw the ACWP curve to timenow and extrapolate to the new end date of the project and EAC. Where EAC = (ACWP / BCWP) x BAC. This equation assumes progress to timenow will continue at the same rate to the end of the project.
Step 4: Draw the SV and CV variances.
Step 5: Determine how far the project is ahead or behind.

Extrapolating: When trying to forecast the trends in the project by extrapolating the *earned value* curves (BCWP and ACWP), the following considerations should be made (see figure 16.4):

- Will the same performance be maintained.
- Will the performance improve because of a learning curve effect.
- Will the performance reduce because of unforeseen problems and re-work as the project nears completion.

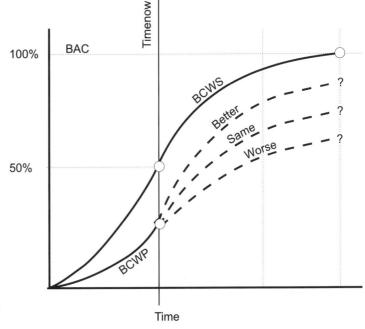

Figure 16.4: BCWP Progress Extrapolations

Exercise: There are thirteen different combinations of planned BCWS vs actual ACWP and earned BCWP. These are shown in the table below (table 16.3), along with a description of each situation. First calculate the EAC, then draw the BCWP and ACWP curves.

Examples	BAC Budget	BCWS Planned Costs	BCWP Earned Value	ACWP Actual Costs	EAC Estimate at Completion
1	$2,000	$1,000	$1,000	$1,000	
2	$2,000	$1,000	$800	$800	
3	$2,000	$1,000	$1,000	$800	
4	$2,000	$1,000	$1,200	$800	
5	$2,000	$1,000	$800	$1,000	
6	$2,000	$1,000	$1,200	$1,000	
7	$2,000	$1,000	$800	$1,200	
8	$2,000	$1,000	$1,000	$1,200	
9	$2,000	$1,000	$1,200	$1,200	
10	$2,000	$1,000	$600	$800	
11	$2,000	$1,000	$800	$600	
12	$2,000	$1,000	$1,400	$1,200	
13	$2,000	$1,000	$1,200	$1,400	

Table 16.3: Earned Value Exercises

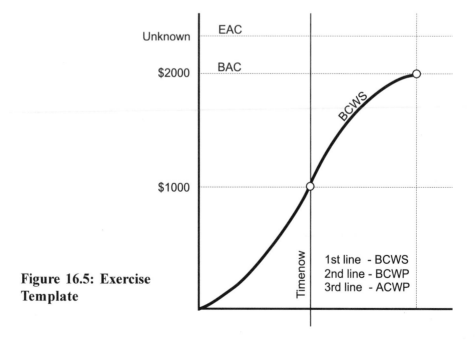

Figure 16.5: Exercise Template

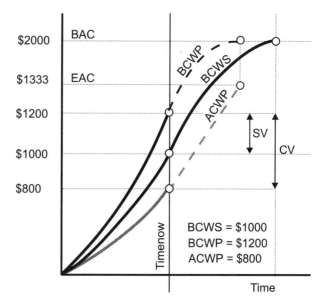

**Figure 16.6:
Solution to
Number 4**

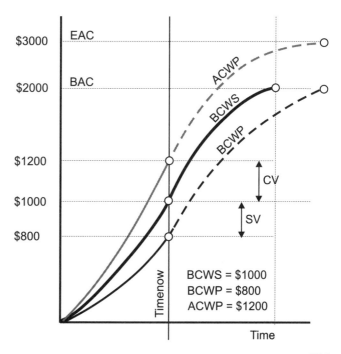

**Figure 16.7:
Solution to
Number 7**

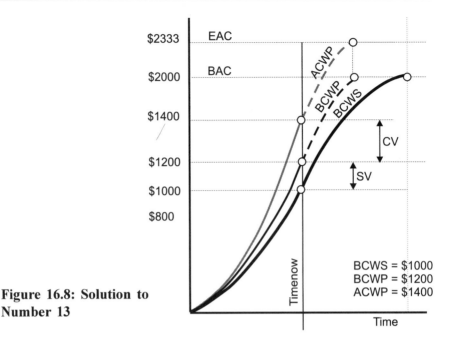

Figure 16.8: Solution to Number 13

Example 1: This is the planned situation, where planned and actual are the same.
Example 2: The project is running late, but the costs are within budget.
Example 3: The project is on time and the costs are under budget.
Example 4: The progress is ahead of planned and the costs are under budget. Retire while you are ahead !
Example 5: The project is running late and the costs are over budget.
Example 6: The progress is ahead of planned and the costs are under budget.
Example 7: The project is running late and the costs are well over budget.
Example 8: The project is on time, but the costs are over budget.
Example 9: The progress is ahead of planned while the costs are on budget.
Example 10: The project is seriously behind and the costs are over budget.
Example 11: The project is behind, but the costs are under budget.
Example 12: The project is well ahead and the costs are under budget.
Example 13: The project is ahead, but the costs are over budget.

5. How to Measure Time Deviation

The schedule variance so far has been measured in money units. This section will show a number of methods to translate the variances directly into time units by measuring distances from the *earned value* graph. Three ways of measuring are (see figure 16.9):
- Horizontally (forwards)
- Horizontally (backwards)
- Vertically

Horizontally (Forwards): The time difference between planned and actual is measured horizontally between the intersection of the planned BCWS at timenow (A) and the horizontal projection to BCWP extrapolated (B).

Horizontally (Backwards): Alternatively the schedule time unit can be measured horizontally from the intersection of BCWP and timenow (C) to the horizontal projection backwards onto the BCWS (D). Note that both of these methods are only an estimate as the actual sequence and timing of the activities are not considered.

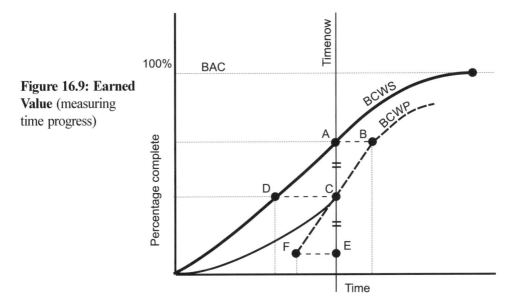

Figure 16.9: Earned Value (measuring time progress)

Vertically: However, even if the sequence and timing of activities were the same as the *baseline plan*, converting the schedule variance to time units on the BCWP curve would be more accurate if based on the tangential rate (CF), where (CA) = (EC). The reason for this is that future progress is more likely to occur at the current actual rate of progress rather than the planned BCWS slope.

Project Accounts: The project manager will need to ensure that the project accounting system will generate costs to timenow. Corporate accounting departments usually base their reports on invoiced costs which may be 4 to 6 weeks behind timenow. When using *earned value* the costs will have to be gathered at the order stage, it is essential to compare like with like. Progress to timenow must be compared with the associated costs (ACWP) to achieve that progress.

Extended Site: If costs are being incurred off site, such as stage payments then the progress (PC) must be reported along with the associated cost (ACWP).

Cash-Flow: The *earned value* technique is not the same as cash-flow. The cash-flow only looks at the timing of the inflows and outflows of money, it does not consider committed costs or progress of work.

Project Control: Beware of managers who constantly revise the BCWS to accommodate their lack of performance (see figures 16.10, 16.11 and 16.12). This may make their weekly progress reports look better, but eventually it will extend the end date of the project. If the contractor continually revises the BCWS from the last BCWP then the contractors lack of progress does not look as obvious as comparing it with the original BCWS. The contractors are only fooling themselves because eventually they will have to perform the remaining work on the last day!

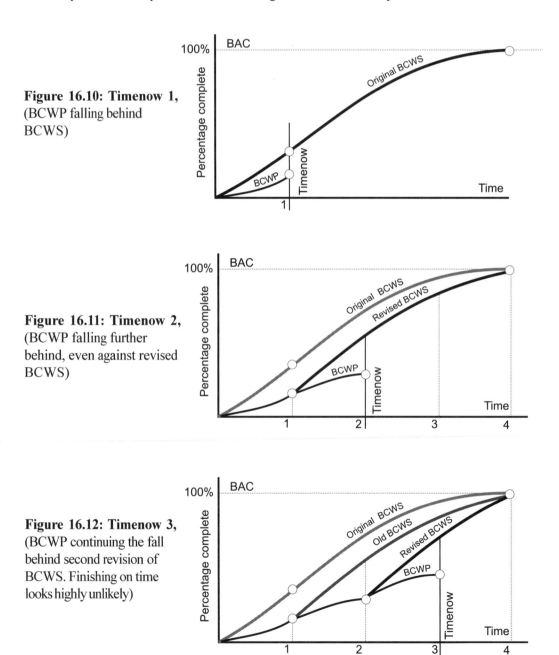

Figure 16.10: Timenow 1, (BCWP falling behind BCWS)

Figure 16.11: Timenow 2, (BCWP falling further behind, even against revised BCWS)

Figure 16.12: Timenow 3, (BCWP continuing the fall behind second revision of BCWS. Finishing on time looks highly unlikely)

6. Client's View of Earned Value

So far the *earned value* technique has only been looked at from the sub-contractors' point of view. This section will consider the client's position.

- If the sub-contractors are working to a fixed price contract then BCWP and ACWP will always be the same.
- The client can effectively use *earned value* to track the progress of their projects in terms of manhours or costs.
- The client must check that sub-contractors do not over claim:

  a) If a sub-contractor has claimed 80% of the contract by value but only completed 50% of the work, there is little financial pressure you can exert. Worse is when it is financially viable for the sub-contractor to walk away without finishing the job. The 10% retention may pale into insignificance.

  b) The sub-contractor's management may not realise their site manager has been over claiming. This could seriously effect the sub-contractor's financial position, which may have a knock-on effect for the project.

- If the sub-contractor under-claims, the client could also be adversely affected because:

  a) By delaying the claim the sub-contractor could increase income by applying higher escalation rates.

  b) The client could have made arrangements to meet a forecast rate of invoice (FRI) payment and released high interest earning bonds only to find a lower claim is made. The funds must now be invested short term at a lower interest rate.

  c) At year end a late claim could effect the client's fiscal budgeting.

This section clearly shows that *earned value* can provide the client with a powerful management tool.

7. Earned Value Reporting

The *earned value* output lends itself to effective reporting for the following reasons.

- The overall status of the project can be seen at a glance on a graph and the tabular reports present more detailed information at the work package and activity levels.
- When reporting to functional management the report should clearly indicate the activities that fall under their responsibility. This information can be separately reported if a responsibility field has been included in the data base.
- The reports can use a ***management-by-exception*** (MBE) technique to identify problem areas. The MBE thresholds can be set using any of the following:-

  a) Threshold variance SV% and CV%. Set upper and lower percentages, for example, -5% to +10%.

  b) Activity float = 0 days, identifies the critical path, or set activity float < 5 days, to identify activities which could go critical in the next week.

- The sign of the variance should influence the management response.

  SV (+) The project is ahead of schedule, move labour off the project if they can be used more effectively elsewhere.

SV (-) The project is behind schedule, move resources on to the project to increase production.

CV (+) The project costs are less than budget, if significant, amend estimating data base for future projects.

CV (-) The project costs are greater than budget, try to increase productivity through increased efficiency and effectiveness.

- Plot trends wherever possible to indicate the direction of the project. Extrapolating trends will give an indication of future events and a quick feedback on recent actions. Even if the variances are negative, but reducing, this will show a positive trend indicating that the project is coming back onto course.

Determining Percentage Complete: The weakest link in the *earned value* calculation is determining percentage complete (PC). If the activity has not started it is zero and if it is complete it is 100%, but all points in between are somewhat of a guess even if you use a structure. A quick way to estimate PC is to use the 50/50 rule, if the job has started give it 50% and when it is finished give it 100%. This rule can be distorted to 40/60, 30/70, 20/80 and 10/90. If the work packages or activities are kept small (less than 50 hours), then this method will work well.

- The *earned value* analysis should not be used in isolation. An activity with a large schedule variance may have plenty of float and not be a problem, while an activity with a small schedule variance may be on the critical path and need prompt action to prevent the project over-running.
- *Estimate-at-completion* (EAC) - is based on the ratio of past performance, but if the original estimate is fundamentally flawed, or performance is significantly different to planned, then the rest of the project should be re-estimated.
- EAC - includes the actual costs to date plus the forecast *cost-to-complete*.
- Cost reserves are budgeted amounts not assigned to any specific work package.
- NASA manager: *"Earned value is only useful if the difference between planned and actual is 10% to 15%, if greater then use other methods."* [Rolling horizon barchart]

If the progress indicates that both SV and CV are negative and significant, then ordering a small contractor to increase their resources may actually put them into liquidation quicker! There is obviously a problem which needs to be investigated - is the contractor's estimate over optimistic or is the contractor's workforce under performing? This concludes the chapter on *Earned Value*, the next chapter will discuss *Quality Management*.

Key Points:

- *Earned value* integrates costs and time or manhours and time.
- The *earned value* graph and table shows the project's present position and forecasts the completion.
- Threshold variances can be set to flag problem areas.

Further Reading:

Fleming, Q., and **Koppelman**, J., *Earned Value Project Management*, PMIC
Turner, R., *Handbook of Project-Based Management*, McGraw-Hill

Case Study and Exercises:

The earned value technique integrates cost and time (or manhours and time) to give the project manager the best of both worlds. For this case study you have been appointed project manager of the drawing office for a military project requiring 1000 drawings. You are required to outline how you will plan, track and control the drawing office project using the earned value technique. Your outline should consider the following:

1. The earned value plan BAC and BCWS.
2. Methods for determining percentage complete.
3. Data capture BCWP and ACWP.
4. Earned value reporting tables and curves.
5. Control of variances.

"Your move"

Quality Management

In today's competitive market companies compete on price, quality and customer service. Over the product's life-cycle the project's initial price is only a short term consideration, whereas the quality of the product and customer service will determine the long term success of the project. **Quality products are only expensive once!**

The PMBOK defines project quality management as; '... *the processes required to ensure that the project will satisfy the needs for which it was undertaken* [by addressing] *both the management of the project and the product of the project.'* And the APM bok defines quality management as; *'... covering quality planning, quality control and quality assurance.'*

You therefore need to consider both the *quality management system* to assure you are capable of building the product, and also consider the *quality control system* which tests and inspects the product, to confirm you have achieved the required condition.

With projects becoming larger, more complex and more technically advanced, the need to assure the product will meet stringent requirements is the focus of quality management. These requirements may be set not only by the client, but also by insurance companies, governmental laws and regulations, together with national and international standards.

The development of quality management systems can be dated back to the large military projects of the Second World War, where they needed to ensure standardisation. Since then BS 5750 (1979) has established the framework for commercial quality management systems and has since been adopted internationally as the ISO 9000 standard.

1. Quality Definitions

Quality is a frequently misused term. Be careful not to confuse quality with degree of excellence or grade, where grade is a category of rank given to products which have the same function but different quality requirements. For example, the Rolls Royce and the Mini are often quoted as being at opposite ends of the quality continuum, the Rolls Royce being built to a much higher quality than the Mini. However, if you wish to buy an economical small car that will do 50 miles to the gallon and is easy to park, then the Mini is the car that '*conforms to the client's requirements*'.

Quality Management Philosophy: The involvement of all project participants to ensure the goals and objectives of the project and resulting product, facility or service meet the needs of the client, project team and other stakeholders.

Quality Assurance: Is a systematic process of defining, planning, implementing and reviewing the management processes within a company, in order to provide adequate confidence that the product will be consistently manufactured to the required condition. The body of knowledge defines quality assurance as; '*... the planned and systematic activities implemented within the quality system to provide confidence that the project will satisfy the relevant quality standards.*'

Quality Planning: Is the process of identifying the quality standards the project needs to comply with, to achieve the required condition and satisfy the terms of the contract.

Quality Control: Is the process companies go through to confirm the product has reached the required condition. Quality control defines the method of inspection, in-process inspection and final inspection to confirm the product has met the required condition. The body of knowledge defines quality control as '*... monitoring specific project results to determine if they comply with relevant quality standards and identify ways to eliminate causes of unsatisfactory results.*' The required condition should be laid down in the *scope of work*, specifications and the *project quality plan*. When a non-conformance has been identified, the resulting non-conformance report (NCR) may trigger a quality audit to gather more information before corrective action is authorised. In some cases the corrective action may call for quality awareness training.

In the past, quality management focused on the inspection of the product after it was built. There was little involvement with the manufacturers. The emphasis was on '*catching*' defects before they were released. But now there is a general acceptance that **you cannot inspect quality into a product** if the product was not made properly in the first place. The emphasis has shifted to the workers at the coalface assuring they have the support to make the job right in the first place.

Quality Control Plan: The *quality control plan* integrates the project schedule with quality control, by listing the sequence of work, performance requirements, inspection requirements and hold points (the *quality control plan* is developed later in this chapter).

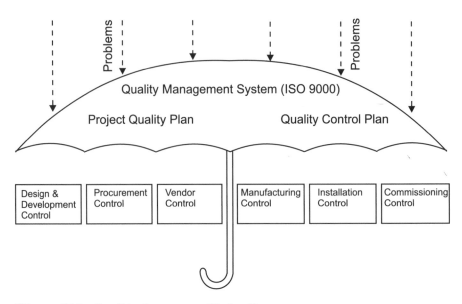

Figure 17.1: Quality Assurance Umbrella

Quality Circles: Quality circles are a management concept the Americans set up for Toyota cars in Japan after the Second World War, to continuously improve their manufacturing process by bringing all the people in a production line together (used in its wider context) to identify and solve problems.

Quality Audit: The body of knowledge defines a quality audit as; '... *a structured review of other quality management activities. The objective is to identify lessons learned that can improve performance.....*' [on this and future projects]. An audit in the project management context should be seen as a search for more information as a basis of the problem-solving and decision-making function.

Quality Training: Quality is a company wide issue, from the CEO to the receptionist. Therefore all employees should undertake quality training so that they can contribute to the quality of the management system and the quality of the product.

Project Quality Plan: The project quality plan is a detailed document explaining how the company will assure that the product will be made to the client's requirements. The 20 subheadings from the ISO 9000 quality management system can be used to structure the document.

Total Quality Management (TQM): TQM considers the wider aspects of quality by amalgamating all of the quality management features. Total quality has a people and outcome focus. It first identifies what the client really wants, how it can best be achieved, keeps an emphasis on continuous improvement, but always wants to keep the *customer satisfied*. For quality to be effective it needs to be introduced to all members and all aspects of the company's operation.

2. Quality Costs

Crosby argues that *quality is free!* It costs less to get the job right first time. However some managers never seem to have the time to get it right first time, yet seem to have the time to re-work the job. The cost of this re-work may be two or three times the original cost in terms of manhours and materials. Consider a weld on a steel fabrication project which has been rejected, the additional costs would include:

- Quality department raise a *non-conformance report* (NCR).
- Planning department schedule the repair and reschedule the remaining work.
- Remove the rejected weld and surface preparation.
- Quality check of surface preparation.
- Re-weld
- Quality check of new weld.

And if the second weld fails this may require the whole section to be replaced, the welder retrained together with additional inspection on all his previous welds. This example clearly demonstrates that the cost of failure can be very expensive.

Quality Costs: Are a combination of management costs, consider these four headings which will be developed:

- Prevention costs
- Appraisal costs
- Failure costs / internal
- Failure costs / external

Prevention Costs: Prevention costs are those expenses associated with steps taken to make sure the product will be made to the required condition.

- Project Quality Plan.
- Quality planning.
- Quality Control Plan.
- Quality auditing.
- Assuring vendor and sub-contractors' quality.
- Reviewing and verifying designs.
- In-process control engineering.
- Design and development of quality measurement and test equipment.
- Quality training.
- Acquisition analysis and reporting quality data.
- Quality improvement programs.
- Product recall and liability insurance.
- Planning of product recall.

Appraisal Costs: Appraisal costs relate to expenses incurred while checking and inspecting the work to confirm that it has achieved the required condition.

- Design appraisal.
- Receiving inspection.
- Inspection and non-destructive testing (NDT).
- Procuring inspection and testing equipment.

- Materials consumed during inspection and testing.
- Analysis and reporting of test and inspection results.
- Field performance testing.
- Approval and endorsements.
- Stock evaluations.
- Record storage.

Internal Failure Costs: These costs relate to expenses incurred within the company due to product failure and inefficiencies.
- Replacement, rework or repair.
- Scrap and waste material.
- Re-inspection and retesting.
- Defect diagnosis.
- Downtime.
- Down-grading.

External Failure Costs: These costs relate to expenses incurred outside the company, usually motivated by the client.
- Receiving and actioning complaints.
- Warranty claims.
- Products rejected and returned.
- Concessions.
- Loss of future sales.
- Increased marketing to replace lost clients.
- Recall costs.
- Product liability.

The lists seems frighteningly long, considering all these items may have a cost associated with them. The criteria for success is that the increase in prevention costs should be less than the reduction in failure costs as shown in figure 17.2.

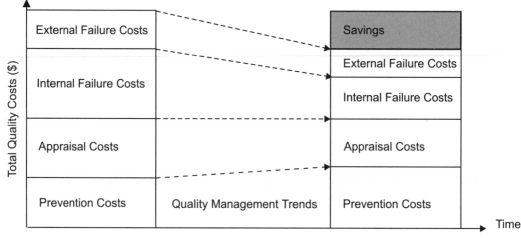

Figure 17.2: Quality Management Costs (showing how increased prevention costs can actually reduce the overall quality costs)

The main problem with the quality management costs diagram (figure 17.2) is that people have a natural propensity to cover up their mistakes, therefore the figures for the cost of re-work may never be accurately known.

Quality Costs: When John Eagan joined Jaguar cars in 1980 the company was losing about $5 million a month. Under Eagan's direction, Jaguar set about developing a quality control programme and four years later the dramatic effect could be seen in the company's sales figures, rising morale and a boost to the workers' wage packets. In addition Jaguar has seen a dramatic reduction in warranty costs, huge gains in productivity and major reductions in finished product defect levels. Once again Jaguar became a profitable company.

3. Quality Planning

The body of knowledge defines quality planning as; '... *identifying which quality standards are relevant to the project and determining how to satisfy them.*' We need to distinguish between a company's quality policy and the *project quality plan.* The company's quality policy applies to the whole company and may be formalised through accreditation to ISO 9000 quality management standard, or the national equivalent. For your project however, it may be necessary to tailor your company's quality management system to meet the needs of the client and the product - this is achieved through the *project quality plan.*

4. Quality Circles

Quality circles are a management concept the Americans set up for Toyota cars in Japan after the Second World War to continuously improve their manufacturing process, by bringing all the people in a production line together (used in its widest context) to identify and solve problems. Quality circles' methodology ties-in well with the *systems breakdown structure* (see *WBS* chapter) where there is a need for a series of trades, departments or people to work together to produce a product, service or solve a problem (see figure 17.3).

Objectives: To improve communication between all parties in the same product line, particularly between planning and production. Also to:
- To identify and solve problems.
- To enhance the product design and manufacturing process, leading to increased productivity.
- To improve working conditions and job satisfaction.
- To empower workers to apply their own creative and innovative skills, leading to peer recognition which will ultimately improve team morale and commitment.

Organisation: Quality circles generally consist of five or six people who select their own leader. The people should be from the same work area or interfacing work areas, for example planning, procurement, HRM and production. Participation is usually voluntary.

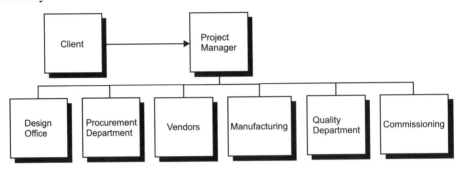

Figure 17.3: System Breakdown Structure (Quality Circles)

Training: To make the most of quality circles the members may need training in; team building, problem-solving techniques and quality management.

Scope of Interest: The quality circle should select its own problems. However, initially the quality circle could be encouraged to select problems from its immediate work area. The problems need not be restricted to quality, they can also include productivity, costs, safety, morale and the working environment.

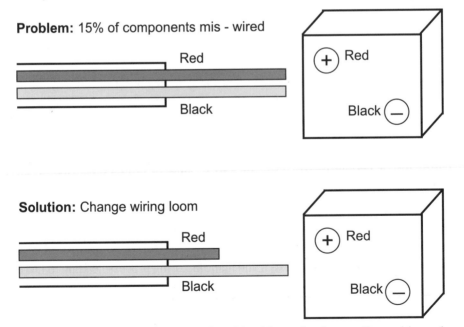

Figure 17.4: Quality Circle Question: Consider this production quality problem where 15% of the electrical components were incorrectly wired, even though the wires were colour coded and the terminals staggered. Solution cut the wires to match the terminals.

Meetings: Usually half an hour per week, held during working hours in a conference room. Use a brainstorming approach to generate ideas and suggestions. Minutes of the meetings should be presented to management for their consideration.

Rewards: Usually no financial benefit. Satisfaction is deemed to be achieved through problem-solving, achieving something worthwhile, observing the implementation of your ideas, having a certain amount of control on your work environment and recognition. Indirectly this may speed up your promotion.

The quality circle approach is becoming more pervasive as the benefits are recognised. People at the workface often see problems and solutions their managers cannot and the best people to fix a problem are usually those who benefit. This working together for the common good of the project creates a dynamic team spirit.

5. Quality Audit

An audit may be defined as an investigation, inspection or survey of a system or product, where the actual or measured condition is compared with the planned condition, required condition or declared condition - the difference or variance being reported in the findings and recommendations. ISO 8402 defines 'quality audit' as; '... *a systematic and independent examination to determine whether quality activities and related results comply with planned arrangements and whether these arrangements are implemented effectively and are suitable to achieve the objective.'*

Audits are not limited to auditing the financial accounts - any aspect of the project can be audited. They can be either internal or external to the company, but should definitely be independent to the project. To achieve this the quality manager would normally report to the managing director and not the project manager or general manager (see figure 17.5). This way the quality manager can be held responsible for assuring both the quality management system and the quality of the product.

Figure 17.5: Project Matrix Structure (showing QA department)

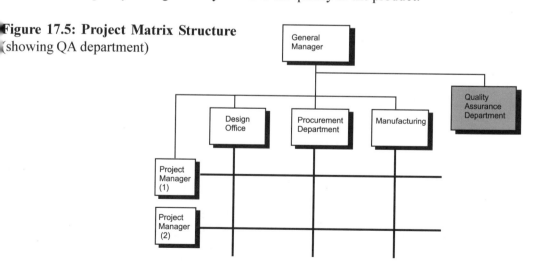

When a non-conformance is reported or suspected, the quality audit provides the project manager or client with an excellent tool for investigating the root of the problem. The right to conduct an audit is usually written into the project's contract, in fact the procurement department often audit their suppliers to pre-qualify them before tendering. Audits should follow a formal structure, consider the following procedure:

- The auditors organise a pre-audit meeting.
- The pre-audit meeting discusses the scope of the audit - why, what, when, who, how and where.
- The audit is carried out by a series of questionnaires, interviews and inspections.
- The audit data is collected and analysed.
- An audit closeout meeting is held where the audit findings are announced and discussed.
- Corrective actions are carried out and re-audited at a later date.

Auditing the Project Management System: The audit of a project management system can be conducted at two levels:

- Audit the project management system against best practices (body of knowledge) to ensure the management function will be able to achieve the project's objectives.
- Audit the implemented project management system against the declared system.

Most small contracting companies will probably not have a project management system, so when you audit these companies you are in fact conducting a double audit of:

- What they intend to do against what they should be doing (best practice).
- What they are doing against what they intend to do.

Audit **benefits:**

- It provides a wealth of information.
- The data collected is actionable.
- The approach is objective.
- The auditor should be an independent expert with no personal agenda.

Audit **problems:**

- There may be an unintentional bias on the part of the auditor.
- The auditor's experience may be unique and provide misleading evidence.
- An audit can only be carried out infrequently due to its complexity, time and costs. A small sample could produce misleading results.
- The results may be too detailed - unable to see the wood for the trees.

Audits are not about punishing people who fail, they should be about helping people achieve the required condition and helping them to do their job better. Part of the quality training should consider training people not only how to conduct audits, but also how to be audited.

6. Quality Control Plan

The *quality control plan* links the quality requirements to the build method and *scheduled barchart*. The *quality control plan* offers you the facility to impose the predetermined work sequence that you want, rather than what the production department may determine as resource efficient at the time. This can be imposed with a *quality control plan* which lists the sequence of work and the level of inspection. The sequence of work is determined by the build method and *network diagram*. The level of inspection is determined by the level of control and risk and this can be imposed as; **surveillance, inspection, witness** or **hold points.** Consider the following project with five key activities to build a warehouse (see figure 17.6):

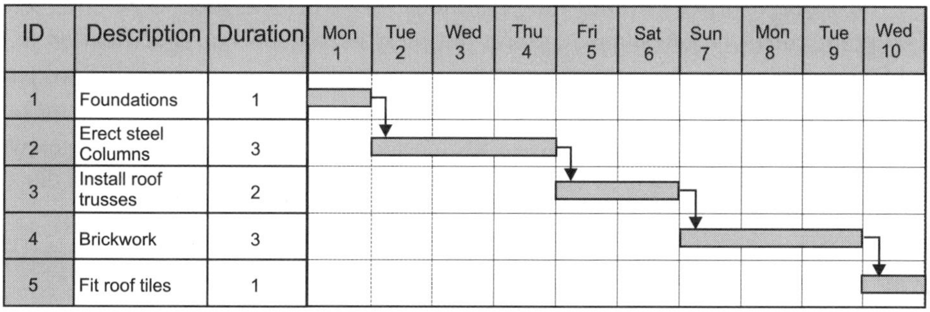

ID	Description	Duration	Mon 1	Tue 2	Wed 3	Thu 4	Fri 5	Sat 6	Sun 7	Mon 8	Tue 9	Wed 10
1	Foundations	1										
2	Erect steel Columns	3										
3	Install roof trusses	2										
4	Brickwork	3										
5	Fit roof tiles	1										

Figure 17.6: Barchart (Building a warehouse)

The plan calls for these activities to be carried out in series, but the site foreman decides it is more efficient to start the brickwork before the roof trusses are installed because the scaffolding is in position. Shortly after starting the brickwork, the engineer stops this activity when he visits the site. The engineer explains to the foreman that the swaying of the unsupported columns will crack the mortar.

When the roof trusses are installed the foreman decides to fit the roof tiles at the same time because all the men are up on the roof - remember the brickwork has not been completed. With the next strong wind many of these tiles are ripped off and besides the cost of damage to property there is a serious risk to life with these giant frisbees flying around.

This example demonstrates a serious lack of understanding between the project office and the production department. The *quality control plan* can be used to ensure and enforce compliance to the *scheduled barchart*. This is achieved by introducing an inspection hold point after each of these key activities. This means no work can commence on a subsequent activity until the previous one has been inspected and approved by the nominated person. Table 17.1 is a typical *quality control plan*.

Activity	Description	Spec	Level of inspection	NC	Sign off
1	Foundations		Witness pouring / hold		
2	Erect steel columns		Hold		
3	Install roof trusses		Hold		
4	Brickwork		Surveillance / hold		
5	Fit roof tiles		Inspection		

Table 17.1: Quality Control Plan (Building a warehouse)

The *scope of work* outlines the operations, tasks or activities to be completed. The requirement or acceptance criteria outlines the standard or specification to be achieved. The inspection outlines who is to inspect; client, contractor or third party and the type of inspection; hold point, witness or surveillance. The signature is to confirm compliance.

This concludes the chapter on *Quality Management*, the next chapter will discuss *Risk Management*.

Key Points:

- Quality management includes both the quality of the management of the project and the quality of the product itself.
- It is generally accepted that the cost of prevention will proportionally reduce the cost of failure.
- The *quality control plan* offers a structure to ensure the production will comply with the planned build method.

Further Reading:

BS 5750 (1979), *Quality Management*
Crosby, P.B., *Quality is Free*, McGraw-Hill
Crosby, P.B., *Quality Without Tears*, McGraw-Hill
Juran, Joseph, *Product Quality - A Prescription for the West*

Case Study and Exercises:

Quality management is the processes required to ensure that the project will satisfy the needs for which it was undertaken, and in today's competitive market companies compete on price, quality and customer service. As project manager of a production line producing DVDs, you are responsible for developing a quality management plan which should consider the following:

1. Quality costs.
2. Quality circles.
3. Quality audit.
4. Quality control plan.
5. TQM.

In process control

Project Risk Management

Company success is achieved by pursuing opportunities to gain a competitive advantage, and projects have typically been setup to take advantage of these opportunities - to make something new, or change (enhance) an existing facility. A key component of change is making decisions - ideally these decisions would be based on complete information with a high degree of certainty of the outcome. However, in the real world most decisions are based on incomplete information with an associated level of uncertainty about the outcome - it is this uncertainty that leads to risk. So risk has always been an intrinsic part of project management.

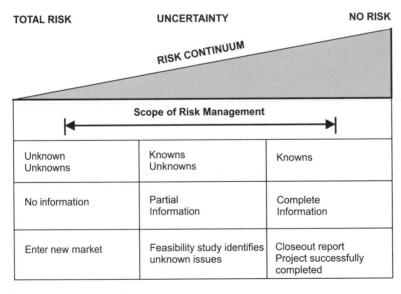

Figure 18.1: Risk Continuum (relating to level of information and uncertainty)

It can be seen that risk, uncertainty and opportunity are closely related. When a risk occurs, with some entrepreneurial ingenuity, this may be turned around to become an opportunity, and conversely when pursuing an opportunity there will be associated risks that could derail your project.

Project Risk Management is defined by the PMBOK as; '... *the systematic processes of identifying, analysing and responding to project risk...* [throughout the project life-cycle]'. It includes maximising the results of positive events and minimising the consequences of adverse events. The APM bok defines risk as; '... *factors that may cause a failure to meet the project's objectives...*' or limits the achievement of your objectives as defined at the outset of the project. The generally accepted risk management model subdivides the risk management process into the following headings (see figure 18.2):

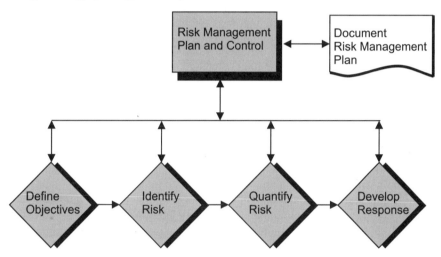

Figure 18.2: Risk Management Model

Risk Management Plan: APM bok; '... *a formal approach to the process as opposed to an intuitive approach...*' The risk management plan documents how you propose to tackle risk on your project.

- **Define Objectives:** Define the context of your work and your plan for success. This defines what you have to achieve to be successful and establishes a basis for dealing with risk and future decisions.
- **Identify Risk:** Identify areas of risk, uncertainty and constraints, which may impact on your project, and limit or prevent you achieving your objectives.
- **Quantify Risk:** Evaluate the risks and prioritize the level of risk and uncertainty and quantify their frequency of occurrence and impact.
- **Develop Response:** Define how you are going to respond to the identified risks (which may be a combination of); eliminate, mitigate, deflect or accept.
- **Risk Control:** The risk control function implements the *risk management plan*. This may involve training team members, and communication to all stakeholders. As the risks and the work environment are continually changing, it is essential to continually monitor and review the level of risk and your ability to effectively respond.

253

1. Project Life-Cycle

The project life-cycle format provides an informative overview of how the level of risk changes as the project progresses through the project phases. Figure 18.3a outlines how the risk and the amount at stake change, while figure 18.3b outlines how the level of influence and the cost to make changes varies through the life-cycle.

Figure 18.3a indicates that risk and opportunity are high at the outset of the project (during the concept and design phases), when there is the greatest degree of uncertainty about the future. As the project progresses these parameters reduce as decisions are made, design freezes are implemented, and the remaining unknowns are translated into knowns. These unknowns are eventually zero when the project is successfully completed. The amount at stake (investment), on the other hand, starts low and steadily rises as capital and resources are invested to complete the project.

Figure 18.3b outlines how the initial phases offer the greatest potential to add value with the least cost, but as the project progresses so the ability to make changes reduces as the cost of changes becomes increasingly expensive.

The highest vulnerability to risk, therefore, occurs during the last two phases (implementation and commissioning). During these phases, problems may occur, particularly during commissioning and start-up.

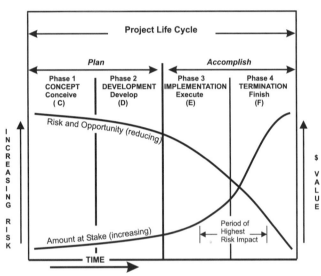

Figure 18.3a: Risk vs Amount at Stake

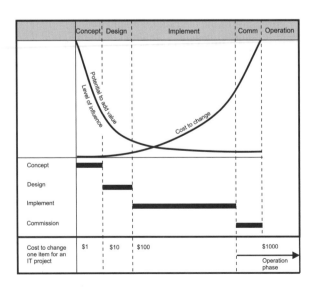

**Figure 18.3b:
Level of Influence vs
Cost to Change**

2. Risk Management Responsibility

Who is responsible for managing risk? The managing director is ultimately responsible to the board of directors and the shareholders for managing risk within the company. However, this responsibility is usually delegated through the corporate hierarchy with the project managers responsible for project risk and the functional managers responsible for their department's risks (see figure 18.4). This process of pushing risk responsibility down the hierarchy is consistent with risk management being a company wide issue (empowerment). The respective managers would then be responsible for developing a *risk management plan* to identify, quantify, respond and control risks that affect their *scope of work*. As with other management techniques, it should be the managers responsibility to ensure that their team members have a working understanding of risk within the context of their *scope of work* and feel accountable for the consequences of their actions.

Disaster Recovery: For the ultimate unplanned catastrophe, that prevents your company providing its critical business functions for a period of time, and results in significant damage or loss, your company needs to develop a *disaster recovery plan*. The objective of disaster recovery planning is to reduce the consequence of a disaster to an acceptable level. The responsibility for developing and implementing the *disaster recovery plan* should be assigned to the selected manager as part of your company's *risk management plan* (see figure 18.4). So that in the event of a disaster the plans will

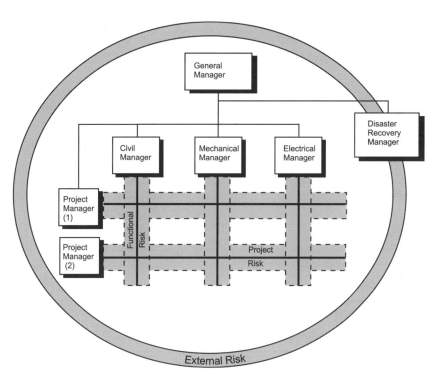

Figure 18.4: Risk Responsibility Organisation Structure

have been developed, updated and a functioning team will be ready to implement them - '*hit the ground running*'. Therefore the project manager should liaise with the disaster recovery manager to establish a disaster recovery plan for the project, particularly for site work, which may not be covered by a corporate disaster recovery plan.

3. Define Objectives

A risk may be defined as any event or constraint that prevents you achieving the project's goals and objectives. It is therefore necessary at the outset to define these goals and objectives in some detail. Consider the project brief, project charter, project proposal, together with the following breakdown structures:

- Subdivide by stakeholders (see the *Feasibility Study* chapter)
- Subdivide by project management knowledge areas (see table 18.1)
- Subdivide by OBS - departments (see table 18.2)
- Subdivide by WBS - work packages (see table 18.3)
- Subdivide by constraints (internal and external) (see *Feasibility Study* chapter)

These structures will provide a logical framework for identifying, quantifying and responding to risk. This systematic approach helps to ensure significant risks and opportunities are not over looked.

The PMBOK knowledge areas can be expanded to include other business operations:

- Sales and marketing
- Design and development
- Education and training
- Computer systems

Project Management Knowledge Areas	Objectives
Scope Management	WBS, Drawing List
Time Management	CPM, Schedule Barchart
Cost Management	Budget, Cash-Flow Statement
Quality Management	Project Quality Plan, Quality Control Plan
Integration Management	Planning and Control
Human Resource Management	OBS, Resource Histogram
Communication Management	Communication Plan
Risk Management	Risk Management Plan
Procurement Management	Procurement Schedule

Table 18.1: Objectives Sub-Divided by Knowledge Area

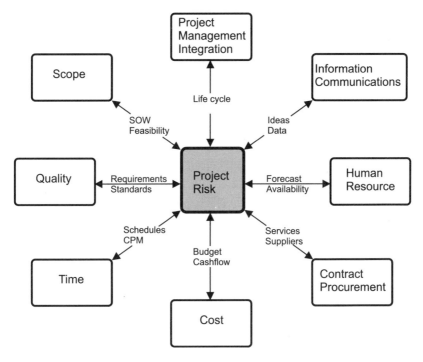

Figure 18.5: Risk Management Integrated
(with the other PMBOK knowledge areas)

Develop **Risk Assessment Criteria** against which risks can be assessed and decisions made. These criteria may be based on operational, technical, financial, legal, social and humanitarian requirements. There will be internal and external constraints which set your boundaries (see the *Feasibility Study* chapter):

- Internal project
- Internal corporate
- External.

Department	Responsibilities and Objectives
Project Office	
Design Office	
Planning Office	
Purchasing Department	
Quality Department	
Accounts Department	

Table 18.2: Objectives by OBS Department

WBS	Objectives
1.1	
1.2	
1.3	
2.1	
2.2	
2.3	

Table 18.3: Establish Objectives by WBS Work Package (proforma)

4. Risk Identification

Having defined your business objectives by one of the above breakdown structures, the next step is to identify what areas of risk and uncertainty could prevent you achieving these stated objectives - plan to prevent failure. Risk identification is probably the hardest and most important part of the risk management process, because if you cannot identify a risk, it will be excluded from further analysis and therefore you will probably not respond to it. The process of risk identification should not be a one time event, but rather a continuous process, its frequency depending on the level of risk on the project and the schedule of meetings.

Using your list of objectives as your starting point, consider adding another two columns to identify cause and effect scenarios. This can be tackled from both directions:
- Cause to effect - if this cause happens what effect will it have on the objectives?
- Effect caused by - what could cause this undesirable effect, or failure?

Risk identification should be a systematic process to ensure nothing significant is overlooked. By adding another column, combinations of risks can also be considered. Seemingly small risks can combine in complex ways, and under a variety of scenarios to produce significant risks; *'it never rains but it pours'*. Walking through the process should give you an appreciation of these interdependencies. Techniques for identifying risk include:
- Analysing historical records and closeout reports (see *Scope Management* chapter)
- Structured questionnaires
- Structured interviews

WBS	Objectives	Cause	Effect
1.1			
1.2			

Table 18.4: Cause and Effect (proforma)

- Brainstorming
- Structured checklists (see *WBS* chapter)
- Flow charts (build method, walk-through)
- Judgement based on knowledge and experience
- System analysis
- Scenario analysis (what-if).

The success of these techniques depends on how the risk management team have been selected and brought together. A balanced team which incorporates; experience, knowledge, judgement, entrepreneurial innovation, creativity, enthusiasm, internal members and external consultants, stands the best chance of success.

Experience: The university of life gives us the experience to identify areas of risk, particularly relating to the problems and situations we have experienced or observed in the past. Greater awareness and appreciation is followed by knowledge and judgement.

Historical Data: Learn from the past - access to a comprehensive data base of relevant experience, both internal and external is invaluable. This information should be available internally from previous projects closeout reports.

Questionnaires, interviews and brainstorming are all ways to generate ideas and feedback from your colleagues, stakeholders, clients, engineers, suppliers, legal eagles and governing agencies. Checklists, breakdown structures and flow charts (CPM) are all ways to group and subdivide information for collation and presentation.

5. Why Projects Fail

Projects fail for many reasons, not least due to lack of professional project management. Project managers are often judged on whether their projects achieved; time, cost and quality targets. Another perhaps more telling criteria is whether the project manager was able to steer the project through a minefield of problems, any one of them just waiting to derail the project. Consider these other items:

- **Innovation:** If your level of innovation is too low your product may not be able to compete in the market, but conversely if your level of innovation is too high you may be forever trying to iron out design problems.
- **Concurrency:** Concurrency is developing your product before your client's requirements are fully defined. The USAF now prefers to *'fly-before-buy'* so that prototypes can be tested before making a production selection. This approach may have prevented the TSR2 (swing-wing bomber) procurement disaster.
- **Stakeholders:** Failing to recognise stakeholders interests, particularly environmentalists. Concorde was an engineering and aviation success, but a commercial disaster because it failed to recognise that the environment lobby would prevent it flying supersonically over land.
- **Communication:** NASA's Mars probe crash landed on the surface of Mars because of a mix up between imperial and metric measurements used by the designers.

- **Scope of work:** Misinterpreting the *scope of work* is a common cause of project failure (states Kerzner). Others include:
  - Mixing and confusing; tasks, specifications, approvals, and special instructions.
  - Using imprecise or vague language, for example; nearly, optimum, about or approximately - can lead to confusion, ambiguity or misinterpretation.
  - The project has no pattern, structure, or chronological order. The WBS and CPM techniques have not been used.
  - A wide variation in size of the tasks and work packages, again caused by not using the WBS to subdivide all the work packages to a common level of detail.
  - Wide variation in how to describe work details.
  - Failing to get a third-party review, or verification from either the client, sub-contractors and suppliers.
- **IT Projects:** (ProjectPro) IT projects have a poor track record for delivering systems within budget:
  - Only 18% of software projects are completed within budget
  - 50% overrun their budget
  - 30% are so expensive that they are abandoned before substantial completion.

Other common reasons for project failure include:
- Not working closely with the client.
- Poor estimating.
- Inadequate planning.
- Insufficient reviews and control.
- A lack of commitment (buy-in of participants and stakeholders) - gain commitment by involving the responsible people in the planning.

"Look before you leap"

- Incomplete information, for example, during the tendering process the contractor is attempting to assess the correct market price for a project not yet built, for a design which is subject to revision, on a site about which there is little information and a labour force not yet recruited.
- Poor planning - material and equipment not available on time.
- Lack of understanding of project management techniques.
- Lack of support from team members.

6. Risk Quantification

Having identified a range of risks, the next step is to quantify the probability (likelihood) of the risk occurring and the impact or consequence to the project, or to the amount at stake. Risk quantification is primarily concerned with determining what areas of risk warrant a response and where resources are limited, a risk priority will determine the areas of risk that should be addressed first.

Probability / Impact Matrix: This matrix plots the probability of the risk occurring against the impact on the project (see figure 18.6). They are quantified as high, medium, or low - this will give a matrix of nine possibilities.

For risks that recur on a regular basis there may be statistical information available (e.g. days lost to inclement weather). For non-recurring risks a more subjective analysis will be required to determine probability of occurrence.

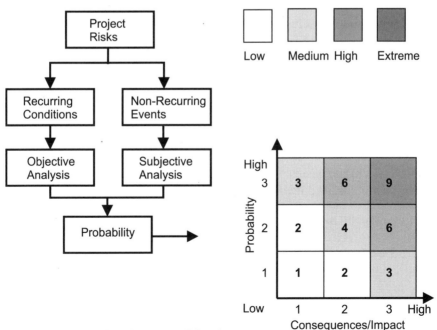

Figure 18.6: Probability / Impact Matrix

Priority: The output from risk quantification should be a WBS table (see table 18.5) which identifies, quantifies and prioritizes the risk. With finite resources it is essential to establish which risks should be addressed first so as to focus your effort.

WBS	Objective	Risk	Probability	Consequence	Priority
1.1					
1.2					
1.3					

Table 18.5: Objective, Risk, Probability, Consequence and Priority (proforma)

7. Risk Response

Having identified, quantified and prioritized the risks, you now need to develop a risk response plan which defines ways to address adverse risk and enhance opportunities before they occur. The levels of risk should be compared against pre-established criteria, then ranked to establish management priorities. There are a range of responses which should be developed in advance during the planning phase:

- Eliminate risk
- Mitigate risk
- Deflect risk
- Accept risk

These are not mutually exclusive - your response may use a combination of them all. A natural sequence would be to first try and eliminate the risk completely - failing that, at least mitigate it. And for the remaining risk the options are to try and deflect it and / or accept it with a contingency. All these responses cost money, so a cost-benefit analysis should be performed as it may be more cost effective to accept a risk rather than taking expensive steps to eliminate it.

Eliminating Risk: Looks into ways of avoiding the risk completely - by either removing the cause or taking an alternative course of action. This should initially be considered during the concept and design phases, where the level of influence is high and the cost to change is low (see the *Project Life-Cycle* chapter).

Mitigating Risk: To mitigate a risk means **reducing** the risk's probability and impact. This could be achieved by using proven technology and standards to ensure the product will work. Developing prototypes, simulating and modelling are three methods which share the notion of using a representation to investigate selected aspects of requirements in order to be more certain of the outcome or suitability. A prototype is a working mock-up of areas under investigation in order to test its acceptance. A model is a miniature representation of physical relationships (often used in ship design).

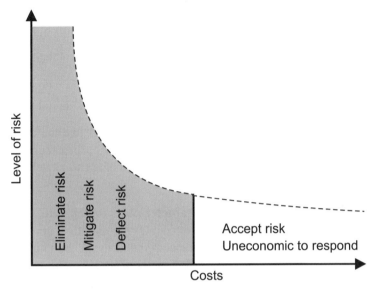

Figure 18.7: Cost Benefit of Reducing Risk

Deflecting Risk: Transfers the risk (in part or whole) to another party. This can be achieved through contracting, retention, bonding and insurance - these are discussed below.

8. Contracting

Project contracts are a means of deflecting risk, usually away from the client to the contractor. Consider figure 18.8 where the contract determines how the client and the contractor share the risk.
- Fixed price contract
- Cost plus contract
- Unit rates contract
- Turnkey contract
- BOOT contract

Fixed Price Contract: Also called **lump sum price**. This contract requires the contractor to complete the *scope of work* for a fixed price which is written into the contract. This contract will include all the costs associated with labour, material, plant, inflation and risk. A detailed *scope of work* is required from the client before the contractor can tender - this effectively prevents *fast tracking* between design and construction. Once the project has started, any changes in the *scope of work* will have to be negotiated. This type of contract is becoming more popular with clients because it passes much of the project risk onto the contractor. The inflation risk, however, is often accepted by the client in the form of an escalation clause.

Cost Plus Contract: Also called **reimbursable, plus-fee** contract. The cost plus contract is considered to be the most flexible type of contract, where all the direct costs are paid by the client plus an agreed fee or percentage profit to the contractor. This type of contract is often used at the beginning of a project when there may be many design changes, requiring close client / contractor liaison, thereby allowing work to proceed while the details are still being discussed. Once the *scope of work* is finalised the type of contract may change, for example, the Channel Tunnel contract changed from cost-plus to a fixed price.

Cost-plus contracts are usually criticised on the grounds that the contractor has little incentive to control costs and increase productivity, since their fee is proportional to the total cost of the project. It is therefore up to the client to closely monitor the contractors performance.

Unit Rates: Also called; **billed rates, parameter costs** or **schedule of rates**. This type of contract works on the basis of negotiated rates for specific work. All payments will be based on measurement of the work completed using the unit rates. At the tender stage the quote will be based on a bill of material (BOM). This type of contract is suitable for projects where the client cannot supply sufficient data for the contractor to give a lump sum quote. Thus the client can start their project sooner than a lump sum price and design the project progressively.

Even on a fixed price contract, unit rates can be agreed at the outset as a framework for costing additional work. Unit rates do offer the contractor an incentive to maximise their profits through efficiency. The client will be responsible for the measurement of the work done, which can be integrated with the planning and control function. This type of contract is appropriate for projects where the *scope of work* cannot be defined at the tender stage - for example, maintenance and ship repair projects.

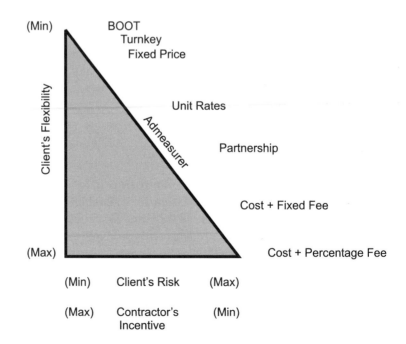

Figure 18.8: Contract Risk

Turnkey Contract: Also known as the **design and construct** contract. Here the contractor is responsible for the project, from the design phase right through to the commissioning phase. This reduces the client's input to a minimum while contractually ensuring that the contractor is responsible for making the project or facility operational.

The contractor takes the undivided responsibility for the design and construction of the project which invariably leads to a pure lump sum principle, but in practice, this is rarely the case due to variations caused by employer interference as the project proceeds. As a general rule, the more expertise the employer has, the more likely they are to interfere!!

Partnership: Or **joint venture** brings client and contractor together to share the risks and benefits on the project.

BOOT Contract (build own operate and transfer): Or BOT contract (build, operate and transfer) or ROT contract (refurbish, operate and transfer), or PPP (public private partnership), transfers the risk completely to the contractor, not only to design and build a facility, but also to finance the building and operation of the facility. The contractor then operates the facility for a period of time and charges the users for the product. For example, a contractor, or consortium would build and operate a power station for 25 years, during which time they will charge their customers for the electricity, and this income will pay for the building of the facility. Also used for toll roads, railways, bridges and tunnels.

Retention: The client retains a percentage of the contractors income against the contractor failing to complete their contractual obligations. The retention is usually 10% of the monthly progress payments until it reaches 5% of the contract value and then it is held until the end of the warranty period.

Bond: The contractor offers the client a bond through a large organisation (bank). The bond could be held against lack of performance or poor quality of work. If the contractor fails to perform, the client is compensated by the bond company, who in turn will take agreed assets from the contractor to cover the bond. Some contractors prefer this arrangement to retention, as they are paid their progress claims in full, thus improving their cash-flow.

Insurance: A third party accepts insurable risks for the payment of a premium. The premium is now the quantified impact of this risk on the project. Insurance could cover:
- Direct property damage
- Indirect consequential loss (business interruption)
- Legal liability
- Personnel liability.

Acceptance: Here you accept the consequence of a risk occurring, also called self-insurance. However, you may develop a contingency plan to protect your business from the risk event. A **contingency plan** defines actions you will take ahead of time - if A happens we will do B. The contingency plan could be established for:

- Minor internal design changes
- Under estimating the BOM, procurement and resources
- Lack of experience (history, knowledge, judgement)
- Unexpected procurement price changes
- Correcting some erroneous assumptions
- Scope - insufficient detail resulting in changes
- Implementing and commissioning problems that lead to schedule delays
- Some unforeseen regulations.

A summary table should be developed to gather together all the identified risks and how you intend to respond (see table 18.6).

WBS	Objective	Risk	Response	Mitigate
1.1				
1.2				
1.3				

Table 18.6: Objective, Risk, Response, Mitigating Risk (proforma)

Risk Management Plan: The *risk management plan*, documents the output from the previous sections; identify, quantify and respond, and assigns responsibility for implementation. The next section - risk control - implements the *risk management plan* and makes it a working document.

9. Risk Control

The risk control function implements the *risk management plan* to make it happen - this is the most important part, but surprisingly is often neglected! The *risk management plan* needs to be communicated to all the project participants and where necessary followed up with appropriate training and practice runs. The training should not only ensure that the *risk management plan* is understood, but also develop a company wide risk management culture and attitude.

The *risk management plan* should be monitored and updated on a regular basis to ensure you learn from recurring risks and that it is relevant to changing circumstances:

- Changes in the scope of work
- Changes in the build method
- Changes in the team members
- Changes in the suppliers.

Risk management may become an item on the weekly progress meetings to prompt discussion, identify new areas of risk and develop appropriate responses.

Figure 18.9: Risk Control Cycle

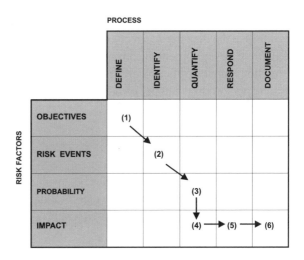

10. Disaster Recovery Planning

A disaster is a sudden, unplanned catastrophe that prevents your company providing its critical business functions for a period of time and could result in significant damage or loss. The time factor will determine whether a problem or service interruption is an inconvenience or a disaster - losing power for a few hours may be an inconvenience, but losing power for a few weeks could be a financial disaster (Auckland's CBD lost power for a month in 1998). The objective of disaster recovery management is to reduce the consequence of a disaster to an acceptable level. This is the ultimate contingency plan!

Disaster recovery planning is essentially a contingency response from your risk management planning, but due to the unique nature and size of the problems it is probably best managed separately - as a project. The management of the disaster recovery plan should be assigned to a manager with responsibility to set up a team to:

- Develop the disaster recovery plan
- Control the disaster recovery plan
- (and when the time comes) - Implement the disaster recovery plan quickly and effectively.

Disaster recovery planning essentially follows the same process as the risk management plan, except now you are focusing on the major risks, which cannot be eliminated, mitigated or deflected. Controlling the disaster recovery plan may involve training, practice and frequently updating the data base of information (for example telephone numbers). The disaster recovery team should meet regularly so that in the event of a disaster they can *hit the ground running*. A fire, flood, earthquake, or hurricane would be a good examples of a disaster where your office, factory, or facility could be completely destroyed, or have restricted access for a long period of time - how are you going to recover?

Disaster Recovery Implementation: When a disaster happens, this is the time to implement your carefully developed and updated disaster recovery plan. The first step is to mobilise the disaster recovery team, maybe at a prearranged office where all the necessary office equipment, information and communications are ready. Communicate the disaster recovery plan to all the key people and stakeholders. Using telephone trees (one person rings ten people), this would include:

- Employees
- Clients
- Suppliers
- Media.

If necessary relocate the project office:

- Move to a prearranged office accommodation
- Recover the critical data bases that should have been regularly backed up and stored off site.

It is essential that you accurately advise your clients how long it will be before you can offer a normal service again. Statistics from America indicate that 43% of American business are closed immediately by disasters, 51% for as long as two years, and of these only 6% survive the experience - these are frightening figures. If your company provides an essential business function, then your clients will have to move to another supplier - certainly in the short term.

This concludes the chapter on *Project Risk Management*, the following chapter will discuss *Project Communication*.

Key Points:

- Risks are inherent in all projects.
- Develop a *risk management plan* to document how you will respond to risk.
- Implement the *risk management plan* and continually monitor and control the risk until the project is completed.

Further Reading:

AS/NZS 4360:1995, *Risk Management* (Australian / New Zealand Standard)
Chapman, C., and **Ward**, Stephen, *Project Risk Management: Processes, Techniques and Insights*, Wiley
Kerzner, H., *Project Management A Systems Approach to Planning, Scheduling and Controlling*, Van Nostrand Reinhold
PMBOK Handbook Volume 6, *Project and Program Risk Management*
Project Management Institute (PMI), *A Guide to the Project Management Body of Knowledge (PMBOK)*
Raftery, John, *Risk Analysis in Project Management*, Routledge

Case Study and Exercises:

Unplanned catastrophes are always waiting just around the corner to derail your project. For this case study you have been appointed project manager, or risk manager to prepare a risk management plan, and a disaster recovery plan for the project office on an IT project. Your risk management planning should consider how you would address natural disasters (flood, power cut, earth quake, fire). Your presentation should include the following:

1. Identify the risks.
2. Disaster recovery preparation - training.
3. Disaster recovery control.
4. Information back-up and post disaster retrieval.
5. Post disaster communication plan.

"That was a lucky escape!"

CHAPTER 19

Project Communications

Communication is one of those subjects that is hard to separate from what we do naturally everyday, so why does it warrant being a knowledge area? For a project to succeed there is a continuous need for communication to issue instructions, solve problems, make decisions, resolve conflicts, and keep everyone supplied with the information they need.

The PMBOK defines project communication management as; '... *the process required to ensure timely and appropriate generation, collection, dissemination, storage and ultimately disposition* [disposal] *of project information. It provides the critical links among people, ideas and information that are necessary for success.'*

The project manager is in the key position to develop and maintain all the communication links, both inside the company and project team, and outside the company with the client, contractors, suppliers and other stakeholders. The project office is like the '*front door*' to the project. It is estimated that project managers spend about 90% of their working time engaged in some form of communication, be it; meetings, writing memos, emailing, faxes, reading reports, or talking with team members, senior managers, customers, clients, sub-contractors, suppliers and stakeholders.

The ability to communicate well, both verbally and in writing, is the foundation of effective leadership. Through communication team members share information and exchange ideas and influence attitudes, behaviours and understanding. Communication enables the project manager to develop interpersonal relationships; inspire team members, handle conflict, negotiate with stakeholders, chair meetings, and make presentations.

It therefore makes sense to rank communication management along with the other knowledge areas, because without effective communication project success will be self-limiting.

It is often stated that *"Information costs money"*, but conversely, *"lack of information could be even more expensive"*. The cost of communication failure may be quantified as; poor problem-solving, poor decision-making based on incomplete information, rework due to the shop-floor using old drawings, downtime due to managers not being advised of late delivery of material, and managers turning up for meetings which have been cancelled. A trade-off needs to be established between the cost of mistakes and the cost of supplying good information.

Projects are particularly prone to communication difficulties because of the unique nature of projects and the matrix organisation through which they are generally managed. There may be overlapping responsibilities, decentralised decision-making and complex interfaces all applying a strain on the communication system. However, if the communication system is well managed it could be the single most important factor determining product quality, efficiency, productivity and customer satisfaction.

The Internet and mobile phones have enhanced the communication mediums - a silent revolution is taking place as we move away from post (snail mail) and faxes. The mobile office and virtual office are now real possibilities for the project team. Consider the facilities:

- Email (one-to-one, or one-to-many)
- Web sites
- B2B procurement
- Real time progress reports
- Video conferences
- Mobile email and internet connections
- Mobile communication nationally and internationally (and with Iridium satellite phones anywhere on the planet).

1. Communication Theory

Communication is essentially the interpersonal process of sending and receiving messages. The key components of the communication process are shown in figure 19.1. They include the sender who encodes and sends (transmits) the message, and the receiver who decodes and interprets the message. The receiver then feeds back a response to the sender and closes the loop. The communication model focuses on each element of the process to identify what should happen and prevent misunderstanding - like the charge of the Light Brigade!!!

WHEN I NOD MY HEAD HIT IT.....

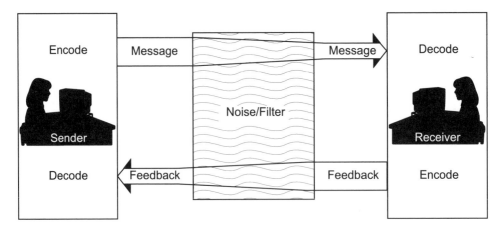

Figure 19.1: Communication Process
(showing the communication cycle as a closed loop)

Sender: The sender is the originator of the message and the starting point of the communication cycle. The sender will have a purpose to communicate. This may be to; request information, send information, ask a question, issue an instruction, encourage team building, marketing or make a courtesy call.

Encoding: Encoding is the process of converting thoughts, feelings and ideas into '*code or cipher*'. In its broader sense code and cipher are the words and phrases we use to express ourselves, which can, if we are not careful, take on the more devious meaning of a disguised secret way of writing.

Medium: The medium is the vehicle or channel to convey the message. Project communications can be transmitted in many forms; formal or informal, written or verbal, planned or ad-hoc. Consider the following:

- Formal written; letters, faxes, email, memos, minutes, drawings, specifications and reports
- Formal verbal; telephone, voice mail, meetings, video-conferencing
- Informal verbal; casual discussion between friends
- Non-verbal; body language.

The choice of medium will influence the impact of the message, for example, another memo or email will not have the same effect as a discussion face-to-face.

The use of written communication should be encouraged because it addresses misinterpretation and forgetfulness. All important agreements and instructions should be confirmed in writing. You will be thankful for keeping a written trail of agreements if (when) problems develop later in the project. Written communications are acceptable for simple messages that are easy to convey and for those messages that require extensive dissemination to all stakeholders. However, verbal channels work best for complex messages that are difficult to convey, may need explanation, and where immediate feedback to the sender is valuable. Verbal communications are also more personal, which helps to create a supportive and inspirational climate.

Non-verbal communication: As the phrases suggest; '*a picture is worth a thousand words*', and '*actions speak louder than words*', tells us that our non-verbal actions are an important part of our communication process. This could be:

- Body posture
- Hand movements
- Facial expressions
- Eye contact
- Use of interpersonal space.

Eye contact and voice intonation can be used intentionally to accent (enforce) certain words or phases. Body language may express your feelings even though you remain silent. It may also send confusing messages if you are saying one thing, but your body is saying something else. In a meeting a person under attack will unconsciously (instinctively) lean away, or sit back on their chair away from the antagonist. Some researchers claim that gestures can make up more than 50% of communication, a consideration as more and more of our communication moves to emails where non-verbal communications are completely lost.

Receiver: The receiver is the person or persons the message is transmitted to. Their ability to receive will depend on their; hearing and listening skills, selective listening, eyesight and reading skills, visual activity, tactile sensitivity, olfactory sensitivity and extra sensory perception.

Decoding: Decoding is the process of converting the message back into an readable format.

Noise, Filters and Perceptions: These are all factors that interfere with the effectiveness of the communication process. Distortions occur during encoding and decoding; communication channels can be blocked by too many messages; and filters and perceptions may influence our interpretations and impressions.

Physical distractions can interfere with your communication, such as; telephone interruptions, drop-in-visitors, or lack of privacy in an open plan office. It is important to have a place where you can shield yourself from any noise - a place where you can conceptually think issues through. For me I like to '*sleep on it*' and I am always pleasantly surprised when I wake up with a more innovative solution than the one I had the night before.

Our backgrounds and personalities introduce communication filters and perceptions - consider the following; Language (*lost in the translation*), semantics, innuendos, intelligence, education, technical experience, knowledge base, cultural background, religion, politics, personal values, ethics, reputation, environment background and organisational position. Consider the OBS block when you tell your boss what he wants to hear, for fear that he will shoot the messenger - this will effectively filter the information.

Other factors which will influence your response are: preconceived ideas, frames of reference, needs, interests, attitudes, emotional status, self-interests, assumptions about the sender, existing relationships with the sender, lack of responsive feedback from previous communications with the sender.

Feedback: It is good manners to not only acknowledge receipt of the communication, but also give the sender a time frame for a reply to any questions. It is important to feedback to the sender so that they can gauge how effectively the message was understood, and also for the receiver to confirm they have interpreted the message correctly. No effective communication has occurred until there is a common understanding. But also consider constructive feedback where you critique and add value to the original message.

2. Communication Plan

Communication planning pulls the project together. The project manager and project office are at the heart of the project's information and control system. It is the project manager's responsibility to not only develop the project organisation structure, but also to develop the project's communication plan and lines of communication. The communication plan should outline the following:

- Who (lines of communication- sender and receiver - responsibility and authority)
- What (scope of communication and format)
- How (email, document, telephone, meeting, presentation)
- When (schedule)
- Feedback (confirm message received and understood - document control)
- Filing (retrieval, storing, disaster recovery).

Lines of Communication: A line of communication may be defined as a formal or informal link between two or more; people, departments, companies, suppliers, contractors or stakeholders. The lines of communication tend to follow the organisation chart, which not only outlines the project manager's position, but also implies responsibility, authority and who reports to whom. Further the stakeholder analysis will identify all the other interested parties, both internal and external to the company (see figure 19.2).

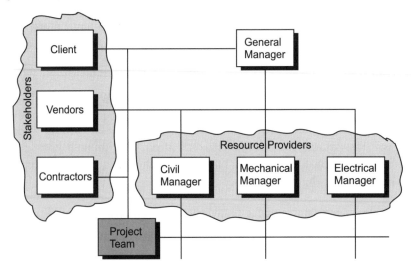

Figure 19.2: Lines of Communication

Every effort should be made to include all the key people in the project's lines of communication. To leave out a key person will not only limit their knowledgeable contribution to the project, but may also result in them adopting a hostile and negative attitude to the project. If senior people are included in your circulation list this will add weight to the document's perceived importance.

Scope of Communication: What should be communicated??? This is a tricky issue - if you filter the information, you may be accused of being manipulative. However, if you give everyone all the information, they will be overloaded and are unlikely to read it. The objective should be to communicate sufficient information for the recipient to solve problems, make good decisions and feel involved and part of the project. Certain information should be controlled - contract, specifications, drawings, instructions and scope changes. The art of good communication is to strike a balance with the value of information supplied against the cost and time it takes to collect, process and disseminate it.

Format: The reporting **format and content** should be discussed with the participants, where possible the client should be encouraged to accept the contractors standard forms, which may have been developed over many projects. The information presented should be in an easy to understand format so that the recipient can quickly assimilate the situation and take appropriate action if required.

Timing: The frequency of reports and turnaround time for responses should be discussed and agreed. An information sequence may be established, for example, the progress may be captured on a Friday, processed on a Monday and reported on a Tuesday at the progress meeting.

3. Project Information and Control System

The project's information and control system is the life blood of the communication plan, and the project's planning and control cycle. This information flow applies to each line of communication, which can be considered as separate cycles within the total information and control system.

For the information flow to be effective, all parties must be aware that they are part of a linked system and that the quality of the information (like cogs in a wheel or links in a chain) will directly relate to the weakest link - further *garbage-in* to the system will deliver *garbage-out* of the system.

With the advances in computer aided data processing and reporting, the weak link in the information flow is probably

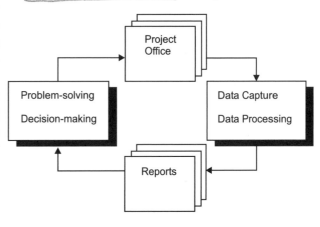

Figure 19.3:
Information and
Control System

275

located at the human interface with the data capture function where the project's status and progress are quantified (see *Project Control* chapter).

The project manager also needs to encourage communication between other parties - both formal and informal. Informal channels are often essential to ensure the smooth operation, particularly in a matrix situation where there can be considerable ambiguity, and formal channels are required to dot the 'i' and cross the 't'.

Effective communication is more than just people talking to each other and transmission of facts, in the project context the communications are mostly going to be using structured reporting forms.

4. Project Reporting

Project data can be collected, processed and reported in many ways, this section will outline a few of the commonly used methods. The format (structure), frequency and circulation of reports needs to be established during the start up phase of the project. The reports should be designed to assist problem-solving and decision-making by the various levels of management so that they can ensure the project will meet its stated goals and objectives.

Status Reports: Status reports simply quantify the position of the project. This data capture function is the first link in the information and control system - all subsequent evaluations are based on this data. Status reports may be specific and focus on the key areas of the project, like time, cost and quality, or they may be general and include a much wider scope (see table 19.1).

Activity	Description	Status
100	Foundation	Material ordered - work started on Monday

Table 19.1: Status Report

Variance Reports: Variance reports quantify the difference between actual and planned. For example the revised budget being compared with the original budget. The variance is simply the difference between the two values (see table 19.2).

Activity	Original Budget	Revised Budget	Variance
100	$10,000	$12,000	$2,000
200	$15,000	$13,500	($1,500)

Table 19.2: Budget Variance Report

When a variance is reported as the difference between two values, it does not take the size of the parameter into consideration. This problem can be addressed by converting the variance into a percentage of the planned value. Now the variance is expressed as a percentage of the original base (see table 19.3).

Activity	Original Budget	Revised Budget	Schedule Variance	Schedule Variance %
100	$1,000,000	$1,010,000	$10,000	1%
200	$400,000	$420,000	$20,000	5%

Table 19.3: Schedule Variance Report

Trend Reports: The status report tells the manager where the project is, but not where the project is going. The trend report uses historical data and extrapolates this forward to give the manager a feel for the direction of the project. Figure 19.3 shows the *earned value* graph where both BCWP and ACWP are extrapolated to show their current trends.

Earned Value: The *earned value* report integrates the variable parameter of cost with time. This technique can also be used to integrate manhours and time. The integration of data enables the planner to model the various parameters more realistically (see figure 19.4 and the *Earned Value* chapter).

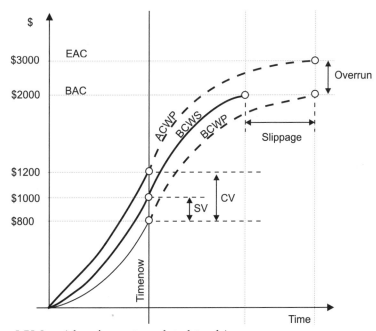

Figure 19.4: Earned Value (showing extrapolated tends)

Exception Reports: Exception reports are designed to flag an occurrence or event, which is outside predetermined control limits. This threshold can be set by the project manager as a guideline for the planner to follow and filter out the important information. For example the planner may be requested to report:

- All activities that have a float less than 5 days. This would highlight all the activities that could go critical in the next week.
- All the deliveries that are due in the next week. This would focus on deliveries that could disrupt the work and resource planning.
- All non-conformance reports (NCR) where the product has not attained the required condition as outlined by the specifications or contract. This would focus on the workforce that may need training, or equipment that may need upgrading.

Monthly Reports: On a long project, monthly reports give the project manager an excellent forum to quantify what is happening on the project and report it to senior management and key stakeholders. The monthly report should roll-up the weekly progress meetings and any other special meetings to give an overall picture of the project. The report should highlight any significant trends or variance, particularly those where the CEOs action is required. It should also identify all major events happening in the next month so that the client, CEO and other stakeholders can plan ahead.

Reporting Period: The agreed timing of the reports should link-in with a schedule of meetings and report roll-ups. This would generally be weekly, but should also include key milestones and be adjusted to accommodate risk and the level of control required.

It is important to use structured reports as much as possible, as ad-hoc reports may not include the information the project manager needs, and people naturally tend to report the good news while they are economical with the bad news. However, if managers are asked to report against a structured format they will generally answer it honestly.

Reports should be quick, easy to prepare and read. The managers should not spend too much time reporting - about an hour per reporting period would be a reasonable amount. If it takes longer then the managers should rightly complain they are being distracted from productive work.

5. Document Control

The purpose of document control is to ensure that key documents are sent timeously to the key people and there is proof of the delivery. The key documents would include; contract, specifications, drawings, schedules, reports and certain correspondence. The key people would be identified by the project organisation structure and lines of communication. An audit trail of transmittals would demonstrate that the controlled documents (usually marked **controlled copy**) have been sent to the right people and there is a signature confirming date of receipt.

On large projects document control would be handled by the configuration department or a document controller, however on small projects this would be covered by the project manager or project team.

Transmittal Note: A transmittal note or delivery note is sent with every controlled document. The addressee must sign the transmittal note and return a copy to the project office to confirm the document has been received (see figure 19.5).

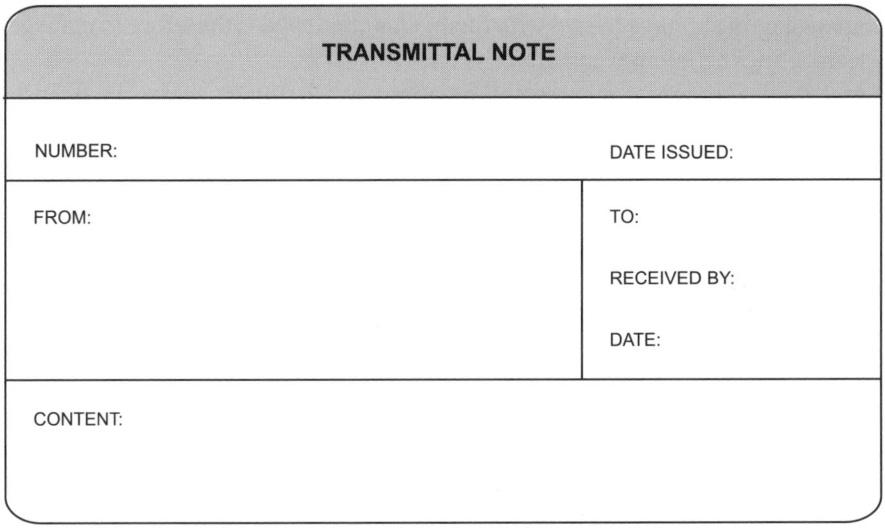

TRANSMITTAL NOTE	
NUMBER:	DATE ISSUED:
FROM:	TO: RECEIVED BY: DATE:
CONTENT:	

Figure 19.5: Transmittal Note (to confirm receipt)

It is the project office's responsibility to control the flow of these controlled documents. The project office must ensure that these controlled documents reach their destination timeously. A control sheet is essential (see table 19.4), each week the document controller should confirm receipt by telephone and ensure the signed transmittals are returned. A list of non-returned transmittals can be tabled at the progress meetings to encourage compliance.

Transmittal Number	Date Issued	Document Type	Document Number	To / Destination	Date Transmittal Returned

Table 19.4: Document Control Sheet or Transmittal Summary

6. Project Meetings

'Meetings Bloody Meetings' you either love them or hate them, but until the management gurus come up with a better method for communicating project information - we are just going to have to live with them. Our challenge is therefore to manage the project meetings efficiently and effectively.

Some managers prefer many small meetings, while others prefer the occasional big meeting with everyone on the project attending. Some managers prefer informal ad hoc meetings, while others prefer formal structured meetings. Whichever type of meeting you use there are five basic reasons for holding a meeting:

- Information sharing; exchange of data
- Problem-solving; brainstorming, generating ideas, options and alternatives
- Decision-making; select a course of action, gain commitment from the team
- Planning; what, who, when, how, where and why
- Evaluation; monitoring, measuring, reviewing and forecasting.

Discussing the project at the coffee machine, may be good team building, but it is not effective control. To make the most of a meeting there needs to be structure to make efficient use of your time. There are two different types of meetings I want to focus on; the handover meeting (to initiate a project phase or contractor - it is important to get off to a good start), and the progress meetings (to guide the project to a successful completion).

As the project manager is responsible for establishing the communication plan, he is also responsible for setting up a schedule of meetings. Successful meetings require good planning to ensure genuine participation from the entire team. So advance notice must be given with purpose and an agenda to enable participants to prepare, together with the venue and time.

7. Handover Meeting

The purpose of the handover meeting is to formally commence the project, phase or subcontract. The attendance would normally include the client, senior management, the project team members and other concerned parties; contractors, suppliers and stakeholders. The purpose of the handover meeting is to set the scene for the project, what it has to achieve and establish how it will be managed. A typical agenda may include:

- **Project Charter:** Outline the purpose of the project, scope of work.
- **Closeout Reports:** Review closeout reports and discuss previous achievements and problems.
- **Project OBS:** Identify all the relevant project participants and stakeholders. Discuss the *scope of work* and contracts - who does what, responsibilities and authority.
- **Communication:** Discuss the lines of communication and the information and control system.
- **Build Method:** Discuss how the product will be made, the required quality and hold points.

- **Schedule:** Discuss the project schedule and milestones.
- **Reporting:** Discuss progress reporting - format, content, frequency and circulation.
- **Meetings:** Discuss the schedule of meetings, required attendance, venue, agenda and minutes.
- **Instructions:** Explain the procedure for issuing instructions, the format and who has authorisation. List the documents that will be used for issuing instructions, these could be; drawings, schedules, minutes, memos, letters, faxes and email.
- **Document Control:** Discuss what documents will be controlled and how they will be transmitted.
- **Configuration Management:** Discuss how changes will be incorporated and communicated. Outline procedures for scope changes and identify the people with approved signing power.
- **Payments:** Discuss how progress will be measured and payments will be made.
- **Contract:** Discuss contractual requirements, retention, bonds, penalties and warranties.
- List of client supplied items.
- List of inclusions and exclusions.
- **Commissioning:** Discuss how the product will be run-up, tested, accepted, or rejected.

It is important to get the handover meetings right to set the framework and tone for the project, and then follow-up with progress meetings to keep the momentum going.

8. Project Progress Meetings

Progress meetings are generally held every week to monitor progress and guide the project to a successful completion. Progress meetings provide an effective forum for the project manager to co-ordinate, integrate and manage the project's participants. Meetings provide a dynamic environment where interaction and innovation will enhance the cross flow of ideas and help solve problems. The meetings should also provide the venue for consensus and decision-making. A typical progress meeting would contain the following:

- **Agenda:** The agenda should be circulated before the meeting to list the participants and action points to prepare for the meeting.
- **Minutes:** Approve minutes of previous meeting.
- **Actions:** Report on actions from previous meeting.
- **Progress:** Report progress by work package.
- **Configuration Management:** Discuss scope changes and concessions - their implications and approval.
- **Document Control:** List controlled documents transmitted and police signing of transmittals.
- **Claims:** Discuss any claims since the last meeting.
- **Quality:** Discuss NCRs and quality issues.
- **Payments:** Approve invoices for payment.

The minutes should be produced as soon as possible after the meeting, preferably the next day. The minutes should document discussions and agreements taken during the meeting, together with actions to be done before the next meeting.

This concludes the chapter on *Project Communications*. The next chapter will discuss *Project Organisation Structures*, particularly the matrix structure.

Key Points:

- All lines of communication should pass through the project office - the project's front door.
- Set up a schedule of progress meetings to plan and control your project.
- Set up a fully integrated information and control system to generate progress reports.

Further Reading:

Bolton, Robert, *People Skills,* Simon & Schuster
Burleson, C., *Effective Meetings*, Wiley
Peace, A., *Body Language*, Sheldon Press

Case Study and Exercises:

Projects are run by good communication. For this case study you have been appointed project manager on an offshore platform. Your presentation should outline how you will approach the following:

1. Communication cycle - data capture, processing, dissemination and storage.
2. Lines of communication.
3. Handover meeting.
4. Progress meetings.
5. Document control.

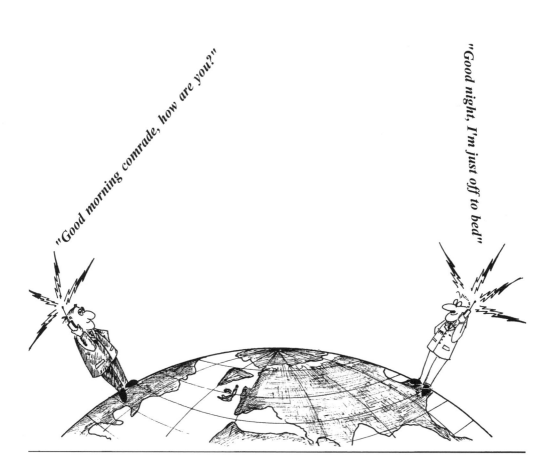

Project Organisation Structures (Matrix)

Projects are performed by people and managed through people, so it is essential to develop an organisation structure which reflects the needs of the project (task), the needs of the project team and just as importantly the needs of the individual (see figure 20.1).

The PMBOK defines project human resource management as; '... *the process required to make the most of the people involved with the project.*' And the APM bok says; '*Issues typically important in the structuring of a project include the degree of project / functional orientation,* [and] *the extent of the project management (office) authority'.*

Organisation Structures: The project organisation structure identifies the relationship between the project participants, together with defining their duties, responsibilities and authority. Because of the dynamic nature of projects it is possible to have a number of organisation structures running concurrently, and over the duration of the project you may well use all of the organisation structures. These structures outline the relationship between the various participants, lines of authority and the lines of communication, consider:

- Project team
- Project interfaces
- Matrix organisation structure
- Responsibility matrix

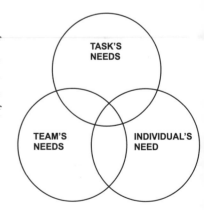

Figure 20.1: Intersecting Needs

Project Team: The project team outlines the relationship between the project manager and the other team members. The membership of this structure may be dynamic, as seconded members move in and out of the project office (see figure 20.2).

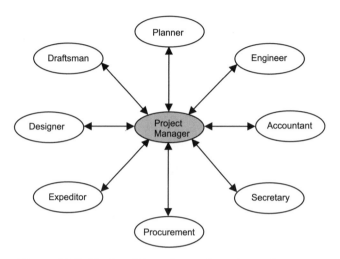

Figure 20.2: Project Team (centred on the project manager)

Project Interfaces: The project interface diagram outlines the contact (communication) between the project manager with the internal and external stakeholders (see figure 20.3).

- Internal contacts - the functional managers and all the other internal departments that may be associated with the project.
- External contacts - the client and all the other outside companies (contractors and suppliers) used on the project.

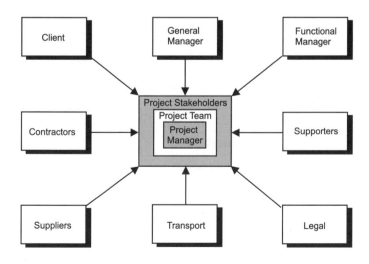

Figure 20.3: Project Interfaces

Matrix Organisation Structure: The matrix structure presents the temporary project lines of responsibility overlaying the functional lines of responsibility, and outlines the relationship between the project manager, functional managers and their subordinates (figure 20. 4).

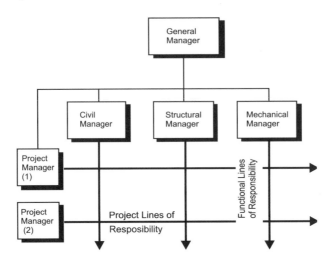

Figure 20.4: Matrix Organisation Structure
(showing lines of responsibility)

Responsibility Matrix: The responsibility matrix is a development of the schedule barchart which clearly links the work (WBS and/or activities) to the responsible person (OBS). This is an easier document to use than the matrix WBS/OBS.

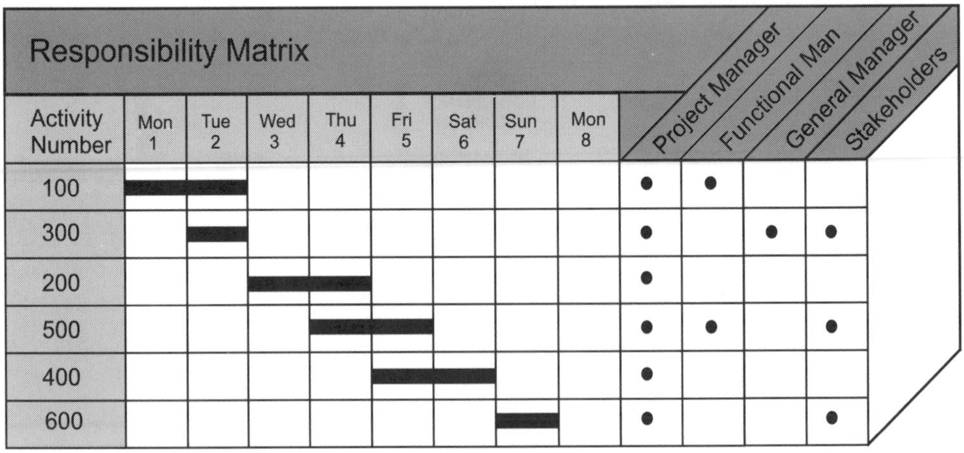

Responsibility Matrix									Project Manager	Functional Man	General Manager	Stakeholders
Activity Number	Mon 1	Tue 2	Wed 3	Thu 4	Fri 5	Sat 6	Sun 7	Mon 8				
100	▬								•	•		
300		▬							•		•	•
200			▬						•			
500				▬					•	•		•
400					▬				•			
600							▬		•			•

Figure 20.5: Responsibility Matrix
(adds a responsibility field to the schedule barchart)

WBS / OBS Matrix: The WBS / OBS matrix is another format outlining the integration of the scope of work (work package) with the responsible person or department. This matrix ensures that the full scope of work is assigned and the responsible person for each work package is identified. The earned value bubble indicates the planning and control function at the work package level (figure 20. 6).

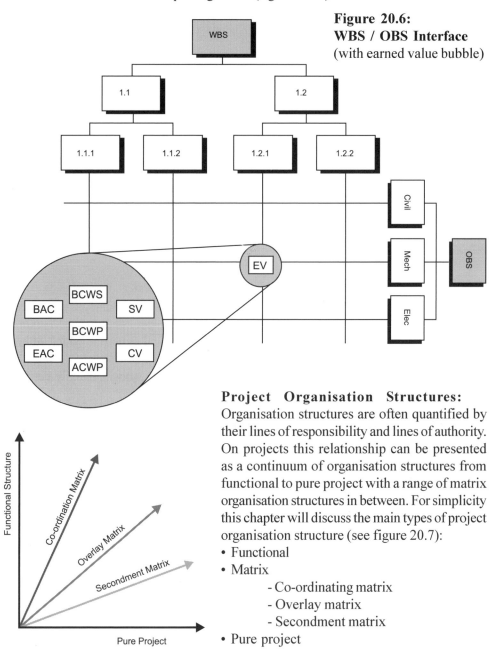

Figure 20.6:
WBS / OBS Interface
(with earned value bubble)

Project Organisation Structures:
Organisation structures are often quantified by their lines of responsibility and lines of authority. On projects this relationship can be presented as a continuum of organisation structures from functional to pure project with a range of matrix organisation structures in between. For simplicity this chapter will discuss the main types of project organisation structure (see figure 20.7):

- Functional
- Matrix
  - Co-ordinating matrix
  - Overlay matrix
  - Secondment matrix
- Pure project

Figure 20.7: Project Organisation Structure Continuum

1. Functional Organisation Structure

This **traditional** organisation structure is based on the subdivision of product lines or disciplines into separate departments, together with a vertical hierarchy. Figure 20.8 outlines a typical structure with a number of functional departments reporting to the general manager. Also called **wedding-cake** corporate structure.

Figure 20.8: Functional Organisation Structure

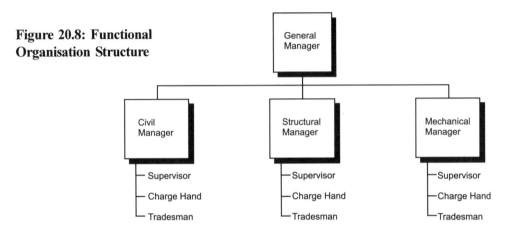

The **advantages** of the functional organisation structure (particularly for projects within a department) are:

- Functional departments provide a **home** for technical expertise which offers technical support and continuing development.
- Functional departments provide good **support** as the work is usually carried out in the department.
- Functional departments can achieve a high degree of flexibility, because people in the department can be assigned to the project, then immediately reassigned to other work. Switching back and forth between projects is easily achieved.
- Functional departments provide the normal **career path** for advancement and promotion.
- Functional department's work is **simpler** to estimate and manage as the scope of work is usually restricted to its own field and the functional data base should contain information from previous projects (closeout reports).
- Lines of **communication** within the department are short and well established.
- There is quick **reaction time** to problems within the department.
- Some employees prefer working in a consistent work routine, rather than the challenge of diverse projects.
- Functional departments offer clearly defined responsibility and authority for work within the department.

The **disadvantages** of the functional organisation structure (particularly when being used on multi-disciplined projects) are:

- No *single point of responsibility* as the project scope moves from one department to another, this can lead to co-ordinating chaos. Without a nominated project manager the co-ordinating and linking role must fall with the general manager, but the general manager should be concerned with corporate issues and not project operations. As projects become larger and more complex, it becomes increasingly difficult for senior management to co-ordinate the day-to-day problems of individual projects.

- On multi-disciplined projects there are no formal **lines of communication** between the workers within the different departments - like a stovepipe, information flows straight up and down. Generally the only formal line of communication is through the functional managers, which will lengthen the lines of communication and slow down the response time. With these long communication cycles, problem-solving and decision-making will be self-limiting. In practice, out of necessity, informal links may be established between the people working on the project.

- Competition and conflict between functional departments may limit effective communication of important project information.

- Departmental work may take **priority** over project work. If there is a resource overload the project's schedule may be pushed out, which could delay the handover to the next department and ultimately delay the project's completion.

- For functional managers the project is not always their main focus of concern, particularly when the work has moved to another department. The client may well feel like a football being passed from one department to another. Clients prefer to deal with one person - the project manager.

- The responsibility for external co-ordination with the client, suppliers and other stakeholders may become muddled because of overlap, underlap and inadequately defined **responsibilities**.

- Without a clear project manager the client may end up **co-ordinating** the different functional departments themselves.

- The department may myopically focus only on their *scope of work* in preference to a holistic view of the project and a departmental solution to a problem may not be the best solution for the project as a whole. For example, the production department may want standardisation, while the marketing department may want to offer a range of products.

- Functional structures are not effective in a **multi-project** environment because of the conflicts associated with assessing the relative importance and priorities as each project competes for limited resources.

- No single department is responsible for the overall project's success, this could lead to decisions by committee.

The functional organisation structure offers excellent facilities within its own department, but where a multi-disciplined *scope of work* calls for interaction with other departments then the system may be found lacking. To address this problem the matrix organisation structure offers an interaction of both functional and project interests.

2. Matrix Organisation Structures

The topology of the matrix structure has the same format as a mathematical matrix, in this case the vertical lines represent the functional department's responsibility and authority, while the horizontal lines represent the project's responsibility and authority, thus giving the matrix structure its unique appearance and name.

The matrix structure is considered by many practitioners to be the natural project organisation structure, as it formalises the informal links (mentioned in the previous section). On multi-disciplined projects employees need to communicate at the operational level to perform their tasks. Where the lines of responsibility intersect, this represents people to people contact, thus providing shorter formal lines of

Figure 20.9: Matrix Organisation Structure

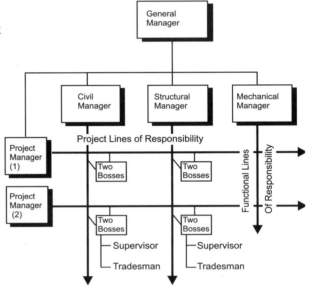

communication.

A characteristic of project management is that it relies on a number of functional departments and sub-contractors to supply the resources to produce the product, each appearing to act autonomously and yet requiring strong communication links with each other. The project manager needs to cut across organisational lines to co-ordinate and integrate specific resources located in different departments. To achieve this the project manager must have appropriate tools, particularly an information system that not only accommodates interdisciplinary tasks but also the cross-functional capability of retrieving data from the different departments. Within this matrix structure there are a number of variants influenced mainly by the distribution of power (authority) - namely:

- Co-ordination matrix (weak matrix)
- Overlay matrix (balanced matrix)
- Secondment matrix (strong matrix)

Consider some of the **advantages** inherent in the typical matrix organisation structure:

- The project has a clear *single point of responsibility* - the project manager.
- The project can draw on the entire resources of the company, when several projects are operating concurrently, the matrix structure allows a time-share of expertise, which should lead to a higher degree of resource utilisation.
- By sharing the use of equipment, the capital costs can be shared between projects and functional departments.
- With seconded resources project termination is not necessarily a traumatic event (worrying about continuing employment), the resources can return to their original functional department.
- Rapid response to the client's needs. The client communicates directly with the project manager.
- The corporate link will ensure consistency with company policies, strategies and procedures, yet give the flexibility to tailor these to the project's needs.
- The matrix structure can be tailored to the needs of the project with respect to; job descriptions, procedures, work instructions and lines of communication.
- Good flow of information (dissemination) within the project as there is a provision for both horizontal (project information) from function to function and vertical (functional information) through the organisation structure.
- The needs of the project and functional departments can be addressed simultaneously by negotiation and trade-off. The project is mainly concerned with what and when (scope and planning), while the functional department is concerned with who and how (resources and technical).
- Problem-solving can draw on a much wider input for ideas and innovative options - brainstorming.
- Teams of experts within the functional department are kept together as the projects come and go. Therefore technology, know-how, expertise and experience are not lost when the project is completed and the project team disbanded. Specialists like to work with other specialists in the same discipline, thus increasing innovation, problem-solving ability and synergy.
- The multi-disciplinary environment exposes people to a wider range of considerations.
- By retaining their functional home, specialists keep their career path. If they work well in a multi-disciplined environment then a new career in the project office may open up.
- The matrix structure is a good training ground for project managers working in multi-functional and cross-functional environments.
- The matrix structure integrates the WBS with the OBS (see figure 20.6).

The following **disadvantages** are inherent with the matrix structure:

- The matrix structure is complex and more difficult for the participants to understand than the simpler functional or pure project organisations.
- More communication links are required to keep the additional number of managers informed and consulted.

- Dual responsibility and authority leads to confusion, divided loyalties, unclear responsibilities, and conflicts over priorities and allocation of resources.
- The two boss situation is a recipe for conflict over the allocation of employees. The conflict could be between the project manager, functional manager and employee.
- Matrix structures do not encourage strong staff commitment to the project, particularly when staff from functional departments are assigned on an as-needed basis. Also the staff may be working on a number of projects, further limiting their commitment to any one project.
- The reward system of a matrix structure does not encourage staff to put in long hours in a project. Why should they when they have no personal stake and no additional payments. Further the project manager does not usually write their appraisal reports.
- Reaction times although faster than the functional structure, may get bogged down in negotiation (there is more negotiation) so decisions could take longer to make as more people must be consulted. This problem is more acute with the weaker matrix structures where the project managers do not have the authority to make decisions on their own.
- A company with a number of projects calling on the same resources faces real problems establishing priorities and resource allocation, as the project manager and functional manager are likely to claim their work should have the highest priority. In this situation the priority will have to be made at a senior management level.
- The cost of running a matrix organisation is higher than a functional or pure project organisation because of the increased number of managers involved in the administration and decision-making process.

- Project integration between departments is more involved and complex than integrating people within one functional department.
- With functional projects and pure projects it is clear who has the power to make decisions, however, with the matrix structure the power may be balanced between departments. If this causes doubt and confusion then the productivity of the project may suffer.
- After a secondment of a few years personnel may find they either do not have a functional department to return to, or their position has been reappointed. *"Someone is sitting at my desk*!!"
- The corporate employees' career path is usually within the functional department. Therefore, while working on projects they may miss-out on functional promotion.
- In the matrix structure the project manager controls the administration decisions, while the functional managers control the technical decisions, this division of power and responsibility could lead to an overly complex situation.
- Where the project and functional lines of influence cross there exists a two boss situation which is a recipe for conflict.
- Where project and functional reporting is required, this double reporting may lead to additional work and therefore additional costs.
- The functional departments are unlikely to give up their best personnel to the project, so team selection may be self-limiting.

For the matrix organisation structure to work successfully the functional departments may have to make some major adjustments in the way they work. The matrix structure introduces new management interfaces and these will increase the potential for conflict. New management skills will be required for the functional managers to accommodate conflicting goals, priorities and resource demands.

3. Co-ordinating Matrix

Referring to the matrix organisation structure (figure 20.9), this is the nearest structure to the traditional functional hierarchy where the project manager (more likely called project co-ordinator, progress chaser, or expediter) co-ordinates the resources across functional departments. The project co-ordinator may come from the department that initiates the project, or the department with the largest scope of work. Although the project co-ordinator is generally in a junior position with little formal power, as titular head of the project they may well be held responsible for the project meeting its objectives.

This arrangement gives little formal authority to the project co-ordinator to manage the project, control resources, or make decisions. Due to this lack of formal authority the project co-ordinator usually ends up performing more project administration work than managing the project. In this situation the best approach may be to offer a co-ordinating service, identify problem areas, and facilitate the project management process through communication skills and interpersonal skills - this way you can earn appreciation and perhaps some power!

4. Overlay Matrix

Also called the **balanced matrix**. This is the commonest type of matrix structure, where the project manager through a project office would negotiate with the functional departments for resources to implement the project. The project manager would be on the same level of seniority as the functional managers which puts the project manager in an interesting position - because the project manager may now be deemed to have sufficient seniority to be held responsible for the project, but at the same time does not have formal authority over the functional managers who **own** the resources.

The onus is on the project manager to practice an appropriate leadership style towards the functional managers, which would certainly include negotiation to address the trade-off between who controls the what, when, who and how.

5. Secondment Matrix

This is the nearest type of organisation structure to the pure project where the project manager has a wide range of powers over the whole project. Although the project manager would usually be senior to the functional managers, they would still need to negotiate with them for the use of their resources. During the secondment the functional personnel would formally report to the project manager.

The project office would develop an information and control system tailored to the needs of the project, together with procedures and work instructions. This ability to either modify existing systems or develop new systems from scratch is a characteristic of project management.

Although the functional personnel will return to their department after their involvement in the project, to help gain commitment and respect from the seconded staff, it is in the project manager's interest to ensure their continuing employment after the project.

6. Pure Project Organisation Structure

The pure project organisation structure is similar in shape to the functional organisational structure except now all the departments are dedicated to the project. It has autonomy from the rest of the company, as a self-contained unit with its own technical staff and administration. This type of structure is typical of large projects - Concorde, NASA and offshore projects (see figure 20.10). The project manager has a high level of authority to manage and control the project's resources and constraints. The **advantages** with the pure project structure include:

- The project manager has full line authority over the project.
- Team members have increased project commitment and loyalty.
- It promotes more effective communication between the project manager and the team members.

Figure 20.10: Pure Project Structure

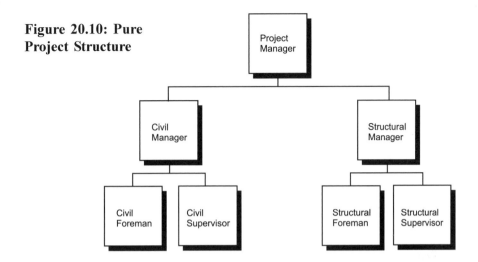

- All members of the workforce report directly to the project manager. There are no functional department heads whose permission must be sought.
- The lines of communication are shorter than the multi-disciplined functional route.
- If there are a series of similar projects, the team of skilled experts can be kept together.
- Because the project team tends to have a strong separate identity, this encourages a high level of communication between members. Inspiration and motivation is high and task orientated.
- With centralised authority, decisions are made quickly.
- With the one boss situation the lines of communication, responsibility and authority are clear and undisputed.
- A pure project presents a simple structure which is easy to understand, implement and operate.
- There is a holistic approach to the project.

The **disadvantages** with the pure project structure include:
- If the parent company has a number of projects running concurrently, with pure project structures this could lead to duplication of effort in many areas and an inefficient use of company resources.
- To ensure access to technical know-how and skills there may be a propensity to stockpile equipment and personnel. This may lead to resources staying on the project longer than required.
- Project team members work themselves out of a job at the end of the project.
- If the project divorces itself from the functional departments and other projects, this could sever the cross flow of ideas and information within the company.
- As the project cannot offer continuity of employment, this may encourage the company to use sub-contractors. If a detailed closeout report is not generated by the sub-contractors the company would lose valuable experience and information.

7. Job Descriptions

The job description develops the organisation structure's positions into a further level of detail. The job description should contain the job title, the supervisor, a job summary, duties, level of responsibilities and authority. A job description should include:

- Who the person reports to, and who reports to that person
- What duties the person is responsible for
- What authority the person has to solve problems, make decisions and issue instructions.

Using this basic framework consider an example of a project manager's job description - reporting to the general manager, the project manager is delegated with responsibility and authority to:

- Achieve all the targets set out in the baseline plan.
- Select and manage the project team.
- Set up the project office and management system to plan and control the project.
- Represent the company at the client meetings.
- Process all project related correspondence.
- Authorise all reimbursable procurement and services required by the project.
- Negotiate and award all the sub-contracts.
- Process all non-conformance reports (NCR's).
- Issue the necessary project procedures.
- Issue weekly / monthly progress reports and financial statements.
- Approve all changes on behalf of the company.
- During the development of the *scope of work* it is the project manager's responsibility to structure and co-ordinate the input and involve all interested parties (internal and external stakeholders). This involvement is required to determine the technical and managerial requirements.
- Some of the qualities the project manager requires include; an ability to communicate, negotiate, deduce, quantify dreams, quantify wish lists and interpret the client's needs correctly.

As the project manager is responsible for selecting the project team it can be assumed that the project manager is also responsible for defining their job descriptions. These would normally include the following positions:

- Project Accountant
- Project Planner
- Project Engineer
- Project QA
- Project Procurement

The size of the project would determine the number of people in the team. On a small project one person may cover all these positions, while on a large project there may be a number of people per position. The bottom line is that the project manager is the *single point of responsibility* and as such has a blanket responsibility for the project. The project manager's authority, however, may be limited. The key word here is to strive for authority **commensurate** with your responsibility.

8. Organisation Structure Selection

Selecting the right organisation structure is essentially a balancing act between addressing the project's needs (scope), the project team's needs (and stakeholders needs) and just as important the individuals' needs (see figure 20.1). On some projects, the client may request or instruct the contractor to use a certain type of management structure.

The choice can be further complicated by an organisation structure which is appropriate for one company, but may be a burden for another. The project could therefore evolve into many different structures running concurrently. The project manager is often selected from a functional department, but which one?

- The department that initiated the project.
- The department with the largest part of the project.
- The department with the initial phase of the project.
- The department with the least work on at the time.

The selection is often influenced in favour of the department with the appropriate technical background. This organisation structure would be called **lead technical**. When the project requires input from a number of different departments the **matrix** structure offers a real solution to the functional division of responsibility and authority. If the project is a large capital project which will run for a few years, setting up a **pure project** structure may be the most expedient and appropriate decision.

9. Responsibility - Authority Gap

A characteristic of the matrix organisation structure is that it relies on the functional departments for resources. Although the project and functional departments may appear to work autonomously, for project success they need strong communication links with each other. The project manager needs to cut across organisational lines to co-ordinate and integrate specific resources located in the functional departments. To achieve this the project manager must have both a fully integrated information and control system and the means of addressing the responsibility - authority gap.

Responsibility may be defined as feeling obliged to perform assigned work, while authority is the power to carry out the work. The authority gap is when you are given responsibility, but do not have sufficient authority to issue instructions to make the work happen. It is often stated that authority should be commensurate with responsibility, but feedback suggests that CEOs are often reluctant to assign sufficient formal power to project managers. In which case the project managers need to address the authority gap in other ways. Consider the following:

Formal Authority: Or position power is automatically conferred on you with your appointment to the project. While position power can be exerted over subordinates, this type of power is very limited in its acceptance and often does little to influence behaviour particularly with the functional managers who own the resources the project manager needs.

Budget Authority: If the project manager holds the purse strings this will confer some financial power over the functional managers, particularly if their departments are run as cost centres. It is certainly powerful when dealing with outside suppliers and contractors who depend on your payments for their existence. Budget authority can lie with both the carrot and the stick - the promise of future business, an incentive bonus and threats of withholding payment for poor work.

Coercive Power: Coercive power uses the fear and the avoidance of punishment and threats to influence behaviour. This may be seen as; power not to reward, or threaten demotion, withholding overtime, limiting salary increase, or transfer to another job. Use of coercive power is linked to organisation position, and if used excessively tends to inhibit creativity and can have a negative affect on team morale.

Information Power: Expert knowledge and technical ability are effective if perceived as valuable and shared appropriately with functional managers and project participants, however it will erode trust and create resentment if hoarded. As project manager you should be at the centre of the information and control system, and therefore in an ideal position to capture, process, file and disseminate useful information.

Reward Power: The ability to provide positive rewards for performance. To be effective, it must properly correspond to participants' values and expectations. Since money is not always available, project managers must consider a variety of potentially satisfying sanctions especially those related to work challenge and recognition (see Herzberg's motivation and hygiene factors in the *Project Leadership* chapter).

Cognitive Persuasion: The logical (cognitive) approach includes the use of reasoned argument, evidence and logical consistency. How can you encourage the functional managers to part with their best people??? Perhaps you can persuade them that their contribution is needed for the success of the project, the success of their department and for the success of the company.

Emotional Persuasion: Beg the functional managers for their assistance, appeal to their sense of compassion. Request a favour, say please, appeal to their better nature - *go down on your knees!*

Personal Power: The charismatic project manager can compel people to listen and follow them. They are natural leaders who can persuade and encourage others to follow a certain course of action. They often have a sense of mission, a sense of purpose, have a good sense of humour, are empathetic to staff needs, enthusiastic and self-confident.

Ideally project managers should be competent in all areas of authority for continuing success. The charismatic manager for example, may have initial appeal, but as problems arise, if they are not able to assist technically, their power will be undermined. The project manager's leadership ability is usually expressed in terms of influencing the behaviour and attitudes of the project team members, the effectiveness of a leader is therefore dependant to some extent on their power.

This concludes the chapter on *Project Organisation Structures*. The following chapters will discuss *Project Teams* and the human factors associated with *Project Leadership*.

Key Points:

- The matrix structure is considered by many practitioners to be the natural project organisation structure.
- Clients prefer to deal with one manager - the project manager as the *single point of responsibility*.
- Acquiring power outside formal authority is the key to successful project management.

Further Reading:

Benedetto, R., *Matrix Management Theory in Practice*, Kendall Hunt
Bryans, P., **Cronin,** T., *Organisation Theory,* Core Business Studies
Davidson Frame, J., *Managing Projects in Organizations: How to Make the Best Use of Time, Techniques, and People*, (Jossey-Bass Management Series)
Dinsmore, P., *Human Factors in Project Management*, Amacom
Project Management Institute (PMI), *A Guide to the Project Management Body of Knowledge (PMBOK)*

Case Study and Exercises:

Projects are performed by people and managed through people, so it is essential to develop an organisation structure which reflects these needs. For this case study you have been appointed project manager for the fabrication and erection of a steel bridge to link a coastal island to the mainland. You are required to design a multi-disciplined OBS which should consider the following:

1. Benefits of a matrix OBS for this type of project.
2. Benefits of secondment OBS for this type of project.
3. Benefits of pure project OBS for this type of project.
4. Job descriptions.
5. Methods of addressing the responsibility - authority power gap.

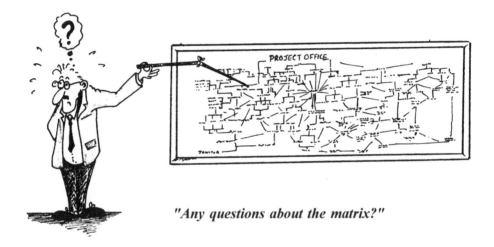

"Any questions about the matrix?"

CHAPTER 21

Project Teams

The PMBOK defines team development [managerial and technical] as; '... *both enhancing the ability of stakeholders to contribute as individuals as well as enhancing the ability of the team to function as a team*.' And the APM bok defines teamwork as; '... *effective teamwork is generally at the heart of effective project management*.'

A project team may be defined as a number of people who work closely together to achieve shared common goals (see figure 21.1). Through interaction they strive to enhance their creativity, innovation, problem-solving, decision-making, morale and job performance. A team implies a number of people working together to achieve results, while a group of people does not. A group implies a collection of individuals who, although they may be working on the same project, do not necessarily interact with each other. This is often the case when the project manager co-ordinates the project with the people individually. Under such conditions, unity of purpose is a myth.

**Figure 21.1:
Project Team
Structure**

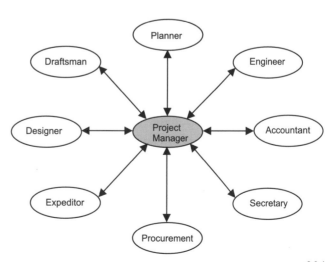

Teams are not always associated with projects, but as companies move to a *management-by-projects* approach, so the link will become better recognised. The implementation of the project planning and control techniques is through people, therefore to effectively implement the system one must gain support and commitment from the project team and other stakeholders. Many projects fail to reach their optimum level of performance, not because of any lack of equipment or project systems, but purely because the human factors were not addressed.

The growth of new technology, increased complexity and competition, has generated a need for multi-disciplined teams to work closely together. Teamwork should aim to bring individuals together in such a way that they increase their effectiveness without losing their individuality - an orchestra is a good example of a team working on this basis.

1. Purpose of Project Teams

Project teams are an efficient and effective way of managing projects, where efficiency implies performing the work well, and effectiveness implies performing the right work. Consider the following points:

- To achieve the schedule the **volume of work** must be distributed (shared) amongst a number of people.
- The scope of the project may require a **range of skills** which any one person is unlikely to have. Consider the orchestra again - this is an excellent example of a set of complementary skills and talents (functional skills) which are required to produce the music.
- **Brainstorming** and discussions are a good example of interactive team work to generate creative ideas and **solve problems**. Through cross-fertilisation and synergy a small team can generate many innovative options and alternatives - a suggestion from one person can stimulate spontaneous ideas from the others (particularly if there is no evaluation).
- Once a project team has made a **collective decision**, the team will be committed to support their course of action.
- Project teams generally take riskier decisions than an individual would on their own. There is a feeling of mutual support.
- Project teams enhance motivation - the members do not want to let the side down.
- Project teams support other team members when they need help both technically and emotionally.

Management tests show that teams repeatedly make better decisions than the team members would make individually with the same information. This has been attributed to the teams' wider range of skills and experiences than any one individual would have.

2. The Individual's Purpose for Team Membership

Why should an individual wish to be part of a project team? Consider the following points:

- It is a means of satisfying an individual's social or affiliation needs, to belong to something or be part of a team.
- It is a means of sharing risk with other team members - spread the load.
- It is a means of establishing self-esteem. People like to introduce themselves as Joe Bloggs from Eurobuilders Ltd. This way they are defining themselves in terms of their relationship to others, as a member of a team or company.
- It is a means of gaining **support** to carry out their particular goals. It also allows you to bounce ideas off other team members who can offer support, constructive criticism and alternative suggestions.
- The team provides a psychological home for the individual.

The above outlines why some people prefer to work in groups. It should be mentioned, however, that not everyone wants to work in a team - many people prefer to work on their own. And with the increasing use of email, the Internet and video-conferencing, working from home or away from the project office is becoming more feasible and popular.

3. Benefits of Teams

In the past, corporations have been preoccupied with the qualities of individual people. Any attempt to list the qualities of a good manager would demonstrate abilities that are almost certainly mutually exclusive to any individual:

- They must be **highly intelligent** but not **too clever**.
- They must be **forceful** but also **sensitive** to people's feelings.
- They must be **dynamic** but also **patient**.
- They must be a **fluent communicator** but also a **good listener.**
- They must be **decisive** but also **reflective**.
- They must be an **expert** on a wide range of different fields.

And if a manager is found with the above attributes, a paragon of mutually compatible characteristics, what happens if they:

- Step under a bus.
- Take up a position with a competitor.
- Go to live in another country.

But if no individual can combine all these qualities, a team of individuals certainly could, for the following reasons:

- It is not the individual but the team that is instrumental in sustaining and enduring management success.
- A team can **renew** and regenerate itself through new recruitment as individual team members leave.
- A team can also build up a store of shared and collectively owned experiences, information and judgement which can be passed on to new team members.

- Many people are **more successful** working within a team or partnership than working alone.
- Team **synergy** generates more output than the sum of the individual inputs.
- The team can offer a wide range of technical support.

Having established the need for a team - what is the appropriate size of the team?

4. Team Size

The appropriate team size depends on a number of factors:

- How many people are required to perform the work for the project and spread the load.
- What variety of technical expertise is required by the project. If the team is too small it may not have the knowledge base and skill depth to meet the needs of the project.
- What is the appropriate level of conflict in a team? Mathematically, the odds of conflict increase with the number of people in the team.
- Large teams tend to be unwieldy and unable to reach agreement, or collect everyone's contribution. If decisions are made by majority vote, an uneven number may prevent 'ties' (although some members could abstain).
- Too large and the team may find communication and agreement difficult, the team may subdivide into cliques.
- The team needs a balance of personalities.

The ideal team size depends very much on its application. Teams tend to grow in size until some magic number is reached - then they subdivide. The experts suggest this is between five and ten people. Sporting teams provide us with some guidelines, consider a rugby team for example, which consists of fifteen players. This number is slightly higher than recommended, and sure enough there is subdivision into a pack of eight and seven backs.

5. Why Teams Win

Research by Belbin at Henley Management College showed that some or all of the following characteristics are present in a successful team:

- The team leader had an appropriate management style for the project, and was not challenged by other team members.
- There was a chairman type person who encouraged all the team members to contribute.
- At least one member of the team generated innovative ideas as a means to solve problems and identify new products and new markets.
- There was a spread of mental abilities.
- There was a spread of personalities which gave the team a balanced appearance.

The person in the chair or team leader will be successful if they gain and earn respect from the other team members. Generally the chairman does not need to dominate the proceedings but should know how to pull matters together and integrate the team. In practice Belbin found the leader always worked closely with the talented members of the team.

Innovation: Innovation and creativity to solve problems and respond to change are essential for continuing project success. Ideas can be generated in many ways from people both inside and outside the team.

Flexibility: In flexible teams the team members play the role or support the role that is in demand or overloaded at the time. Successful teams exhibit flexibility where members are able to move around in the team to find the best match between people and jobs. They also realise that if they did not have a balanced distribution of team roles they would have to appoint members to play those missing roles.

Belbin (*Management Teams*) said that; '... *the essence of a team is that its members form a co-operative association through a division of labour that best reflects the contribution that each can make towards the common objectives.*'

6. Why Teams Fail

Belbin found that the single factor evident in all unsuccessful teams was low mental ability. If this is compared with the innovation and creativity of winning teams, then it would imply that low mental ability teams were not able to:

- Take advantage of **opportunities**
- Were poor at **problem-solving**
- Unable to **change** with the times.

Negative Selection: The failure of companies to produce teams which have an adequate proportion of managers with good mental ability must surely not be due to any conscious search for such people, but rather the unintended by-product of negative selection. Negative selection refers to the recruitment process designed to filter out the type of people the company really needs. Consider the company which is looking for a good manager to reverse their present decline, but will not increase the current salary package offered. This low salary will unintentionally exclude the quality manager the company needs.

7. Team Development Phases

Project teams pass through a number of distinctive development phases or stages. It is important to be aware of these phases so that you can guide the team through the stages, particularly the conflict phase to the productive phase:

Forming	The team members form a team, there is a sense of anticipation and commitment. Their motivation is high, but their effectiveness is moderate because they are unsure of each other and the purpose of the project.
Storming	Disagreement and conflict over task and ways of working as a team. Clash of personalities.
Norming	Consolidation differences are accepted and agree to work together.
Performing	Effective teamwork - work well and interact together as a team.
Maturing	Getting old gracefully, more interested in maintaining situation, rather than trying out new ideas.
Declining	Market has changed, team has no new products. The team are really over the hill, just hanging in there waiting for their pension.

Table 21.1: Team Development Phases

8. Role of the Project Manager

The project manager's position evolved in the 1950s as the *single point of responsibility* to co-ordinate multi-disciplined projects and make the best use of the company's resources. The role of the project manager is influenced by the size of the project - on a small project for example, the project manager may be expected to be a technical expert as well. Consider the following points in favour of the project manager being a **technical expert:**

- Companies prefer their managers to be technical experts in the field of the project, as it enables the managers to confirm technical decisions themselves. This view is supported by the fact that most project management positions advertised require the managers to be technically competent in field of the project.
- If the project manager knows and understands the technical issues of the project they will be in a better position to apply judgement and forecast problems.
- Team selection can be based on both human compatibility and technical ability. The technical ability and demonstratable skills they would be able to verify directly.

- They can be effectively involved up-front during the feasibility study, estimating and quotation stage of the project.
- They will be able to gain respect from the team by demonstrating not only good management but also technical expertise (see *Herzberg's* motivation and hygiene factors in the *Project Leadership* chapter).

Now for the other side of the argument in favour of the project manager being a **generalist** in the field of the project:

- As a manager moves up the corporate ladder they will be concerned more with people, costs and co-ordinating multi-disciplines and less with technical issues.
- It may not be desirable to have the technical expert leading the team, as they could suppress innovation from the other team members, particularly in their area of expertise.
- Effective project management requires many non-technical skills such as human resource management, team building, financial accounting, negotiation, integration and co-ordination.

It would seem from commercial feedback that initially to embark on a career in project management you need experience in the field of the project, but once established you will slowly become more of a generalist in project management.

Key Points:

- Project teams are characterised by positive interaction.
- The ability to generate innovative ideas is essential for problem-solving and the success of the project.
- Employers prefer the project manager to have technical ability in the field of the project

Further Reading:

Adams, J., and **Campbell**, B., *Roles and Responsibilities of the Project Manager*, PMI
Belbin, M., *Management Teams,* Butterworth
Handy, Charles, *Understanding Organisations*

Case Study and Exercises:

Project teams work together to achieve common goals. Through interaction they strive to enhance their creativity, innovation, problem-solving, decision-making, morale and team performance. As team leader of a motor racing team you are responsible for designing and building the team. There are many challenges building a team, your presentation should consider the following:

1. Team selection techniques.
2. Ideal team size before subdivision.
3. Why teams win, why teams fail.
4. Team development phases.
5. Does the team leader need to be a technical expert.

Project Leadership

For project managers to be effective and successful they must not only demonstrate efficient administrative skills and technical know how, but must also practice an appropriate style of leadership. The leadership style used can profoundly effect employee morale and productivity, so that the success of a project may be directly dependent on good leadership. The APM bok says; '... *leadership is about setting goals and objectives and generating enthusiasm and motivation amongst the project team, and stakeholders, to work towards those objectives.*'

1. Leadership Styles

Leadership styles may be considered as a continuum from autocratic to democratic. The leadership style used by the manager may depend on the type of decisions required, the pressures prevalent at the time and the type of people they are working with. The continuum of leadership styles relating to decision-making may be conveniently subdivided into a number of categories as shown in figure 22.1:

**Figure 22.1: Decision-Making
Continuum**

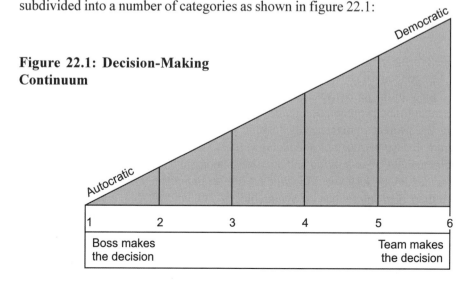

The six stages from autocratic to democratic leadership are:

1. **Autocratic (isolated decision):** The project manager solves the problem or makes the decision on his own, using information available to him at the time. There is no communication with the team members.

2. **Autocratic (informed decision):** The project manager obtains the necessary information from the team members then decides on the solution to the problem on his own.

3. **Consultative Autocratic (discuss with individuals):** The project manager shares the problem with the team members individually, gathering their ideas and suggestions. Then the project manager makes the decision on his own.

4. **Consultative Autocratic (discuss with team):** The project manager shares the problem with the team members as a group. Then the project manager makes the decision on his own.

5. **Democratic:** The project manager shares the problem with the team members. Then together they make the decision as a group - majority vote.

6. **Laissez-Faire:** The project manager gives the problem to the team and lets them make the decision themselves. This is a policy of non-interference.

Even though the project manager may make the decision on his own, how he sells his decision to the team is important. There is a big difference between telling someone what to do and using persuasive argument. The following questions are a guide to selecting the appropriate leadership style.

- Is one decision likely to be better than another? If not, go for number 1.
- Does the leader know enough to make the decision on his own? If not avoid number 1.
- Is the problem clear and structured? If not use numbers 4 or 5.
- Must the team members accept the decision? If not then numbers 1 and 2 are possibilities, if they do then use numbers 4 or 5.
- Will the team members accept the manager's decision? If not then number 5 is preferable.
- Do the team members share the manager's goals for the organisation? If not then number 5 is risky.
- Are the team members likely to conflict with each other? If yes then number 4 is better than 5.

The project manager may use all of the above methods on a project as the circumstances dictate. The concept of shared leadership is fundamental for project management and effective team building because it requires participation and involvement of all the team members. The project manager must delegate some authority to the team and in so doing the project manager will become more of a team member and the team members will assume more of a leadership role. This encourages the team members to participate in problem-solving and decision-making and accept the responsibility for the project achieving its goals. This will not only enhance the team's commitment, but also give them a strong feeling of ownership.

2. Action-Centred Leadership

Action-centred leadership was originally developed by **John Adair** for leadership training at Sandhurst Military Academy. It is now widely applied to the commercial environment. John Adair has published a number of books on leadership and team work, which are reported to have sold over 300,000 copies world wide. *Action-centred leadership* focuses on the three basic project needs:
- Individual's needs
- Team's needs
- Task's needs.

Figure 22.2: Action Centred Leadership

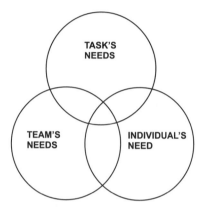

These needs are presented as intersecting circles to indicate the separate needs and mutually overlapping needs. *Action-centred leadership* neatly combines the **motivation** theories for the individual's needs with the **team building** theories for the team's needs and the **project planning and control techniques** for the task's needs.

Individual's Needs: The individual's needs should be considered first, because if the individual's basic needs are not being satisfied then that person is unlikely to be able to contribute effectively to the team or task. A person with a serious problem at home, for example, will be mentally preoccupied. Only when the individual's problems have been resolved can they apply themselves effectively through the team to perform the task.

Team's Needs: For the team to be effective the individual team members must work together and interact as a team under a *single point of responsibility*, the team leader or the project manager.

Task's Needs: With both the individual's needs and the team's needs addressed, the project team is now in a position to effectively apply themselves to address the task's needs. The task's needs are to deliver the project's objectives; scope, time, cost and quality through an effective planning and control system that includes integrating the project process, communication, organisation structures and risk management.

At the end of the day the success of the project may be determined by the team's ability to effectively solve problems and be committed to their decisions.

3. Motivation

The term motivation is often misunderstood and misused in the managerial context. Motivation is an inner force that causes or induces someone to be inspired to do something. However, what inspires one person may not inspire another. And what inspires an individual in one set of circumstances may not inspire him in another. The manager's task is to influence the work situation in such a way as to encourage the individuals to inspire and motivate themselves to achieve the project's goals. When we assess a person's ability to complete a job successfully it can be subdivided into ability and commitment.

Performance = Ability x Commitment

Ability: Ability describes the personal qualities and competency a person brings to the job. These are qualities of skill (welding or programming for example) that enable a person to perform a task, and give them the capacity to cope with the demands of the job. A person's level of calibre is associated with their innate ability and the amount of training and experience they have acquired.

Commitment: The performance of an individual, however, also depends on their willingness and drive to complete the task, in other words their commitment. Unlike ability, commitment is not a fixed commodity. It may change in response to conditions and situations the individual encounters.

To this extent, the manager must use an appropriate style of leadership to control the working environment in such a manner that the workforce will be committed to the task and so inspire and motivate themselves to achieve the objectives of the project. Therefore to achieve maximum output from the workforce the manager must address both ability and commitment.

4. Maslow's Hierarchy of Needs

Maslow's experiments in a Californian electronics factory, promoted theory Z, which outlined that workers needed secure structures and a sense of direction to maintain high standards and goals. The corner stone of motivation theory is Maslow's *hierarchy of needs*, which was first published in 1954. Maslow made the assumption that people work in order to satisfy various needs. Maslow stated that motivation is an unconscious attempt on behalf of the individual to satisfy certain inner needs. He expressed this in the form of a hierarchy.

The hierarchy illustrates a priority of needs (see figure 22.3). Maslow indicated that one is always striving to achieve the higher order needs, but this can only be achieved once the lower order needs have been satisfied.

Physiological Needs: This refers to the needs of the body to survive and self-preservation - the most fundamental need of all. If you were to be deprived of air to breath or food to eat, you would become totally preoccupied trying to acquire these lower order needs in preference to any other need. People who are addicted to cigarettes and drugs may adopt antisocial behaviour to satisfy these needs (stealing). However, once these needs have been fulfilled offering them more would have no motivational value.

Security and Safety Needs: This refers not only to the obvious immediate concerns for the continuity of job, income and protection from accident and physical danger, but also concerns fear of disapproval, comments against your personality and character, risk of failure and unfair criticism, which may be seen as psychologically damaging. When one has reached a level of economic security that satisfies, one will only want to ensure that they stay there. When the security needs are reasonably well satisfied you are unlikely to be motivated towards activities aimed at increasing security still further.

We generally prefer a safe, predictable environment to one plagued by unforeseen events. This protective desire may prompt us to be concerned with insurance and with jobs that offer security. Working on projects is a moot point - what are the persons feelings as the project moves to completion and their contract is terminated. If there is not another project in the pipeline, then this security need will prevail. Security needs do not dominate our lives except in times of emergency or danger.

Social and Love Needs: This refers to the need to associate with other people, our need to be accepted by others and belong to a team or group. Sharing our lives with others is important to most of us, and we generally react quickly to the possibility that this need will be denied. We satisfy our love needs through our family and close friends. We desire the approval and acceptance of our fellow workers and the many groups of people we associate with and with whom we tend to identify ourselves. We alter our behaviour and even our standards in order to be accepted by our chosen friends and groups. The lonely hearts clubs of this world owe their existence to this powerful need to give and share love.

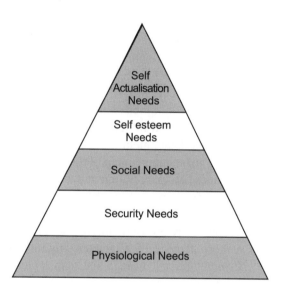

Figure 22.3: Maslow's Hierarchy of Needs

Self-Esteem Needs: This refers to a person's **ego** needs, which drives the person to feel wanted and important within their own working group. This need for recognition, respect, prestige and status is a higher order need. This need goes beyond the more passive need to belong to ..... or to be loved by....... - to a more active desire for recognition and self-respect. Self-esteem needs involves self-evaluation, the desire for reputation or prestige, recognition, attention, importance or appreciation. In our culture self-esteem needs are particularly important. Satisfaction of self-esteem needs leads to self-confidence and a feeling of personal worth.

Self-esteem needs are often accompanied by many frustrations and personal conflicts, since people desire not only recognition and attention by their chosen groups but also the self-respect and status that their moral, social, and religious standards call for. When the chosen group calls for behaviour that conflicts with a person's standards, that person must make heroic choices in order to remain well adjusted. People play many roles in order to satisfy some of the different groups and team cultures to which they belong.

Self-Actualisation Needs: This refers to a person's own self-fulfilment and self-realisation - our desire to reach the height of our personal abilities and talents. In Maslow's words, *"What a man can be, he must be."* This category of need includes creativity, achievement, competence and productivity. This is the highest of all the needs. This need becomes increasingly important as the previous needs are satisfied. Maslow described self-actualised people as having the following characteristics:

- A more efficient perception of reality.
- Increased acceptance of self, of others and of nature.
- Spontaneity, simplicity and naturalness.
- Problem-centred rather than ego-centred.
- Increased detachment and desire for privacy.
- Ability to be independent of their physical and social environment.
- Freshness of appreciation and richness of emotional reaction.
- Higher frequency of *'peak'* mystic, or transcendent experiences.
- Increased identification with and feeling of mankind.
- Deeper, more profound interpersonal relationships.
- A more democratic character structure.
- Strongly ethical - able to distinguish clearly between means and ends.
- A natural, spontaneous creativity.

The rank and practical importance of these needs depends on the degree to which each is satisfied. Because this degree of satisfaction is constantly changing. Maslow believed people have a need to grow and develop (self-actualise). By using and developing their capacities people begin to self-actualise, they experience satisfaction and enjoyment. As self-actualisation is the highest need - as this need is satisfied, it is replaced with new areas or targets to achieve, so causing a continuous process. Self-actualisation, therefore differs from the other needs, because it can never be satisfied!

The hierarchy of needs has an important impact on management thinking because it provides a powerful instrument for predicting the outcome of responses by individuals within the organisation. In organisations this self-actualisation need can exhibit a high desire for promotion. Large companies provide career opportunities through career development and training, this can satisfy a need of self-development and improve promotion prospects. Self-actualisation seems to be an intrinsic desire and not directly related to rewards of money.

Motivation Cycle: The motivation cycle outlines the dynamic and changeable nature of motivation. When a need becomes unsatisfied it creates within the individual a kind of tension, which in turn creates a driving force or impetus towards certain actions or behaviour. This behaviour will be aimed at satisfying the need and when the need is satisfied the tension is relieved, but now the cycle starts all over again with respect to another need.

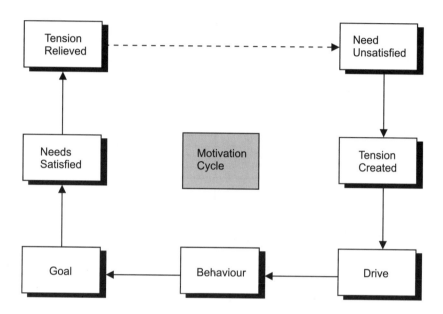

Figure 22.4: Motivation Cycle
(from unsatisfied need to tension relieved)

5. Herzberg's Motivation and Hygiene Factors

Frederick Herzberg, a consultant for AT&T, preached "*Job enrichment and individual development*". Herzberg's theory was designed to improve our understanding of working people, what factors determine job satisfaction and what determines job dissatisfaction. Herzberg found these were separate independent factors operating at the same time. Here the term motivation indicates factors that increase your commitment to the job, while hygiene factors will cause a sense of grievance leading to your job dissatisfaction and hence a reduction of motivation and commitment.

A hygiene factor can be likened to a sewer, when it fails it becomes extremely important to people in the vicinity that it should be repaired as quickly as possible!!!! However, once repaired the sewer now loses importance to those people concerned, and improving its efficiency still further is of little interest.

Herzberg presented his motivation and hygiene factors in figure 5 where the x axis indicates the frequency with which the factor was reported as causing high morale or causing a sense of grievance. The factors are listed vertically, sorted by high morale, while the depth of each box indicates how long the feeling lasted.

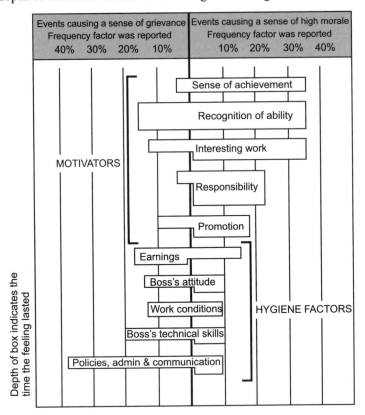

Figure 22.5: Herzberg's Motivation and Hygiene Factors

The analysis indicates some interesting findings:

- Earnings, although a motivator for a short period of time were mostly reported as a hygiene factor. This means that even if the employees are paid above average salary, they will only be motivated for a short period of time, until their new salary becomes their norm. If, however, they are paid less than their colleagues they will quickly become dissatisfied.
- Once the working conditions are at an acceptable level, improving them further will not necessarily stimulate additional effort or commitment.
- On the positive side there can be no substitute for factors like opportunity to gain a sense of achievement, recognition of ability, more interesting work, greater responsibility and opportunities for promotion.

The motivation theories outlined have the benefit of being mutually supportive. Herzberg's motivators for example, relate closely with Maslow's hierarchy of needs.

6. Conflict

All projects are subjected to some degree of conflict, so it is important for the project manager to recognise the *symptoms* of conflict:

- Poor communication laterally and vertically. Decisions taken on incomplete information. Two levels in the same company are moving in different directions on the same problem.
- Inter-group hostility and jealousy expressed as; *"They never tell us anything"* or *"They expect us to know by intuition"*.
- Interpersonal friction affects the relationships between individuals where it can deteriorate to icy formality or argument. Problems seem to focus on people and personalities.
- Escalation of arbitration by senior management.
- Proliferation of rules and regulations. It becomes more and more difficult to do anything without riding roughshod over somebody's regulations.
- Low morale expressed as frustration and inefficiency.

Control of Conflict: When symptoms have been identified that cannot be addressed by rearranging the ecology to create an amenable working environment, then consider the following:

- **Arbitration:** Conduct arbitration at a low level. This solution is useful when the conflict is apparent and specific, but not very useful in episodic or continual conflict. Try and agree on an arbitrator at the outset of the project, because later when there is conflict the parties will each nominate a person sympathetic to their own view.
- **Co-ordination Device:** A position is created in the company between the conflicting parties. This eliminates the contact and so the conflict. There are, however, additional administration costs for the company. This device is not an effective solution for episodic or occasional conflict, but useful where the conflicting pressures are continuous.
- **Negotiation:** An interesting variation on confrontation is an approach called role negotiation, where conflicting parties negotiate and trade items of behaviour, e.g. *"I will stop doing X if you stop doing Y"*. This method goes a long way to reduce the pains of conflict, particularly between individuals, although it may leave the underlying problem untouched.

317

- **Separation:** If interaction increases the depth of the sentiments then separation should cool them down. This solution will work if the true cause of the conflict is two incompatible individuals, incompatible in personality, or more often with relative status inappropriate to the situation. To separate the individuals, transferring one to another department may be a successful strategy. This will at least allow both parties to be productive in their different areas.
- **Withdrawal and Neglect:** Retreating from an actual or potential conflict situation. This is not a solution in itself unless it is trivial, but it could provide a cooling off period while a better solution could be found.
- **Smoothing:** Smoothing emphasises the use of agreement rather than focusing on the differences of opinion. Smoothing allows the work to continue and can smooth ruffled feelings and defuse the situation, but is only a temporary solution.
- **Rules and Regulations:** Strive to compile rules, regulations and procedures by negotiation and agreement. This approach is useful when the conflict is recurrent and predictable, but should not be regarded as a permanent solution.
- **Compromising:** Searching for solutions that bring some degree of satisfaction to both conflicting parties.
- **Confrontation:** A technique much favoured by those who believe in openness. This strategy will be effective, if the issue can be clearly defined and is not a symptom of more underlying differences. Confrontation and inter-group meetings can greatly increase understanding of people's views, but they cannot be a complete substitute from the ecological point of view.
- **Forcing:** Pushing one's point of view at the potential expense of another.
- **Problem-Solving:** Treating conflict as a technical problem to be solved by reasoned argument and examining the alternatives.

Permanent solutions are generally only reached by compromise, confrontation or problem-solving. Research by Thamhain and Wilemon suggest that forcing and withdrawal appears to increase conflict with functional support departments, while confrontation, compromise and smoothing tends to reduce conflict.

7. Delegation

Skilful delegation is the key to effective project management. Through delegation the project manager can improve project team efficiency, develop employee ability and contribute to the growth of the company.

Feedback from commerce and industry suggests, however, that delegation is not a widely practised technique and that project managers are held back by performing trifling tasks themselves. The project managers become overworked, overtaxed, and at the same time miss the opportunity to encourage initiative and motivate growth among their employees. Delegation has three basic elements:

- Assign a function, duty or task to an employee.
- Allocate sufficient authority so that the employee can command the resources necessary to accomplish the assignment.
- Gain commitment from the employee for the satisfactory completion of the task.

The employee must know that they will be held accountable for the work delegated, but bear in mind that under performance may indicate that further training of the employee is required. It should always be remembered that delegating work will not reduce the project manager's ultimate responsibility and accountability for the task - this is not transferable. However, although it is unreasonable to imply that the project manager should be responsible for the actions of a team worker, it does mean the project manager is responsible for setting up the system to ensure that the team worker can do the job correctly.

Method of Delegation: The following list is a managerial guide to delegate a task and authority to a subordinate.
- Accept the need to delegate.
- Develop a detailed plan for delegation.
- Obtain the supervisor's approval for your delegation plan.
- Establish a climate of mutual confidence and trust (this will not happen over night).
- Select the function, duties and tasks to be delegated and assigned.
- Establish clear lines of authority and responsibility and ensure that they are understood by all.
- Adopt a constructive attitude, demonstrate patience when a subordinate makes a mistake.
- Monitor performance and provide frequent feedback.
- Reward effective delegation.

The crunch comes when the subordinate makes a poor decision, how do you react? Try not to reverse the decision without discussing it with them first, otherwise they are unlikely to be motivated to make another decision - they will rather refer decisions to you instead - and now you are back to square one.

Key Points:

- The decision-making continuum outlines how teams make decisions.
- Herzberg's motivation and hygiene factors outline what factors motivate team members to perform, while also identifying what causes a sense of grievance.
- As the work load increases the project manager must delegate or risk becoming bogged down performing trivial tasks.

Further Reading:

Adair, John, *Action-Centred Leadership,* Pan
Adair, John, *Team Building,* Pan
Hans, J. **Thamhain** and **David,** L. **Wilemon,** *Conflict Management in Project-Orientated Work Environments*, Project Management Institute
Herzberg, F., *Work and the Nature of Man*
Maslow, A., *Motivation and Personality*
Blake, Peter, *How Team New Zealand won the America's Cup,* Management

Case Study and Exercises:

Is there a difference between a leader and a manager??? The Economist says '*A leader challenges the status quo; a manager accepts it. A manager's prime role is to prevent the complexity of a modern company degenerating into chaos. Managers take details - like financial planning, quality, stock levels, staffing and market research - and bring order, consistency and control to them. To managers, systems and structure are all. Because the abilities needed to lead and manage are so different, an aptitude for both is rarely in one larger-than-life individual. But because their kind are hard to find, companies cannot rely on locating a born leader-manager. Instead, firms may find it easier to build 'leadership teams', combining the talents of their best leaders with those of their top managers. This does not mean simply lumping them all together on the company board and crossing corporate fingers - there must be a conscious effort to get leaders and managers to influence each other.*'

Are you a leader or a manager??? Give your answer with respect to the following:

1. Decision making.
2. Action centred leadership.
3. Motivation.
4. Conflict resolution.
5. Delegation.

"Delegation doesn't always explode in your face"

CHAPTER 23

Project Management Computing

A revolution has taken place in the field of project planning and control - up until the 1980s all the data processing was performed by either large mainframe computers or by hand, but now with the introduction of powerful yet inexpensive personal computer hardware and computer software, there is a dramatic shift of information processing power away from the data processing department to the desk of the project manager or project team. This falling cost of computer power is also driving a new age of experimentation with management systems and how we do business.

The PMBOK says '*Project management software is widely used to assist with schedule development. These products automate the calculation of mathematical analysis and resource levelling and thus allow for rapid consideration of many schedule alternatives. They are also widely used to print or display the outputs of schedule development.*'

There used to be discussion about the resistance to change caused by introducing computer systems, but now computers have become an essential tool for the project manager to plan and control their projects, and there is universal acceptance of this new technology. Even small projects benefit from simple barcharts which clearly outline the scope of work, the timing of the work, and who is responsible. Accurate information will always be a prerequisite for good problem-solving and decision-making.

The use of computers is now a central component of the information and control system, the focus should therefore not only include the hardware and software components, but also the project office environment as the centre of the project management system.

1. Project Office

The project office enshrines the project management approach as the central point for managing projects. The project office provides a location for project management excellence, particularly for the development of project management systems, their operation, reporting and maintenance. The formation of the project office is often a recommendation from closeout reports which have identified project failure associated with;

- Information delays
- Cost overruns
- Confusion caused by inconsistent standards.

The formation of the project office is also seen as a means to introduce a new (project management) culture into the organisation, particularly with the move to *management-by-projects*.

A common information and control system ensures uniformity and standardisation of management systems. This becomes increasingly important as companies grow and their associated systems need to be supported. With standard systems collecting performance data, processing, storing (filing and retrieval) and reporting become highly efficient and effective. The project office also becomes the knowledge base and library of project management and project specific information.

Projects are run by communication. The project office becomes the front door to the project and hub for the project's communications. Clients are not passed around like a football from functional manager to functional manager, now they have a single point of responsibility and lines of communication to the project team, the contractors, the suppliers and other key stakeholders.

The project office should provide a good working environment - comfortable and quiet with few distractions. Whether it is open plan, many small offices or something in between seems to depend on company culture. And with the growing power of the Internet the **virtual office** can connect the project team members electronically by email, video conferencing and virtual reality. This enables the members team to develop a mobile office approach where they can work from site, the clients office or reduce their travelling and work from home. It is as if we are experiencing the industrial revolution in reverse - the steam age moved production from the home to the factory - now the Internet is moving people back from the factory to their homes.

2. Education and Training

To make the most of your project management software you need to understand and be able to apply the principles and techniques of project management. The software will not tell you what decisions to make or how information should be interpreted, but it will speed up data processing if the information system has been well designed.

Companies running planning software courses on packages like *Microsoft Project,* invariably have to explain the project planning techniques before they can begin the computer skills training. You need to beware of ***mistaking the tool for the solution***. A project management package alone, *does not a project manager make* - it is the difference between teaching someone how to use a fishing rod and fishing.

This book has focused on the manual techniques of processing project information. This is deliberate, because now you are in an excellent position to understand how the software performs its calculations and make the computer system work for you. The techniques covered in the text are the same as those used by the project management software packages.

Feedback from lecturers running short courses suggests that many managers who are moving into project management start by buying a project management software package in the belief that the computer will manage the project for them - "*Hey, look at these professional barcharts!*"
However, the managers soon find out that managing projects is a little bit more complicated and enrol on a short course in project management, where they receive a sound introduction to project management planning and control techniques. It therefore makes sense if you are getting started to go for the locally supported software - this way help is only a telephone call away.

As the world of project management continues to grow and develop, and incorporate computer systems, so the project management profession requires more highly skilled and better qualified managers. Hence education, industry and commerce continually work together to establish internationally recognised standards and professional qualifications. Project managers of the future are, therefore, more likely to follow an academic route to enhance their career opportunities.

3. Planning Software

Project planning software is used in conjunction with word processing and spreadsheets. Spreadsheets in particular offer simple control sheets. The planning software can be broadly separated by the cost of the package. Although it is tempting to associate higher prices with richer functions and better quality, some of the lower priced software packages can offer similar capabilities. In general, the higher priced programs are able to manage larger projects, define constraints in greater detail (more precision) and will produce more flexible reports. In contrast, the cheaper programs are easier to use, have better designed screens, are more interactive and process the data much faster.

The higher priced programs tend to handle the project cost requirements more effectively, offering more cost fields, earned value schedule cost integration and a wider range of management reports. Reporting is another area of difference, with the higher priced programs offering full report writers, which let the user generate almost any kind of management report. The low budget packages usually have a restricted number of report formats available with limited customisation. However, if you are entering the market I would suggest that you use the market standard which can be locally supported with computer skills training and hotline help.

4. Benefits of Using Project Management Software

In the past we may have had to substantiate why we need computers - now that they are part of the project office, you may have to substantiate why you are not using a computer! Consider the following benefits:

- Project management software offers fast calculations. This can be demonstrated on a spreadsheet where changes are processed almost immediately, whereas hand calculations would be very laborious.
- The calculations are always correct, the accuracy of the output being directly dependent on the accuracy of the data input. Validation of data entry is also possible, which will reduce human errors.
- Editing is very quick once the database has been established.
- The application packages typically offer well thought out information structures which, if used, will help standardise methods and enforce a disciplined approach.
- The software has the capacity to process large projects with 10,000 + activities.
- Select and sort functions enable the operator to present the information in a structured format.
- *Management-by-exception* and variance reports are easily obtained, e.g. where float = zero, this will highlight the activities on the critical path.
- Once the database has been established, **what-if** analysis can be performed quickly.
- The project database can be linked to the corporate database.
- The software can offer centralised or distributed reporting which is flexible to suit the organisation structure.

324

- They have better quality reporting; the documents and graphics can be customised to facilitate easier dissemination of information within the project team.
- Quicker calculations can lead to a shorter reporting period which gives greater control and more accurate trend analysis. It will also be quicker to respond to a changing situation.
- Reports can be structured by the *work breakdown structure* (WBS) or *organisation breakdown structure* (OBS).
- The software will release the managers from processing large amounts of data manually, which should give them more time to concentrate on managing the project and the people involved on it.
- It is relatively simple to make back-ups of the project data. This addresses the risk management need for disaster recovery.
- Managers can type their own reports, faxes and emails.

There are, however, a number of **disadvantages** which include:

- Additional costs associated with education and training, hardware and software procurement and loss of production while implementing the new system.
- The additional cost of maintenance and up-grading.
- The organisation may need to be restructured.
- The new system may cause a *resistance to change* which could affect company morale and productivity.
- If the computer goes down this could stop the company's operation, especially if effective back-up systems have not been established.
- If data safety precautions are not taken it is possible to lose vast amounts of data, caused by; virus attack, hard disk crash, fire, or theft.

"Would you like to take a bite of my Apple???"

5. Planning Software Examples

Although there are over 200 software packages, there are only so many ways to present the project management techniques. Here are a few examples from *Microsoft Project* and *Primavera*. In figures 23.1 and 23.2 the activity boxes can be setup to display more information and the links can also be setup diagonally. The *network diagram* can be developed either on the screen in the PERT view or from the precedence table in the Gantt view. Figures 23.3 and 23.4 show linked barcharts and resource histograms with activity float, timenow and progress. In both cases the resource is overloaded and would need to be either increased to meet the end date, or rescheduled.

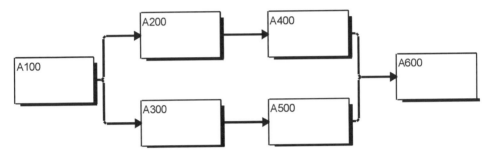

Figure 23.1: Network Diagram [*Microsoft Project* - PERT view] (this is a repeat of figure 10.4 in the *Critical Path Method* chapter

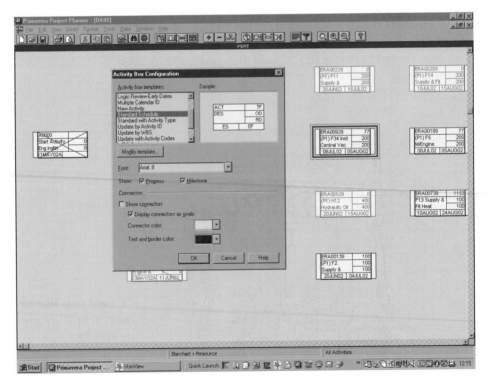

Figure 23.2: Activity Boxes [*Primavera*]

326

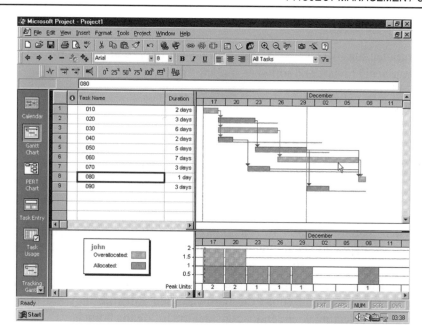

Figure 23.3: Linked Barchart and Resource Histogram [*Microsoft Project* - Gantt view]

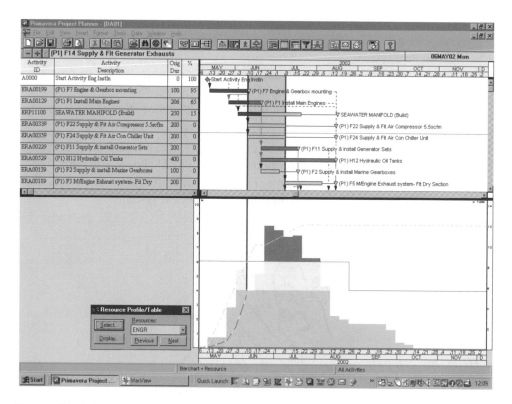

Figure 23.4: Linked Barchart and Resource Histogram [*Primavera*]

6. Vendor Selection

The computer supplier or vendor can play a very important part in the selection of your computer hardware and software, making them work effectively for you. Consider the following points:

- System design
- Training
- Getting the system up and running
- System compatibility
- Maintenance and repairs
- Upgrading.

If you have purchased the market standard hardware and software then many of the above will be widely available from a range of supporting companies, but if you have purchased one of the 200 lesser known planning packages, then you will be reliant on the vendor for the above. If they are situated in another country, the software may become self-limiting. In fact some practitioners argue that you should **select the vendor first** and let them chose the hardware and software they are prepared to support. When selecting your vendor consider the following points:

- **Expert Hot Line:** This is a telephone service where problems can be discussed. Some of the international companies will redirect your local call to offer a worldwide 24/7 hour service.
- **Training:** The training should cover a range of courses, particularly hands-on computer skills, but also project management training to help setup the information and control system.
- **Vendor Stability:** Will the vendor be in business next month, or next year when you may urgently need them?
- **Cost of Service:** Determine what is included in the one to three year warranty, what is not included, and how much any additional service will cost?

As the management systems have become more complicated it is important to ensure that the well chosen hardware will support the equally well chosen software. Again the vendor's assistance here is invaluable. The vendor must confirm that their product is compatible with your existing and proposed management systems.

"Hello, my computer won't work"

7. Implementation

Implementing a new project management system is always a dilemma, *"Do I use the old system I'm familiar with?"*, or *"Do I risk using the new more powerful system that I've just bought?"* Ideally you want to get up to speed without production pressure, however the live situation does accelerate learning. This is where a small pilot project is ideal to develop and test new equipment or systems. There are four basic implementation methods which can be used on their own or in combination:

Pilot System: A pilot system is essentially a mini version of a large project's management system. The pilot project is used to carry out a heuristic development process, to progressively develop, implement and iron out all the teething troubles. Ideally it should be used on a small project alongside the old computer system or manual system, so that if there are any problems the manager can quickly switch back to the old system.

Parallel Systems: Parallel systems operate the new management system and old management system at the same time. This effectively doubles the management work load, but if there are problems with the new system then the old system (computer or manual) is always available as a backup. This method would be preferable for a company who could not risk having a system down for an unknown period of time, e.g. emergency services, hospitals, power stations or even the daily newspapers.

Phase-in / Phase-out: This method uses a slice by slice approach, implementing the new management system one section at a time - getting each section up and running before moving on to the next part. This method has the advantage of allowing the project team to set their own pace and keep control of the changes so that, if there are any problems, they will only have to address a small area of the new management system rather than the whole system.

Cut Off: The cut off or **big bang** approach is to change from the old management system (computer or manual) to the new management system overnight. The advantage here is that the extra cost of running parallel systems is removed and the new management system is up and running quicker, but of course you do run the risk of the new management system failing with all its associated lost production costs. Only use this method if you are confident the new management system will work first time without any significant debugging. The London stock exchange used this method in the 1980s, and although they were very confident and had spent years planning the new system, the news for months after the '*big bang*' was of interrupted service and frustrated dealers.

In reality implementation tends to be most effectively achieved by combining all the different methods and using the one that is most appropriate to the management system and your management style.

This concludes the computer chapter and the last chapter of the book. The following appendices include a few worked examples which demonstrate how the key project management techniques can be applied.

Key Points:

- The computer has become an integral part of the project office's information and control system.
- The vendor could be the key person to make your computer system work effectively.
- To make the most of project management software you need to fully understand and be able to apply the principles and techniques of project management

Further Reading:

Gibson, C.F., and **Nolan**, R.L., *Managing the Four Stages of EDP Growth*, Harvard Business Review

Catapult, *Microsoft Project 98 Step by Step (Step by Step Series)*

Davidson Frame, J., *The Project Office (Best Management Practices)*, Crisp

Drigani, Fulvio, *Computerized Project Control*

Johnston, Andrew, *A Hacker's Guide to Project Management,* Computer Weekly

Palfreman, J., and **Swade**, D., *The Dream Machine*, BBC Books

Case Study and Exercises:

This case study is to get you started using project planning software. Many software companies offer free trial packages of their software - these may have either a limited ability and/or be for a limited period of time. Your case study for this chapter is to use the locally available software to setup the following presentations on a small project you are familiar with.

1. CPM network diagram showing activity logic and critical path.
2. A scheduled barchart showing, activities, events and hammocks.
3. Sort your database and reprint your barchart per responsibility or location.
4. Add resources and show resource loading.
5. Add progress and show the revised barchart.

"Let's get connected"

Appendix 1 will develop the *critical path method* and *network diagram* . Please note the solution is detailed for the beginner - if this is understood I suggest you move on to appendix 2 where this worked example is developed further:

Preceding Activity	Succeeding Activity
Start	100
100	200
100	300
100	400
200	500
300	600
400	700
500	800
600	800
700	800
800	Finish

Activity	Duration
100	2
200	3
300	6
400	2
500	5
600	7
700	3
800	1

Table 1: Logic Table and Activity Data

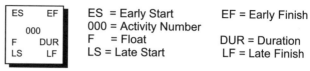

Figure 1: Activity Box

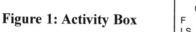

ES = Early Start   EF = Early Finish
000 = Activity Number
F = Float   DUR = Duration
LS = Late Start   LF = Late Finish

The logical relationship between the activities are shown as lines between the boxes, for example, from the logic table 1, activity 100 precedes the constraint while activity 200 succeeds the constraint. The lines are generally drawn horizontally or vertically, leaving or entering from the side of the box. The start of the project is from the left side of the page, moving right and downwards (figure 2).

Figure 2: Logic Relationship

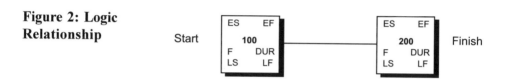

Step 1: Draw the *network diagram*. From the logic table, look at the first four lines (table 2):

Table 2: Logic Table
(extract from table 1)

Preceding Activity	Succeeding Activity
Start	100
100	200
100	300
100	400

Activity 100 is drawn first, because this is the start activity, the other three activities (200, 300, 400) follow, finish-to-start (see figure 3).

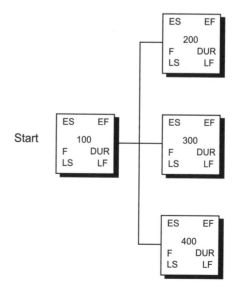

Figure 3: Network Diagram

Step 2: The next three lines from the logic table 1 are (table 3):

Table 3: Logic Table
(extract from table 1)

Preceding Activity	Succeeding Activity
200	500
300	600
400	700

This means that activity 500 follows 200, activity 600 follows 300 and activity 700 follows 400 (figure 4).

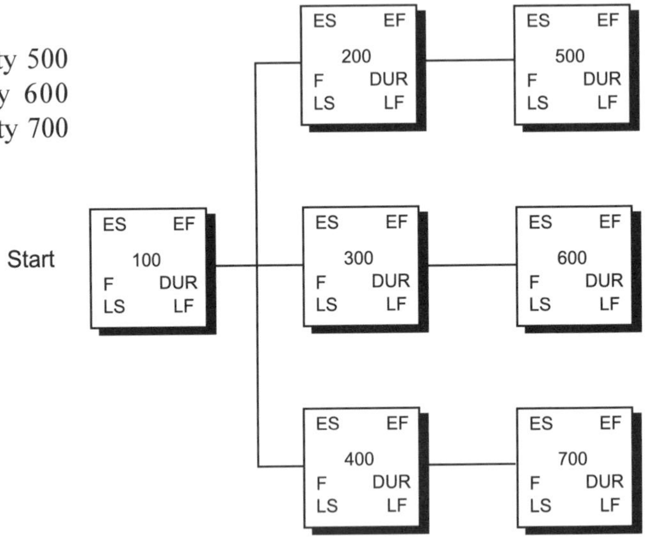

Figure 4: Network Diagram

Step 3: The last four lines of the logic table 1 are (table 4):

Table 4: Logic Table
(extract from table 1)

Preceding Activity	Succeeding Activity
500	800
600	800
700	800
800	Finish

This means activities 500, 600 and 700 must be completed before 800 can start and activity 800 is the last activity of the project (figure 5).

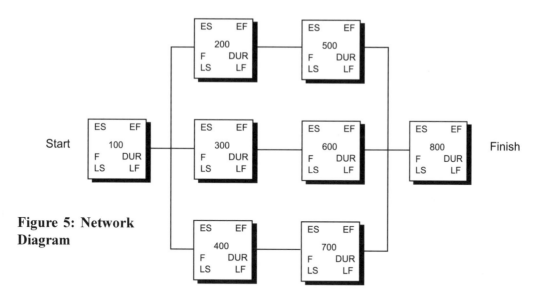

Figure 5: Network Diagram

The *network diagram* showing the logical relationships is now complete (figure 5). The *network diagram* on its own is an important presentation because it shows the sequence of work, besides the *critical path method* this is also a key input document for the *quality control plan*.

Step 4: The next step is to transfer the activity durations from the activity table (see table 1) to the activity boxes in the position marked **'dur'** (figure 6).

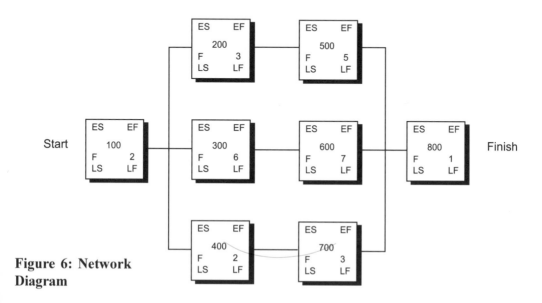

Figure 6: Network Diagram

Step 5: We now perform the forward pass to determine the *early start* (ES) and *early finish* (EF) of each activity. Activity 100 starts on day 1 or in calendar notation (say) 1st May. The activity has a duration of 2 days, so it will finish on day 2, or 2nd May. The equation is: EF = ES + duration - 1

Step 6: If the EF of activity 100 is 2nd May, then the ES of activities 200, 300 and 400 is the following day 3rd May. Calculate the EF for 200, 300 and 400 (figure 7).

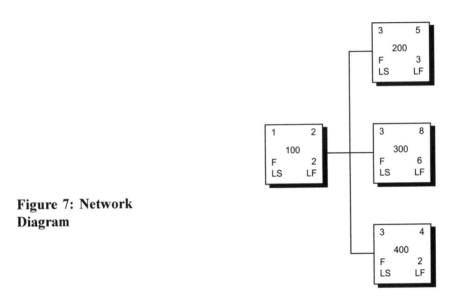

Figure 7: Network Diagram

Step 7: Calculate ES and EF for the activities 500, 600 and 700 (figure 8).

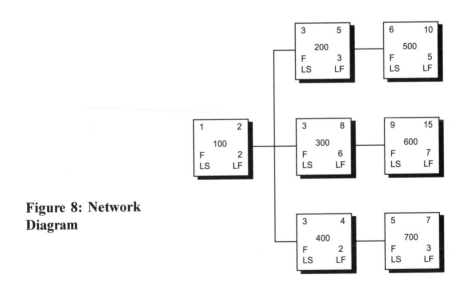

Figure 8: Network Diagram

336

Step 8: We now have an interesting situation, when there are many activities leading into one activity, select the highest EF value to give the ES for the following activity. This means activity 800 cannot start until all the preceding activities have finished (figure 9).

Figure 9: Network Diagram

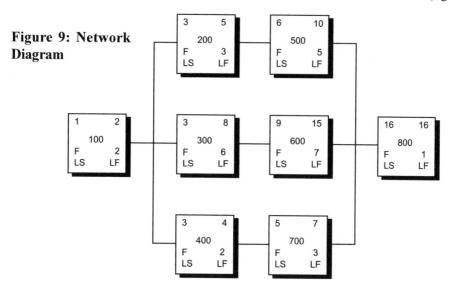

Step 9: The EF of activity 800 is a keydate, as this indicates the earliest date it is possible to complete the project, in this case 16th May.

Step 10: We now perform a **backward pass** to determine the LS and LF of each activity. Starting with activity 800 set the LF to be the same as its EF (16th May), then work backwards to find the late start for each activity. The equation is:
LS = LF - duration + 1 (figure 10).

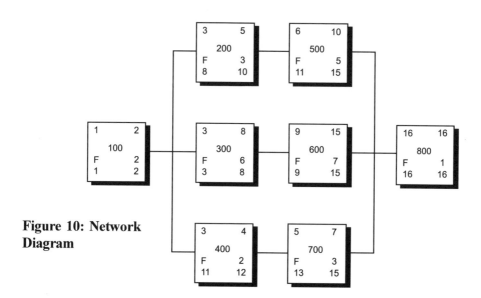

Figure 10: Network Diagram

Note: On the backward pass where there are many activities leading into one activity select the lowest number or date. This ensures that all the preceding activities have finished before the succeeding activities start.

Step 11: The next step is to calculate the activity float. Use the following equation:
Float = LS - ES
Float = 1 - 1 = 0 (for activity 100)

Using this equation the float for all the activities can be calculated.

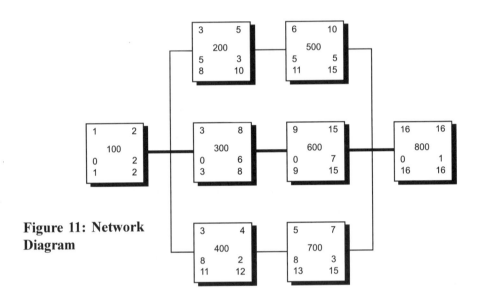

Figure 11: Network Diagram

The critical path by definition links all the activities with zero float. It is important to identify the critical path, because if any of these activities are delayed the end date of the project will be extended. In this case the following activities have zero float; 100, 300, 600 and 800. It is normal practice to highlight the critical path in heavy print, double lines or red ink to make them standout.

This worked example is a continuation from appendix 1 which developed the *network diagram*. Here the *critical path method* model will be developed further, to include; project acceleration (crashing resources), the expenditure S curve, the *cash-flow statement* and the revised barchart. To calculate the above, additional activity information is required together with data capture at timenow 4 and 8.

Activity Number	Normal Time	Resource per day	Total Normal Cost $	Crash Time	Total Crash Cost $	Additional Crash Cost per day
	A		B	C	D	(D-B)/(A-C)
100	2	2	$100	1	$200	$100
200	3	3	$150	2	$200	$50
300	6	3	$60	3	$120	$20
400	2	2	$100	2	$100	-
500	5	3	$50	4	$60	$10
600	7	2	$210	4	$255	$15
700	3	3	$90	2	$145	$55
800	1	2	$50	1	$50	-

Table 1: Activity Data (project acceleration)

Step 1: Appendix 1 analysed the network to give completion on day 16. Consider the situation where the client requests the contractor to advise the cost implication to complete the project in 10 days, or shorten the project by 6 days (see figure 1).

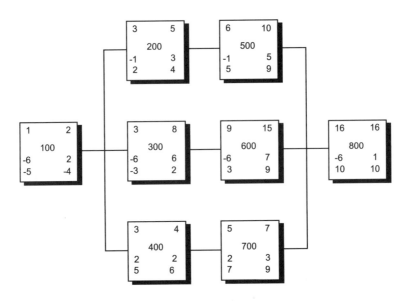

Figure 1: Network Diagram

The *network diagram* is first re-analysed by setting the LF of activity 800 to day 10, or 10th May and then performing a **backwards pass** to calculate the new LS, LF and float for all the activities. The negative float will indicate which activities need to be crashed and by how much. A priority list is then established (see table 2) with least cost to crash, first.

Activity	Cost to Crash	Priority
600	$15	1
300	$20	2
100	$100	3

Table 2: Priority List of Critical Activities

After crashing an activity the network should be reprocessed to see if any other paths have gone critical. Note here how the network arm (200, 500) also goes critical when the target completion date is reduced to 10 days. For this example, the client decides not to crash the project.

340

Crash by	Cost	(days x activity no)
3 days	$45	(3 x 600)
4 days	$65	(3 x 600) + (1 x 300)
5 days	$85	(3 x 600) + (2 x 300)
6 days	$115	(3 x 600) + (3 x 300) + (1 x 500)

Table 3: Cost to Crash the Project by 3 to 6 days

Step 2: The information from the forward pass, backward pass and float calculations (see appendix 1) are usually presented in a tabular format (see table 4).

Activity Number	Duration (days)	Early Start	Early Finish	Late Start	Late Finish	Float (days)
100	2	1 May	2 May	1 May	2 May	0
200	3	3 May	5 May	8 May	10 May	5
300	6	3 May	8 May	3 May	8 May	0
400	2	3 May	4 May	11 May	12 May	8
500	5	6 May	10 May	11 May	15 May	5
600	7	9 May	15 May	9 May	15 May	0
700	3	5 May	7 May	13 May	15 May	8
800	1	16 May	16 May	16 May	16 May	0

Table 4: Activity Data (transferred from appendix 1, figure 11, network diagram)

Step 3: The data can now be used to produce a graphical barchart. For this example the barchart will be ordered by activity number, however, in industry it is common to order by *early start* (ES) (see figure 2).

The barchart is further enhanced by including the number of resources required per day which are summed daily to give the resource histogram. The resource histogram indicates the number of men required per day. For this example the company only has six men available, this means there will be an overload on days 3, 4, 5, 6 and 7th May.

	DAYS															
Activity list	1	2	3	4	5	6	7	8	9	10	11	12	13	14	15	16
100	2	2														
200			3	3	3	-	-	-	-	- ♦						
300			3	3	3	3	3	3								
400			2	2	-	-	-	-	-	-	-	- ♦				
500						3	3	3	3	3	-	-	-	-	- ♦	
600									2	2	2	2	2	2	2	
700					3	3	3	-	-	-	-	-	-	-	- ♦	
800																2
Total	2	2	8	8	9	9	9	6	5	5	2	2	2	2	2	2

Manpower Resource Histogram

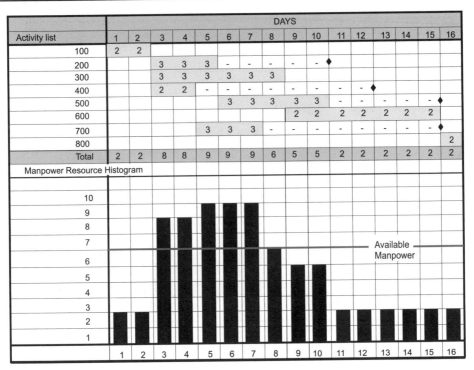

Figure 2: Early Start Barchart (showing resources)

Step 4: Resource overload is initially addressed by moving activities within their float. Try moving activities 400 and 700 to their LS (see figure 3).

	DAYS															
Activity list	1	2	3	4	5	6	7	8	9	10	11	12	13	14	15	16
100	2	2														
200			3	3	3	-	-	-	-	- ♦						
300			3	3	3	3	3	3								
400 >>>			-	-	-	-	-	-	-	-	2	2 ♦				
500						3	3	3	3	3	-	-	-	-	- ♦	
600									2	2	2	2	2	2	2	
700 >>>					-	-	-	-	-	-	-	-	3	3	3 ♦	
800																2
Total	2	2	6	6	6	6	6	6	5	5	4	4	5	5	5	2

Manpower Resource Histogram

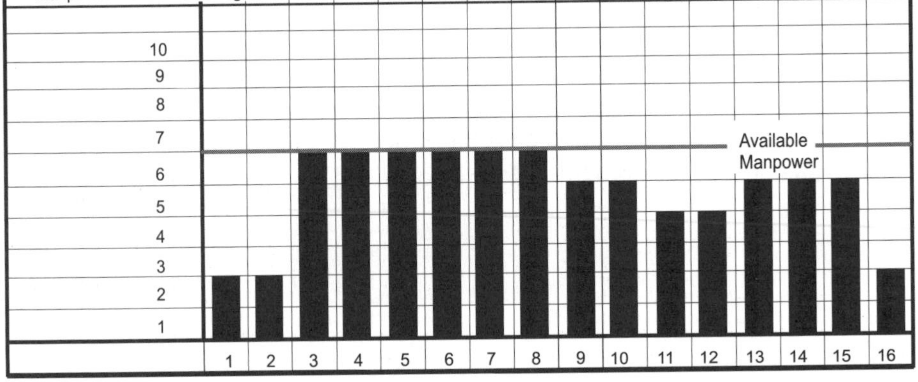

Figure 3: Barchart and Resource Histogram (after moving 400 and 700)

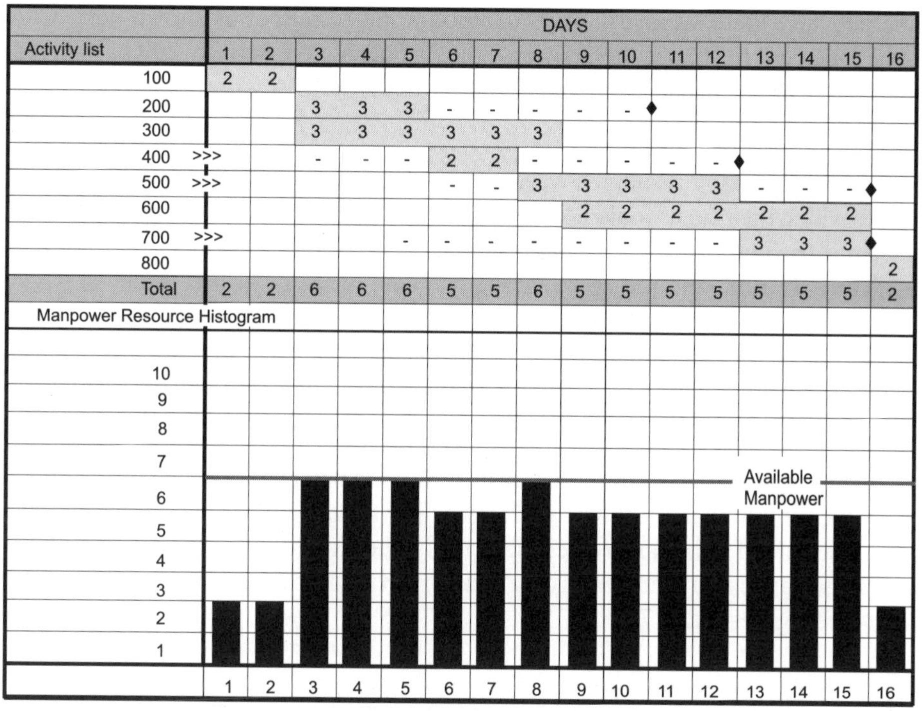

Activity list	DAYS															
	1	2	3	4	5	6	7	8	9	10	11	12	13	14	15	16
100	2	2														
200			3	3	3	-	-	-	-◆							
300			3	3	3	3	3	3								
400 >>>			-	-	-	2	2	-	-	-	-	-	-◆			
500 >>>						-	-	3	3	3	3	3	-	-	-◆	
600									2	2	2	2	2	2	2	
700 >>>					-	-	-	-	-	-	-	-	3	3	3◆	
800																2
Total	2	2	6	6	6	5	5	6	5	5	5	5	5	5	5	2

Manpower Resource Histogram

Figure 4: Resource Histogram (A second way to smooth the resources is to move activity 400 to 6th May, 500 to 8th May and 700 to 13th May)

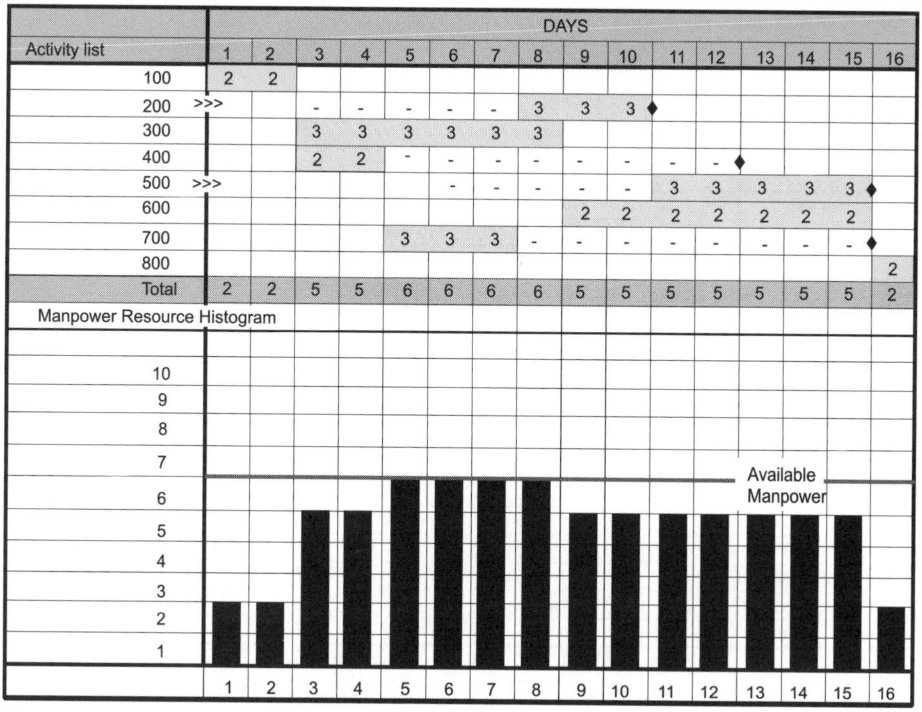

Activity list	DAYS															
	1	2	3	4	5	6	7	8	9	10	11	12	13	14	15	16
100	2	2														
200 >>>			-	-	-	-	-	3	3	3◆						
300			3	3	3	3	3	3								
400			2	2	-	-	-	-	-	-	-	-◆				
500 >>>						-	-	-	-	-	3	3	3	3	3◆	
600									2	2	2	2	2	2	2	
700					3	3	3	-	-	-	-	-	-	-	-◆	
800																2
Total	2	2	5	5	6	6	6	6	5	5	5	5	5	5	5	2

Manpower Resource Histogram

Figure 5: Resource Histogram (A third way to smooth the resources would be to move activities 200 and 500 to their LS)

343

Mathematically there are many ways to smooth the resources as shown here. Care must be taken not to change the activity logic, for instance if activity 200 has moved, then activity 500 must also be moved because of their *finish-to-start* relationship (see *network diagram* figure 1).

Step 5: If the company resources were to be reduced further to 5 men, then moving activities within their float would not be sufficient, other methods need to be considered:

- **Split the activity** - this option is not always feasible or efficient.
- **Time-limited smoothing** - here the end date of the project is fixed, so where the resources are overloaded more men must be assigned.
- **Resource-limited smoothing** - here the maximum number of a resource is fixed, in this case it is 5 men. To achieve this lower resource level it will be necessary to move an activity on the critical path, thus extending the end date of the project.

Step 6: The next step is to consider the cash-flow. This will be influenced by the timing of the costs, for this example the two extremes, ES and LS will be considered. The cost per day is assumed to be linear over the activity, the expenses are shown in the bars. The expenses are calculated per day by adding vertically, then accumulated from left to right (see figures 6 and 7).

Activity list	DAYS															
	1	2	3	4	5	6	7	8	9	10	11	12	13	14	15	16
100	50	50														
200			50	50	50	-	-	-	-	- ◆						
300			10	10	10	10	10	10								
400			50	50	-	-	-	-	-	-	-	- ◆				
500						10	10	10	10	10	-	-	-	-	- ◆	
600									30	30	30	30	30	30	30	
700					30	30	30	-	-	-	-	-	-	-	- ◆	
800																50
Expenses per day	50	50	110	110	90	50	50	20	40	40	30	30	30	30	30	50
Accumulated expenses	50	100	210	320	410	460	510	530	570	610	640	670	700	730	760	810

Figure 6: Early Start Barchart (showing expenses)

Activity list	DAYS															
	1	2	3	4	5	6	7	8	9	10	11	12	13	14	15	16
100	50	50														
200		-	-	-	-	-	50	50	50 ◆							
300			10	10	10	10	10	10								
400			-	-	-	-	-	-	-	-	50	50 ◆				
500						-	-	-	-	-	10	10	10	10	10 ◆	
600									30	30	30	30	30	30	30	
700								-	-	-	-	-	30	30	30 ◆	
800																50
Expenses per day	50	50	10	10	10	10	10	60	80	80	90	90	70	70	70	50
Accumulated expenses	50	100	110	120	130	140	150	210	290	370	460	550	620	690	760	810

Figure 7: Late Start Barchart (showing expenses)

The two expense curves can now be plotted cost against time. The expense curve, also called *budgeted cost for work scheduled* (BCWS) is the link between the CPM and the budget (see figure 8).

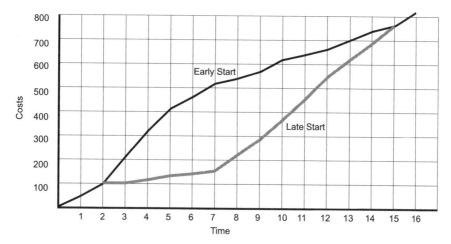

Figure 8: BCWS (S Curve of early start and late start expenses)

This double curve between ES and LS is often called the **banana curve** because of its shape. The important feature here is to appreciate the affect scheduling has on the cash-flow.

Step 7: This step will show how the *cash-flow statement* is linked with the *scheduled barchart*. Using the following information a *cash-flow statement* will be developed for every period (for this example make every four time units or days equal to one period), also assume you are considering the cash-flow from the contractor's perspective.
- For period 1 the brought forward amount is zero.
- Income is calculated at cost plus 30% as they occur on the ES barchart.
- The client takes 1 period to pay and a completion bonus of $200 will be paid with the final invoice.

Time Units	0-4	5-8	9-12	13-16	17-20
Periods	1	2	3	4	5
Costs	$320	$210	$140	$140	
Income (times 1.3)		$416	$273	$182	$182
Bonus					$200

Table 5: Cash-Flow (income)

- Cost of sales:
    - [1] Overheads are $50 per period
    - [2] Activity costs from the ES barchart (assume costs are split 50:50 between labour and materials). The labour costs are paid in the period they occur (see table 6).
    - [3] The material supplier gives 1 period to pay, therefore the cash-flow is moved forward 1 period.

Time Units	0-4	5-8	9-12	13-16	17-20
Periods	1	2	3	4	5
Total Costs	$320	$210	$140	$140	
Labour Costs	$160	$105	$70	$70	

Table 6: Cash-Flow (Labour costs)

Time Units	0-4	5-8	9-12	13-16	17-20
Periods	1	2	3	4	5
Total Costs	$320	$210	$140	$140	$0
Material Costs	$0	$160	$105	$70	$70

Table 7: Cash-Flow (Material costs)

[4] If the closing statement is negative the funds can be borrowed @ 10% per period, these bank charges are then levied in the following period. Round up 0.5 and above if necessary.

Time Units	0-4	5-8	9-12	13-16	17-20
Brought forward	$0	($210)	($130)	($95)	($113)
Income	$0	$416	$273	$182	$182
Completion Bonus					$200
Total Available (A)	$0	$206	$143	$87	$269
Overheads	$50	$50	$50	$50	$0
Labour	$160	$105	$70	$70	$0
Material	$0	$160	$105	$70	$70
Interest	$0	$21	$13	$10	$11
Total Payment (B)	$210	$336	$238	$200	$81
Closing Amount (A-B)	($210)	($130)	($95)	($113)	$188

Table 8: Cash-Flow Statement

From the *cash-flow statement* it is obvious that the project will require up-front financing, but will, however, go positive during the last period.

Step 8: The above calculations form the main part of the **baseline plan**, once this information is available the project can be executed. Using the data capture at timenow 4 the revised barchart can be drawn in conjunction with the *network diagram*, see appendix 1.

Activity Number	Actual Start	Actual Finish	Percentage Complete	Remaining Duration
100	1 May	2 May	100%	-
200	2 May	4 May	100%	-
300	3 May	-	-	5
400	4 May	-	50%	-

Table 9: Data Capture at Timenow 4

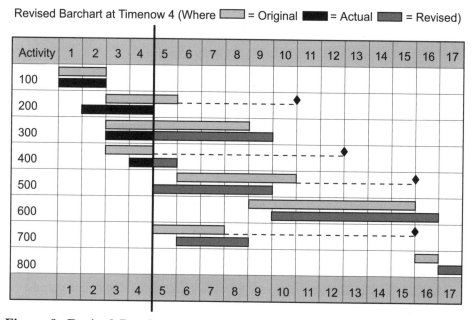

Revised Barchart at Timenow 4 (Where ⬜ = Original ⬛ = Actual ▨ = Revised)

Figure 9: Revised Barchart at Timenow 4

Timenow 4: The analysis at timenow 4 shows that activity 100 has started and finished as planned, but 200 started and finished 1 day early. Because 200 and 500 have a *finish-to-start* relationship, 500 should be able to start 1 day early assuming resources are available. Activity 300 started on time but is going to be finished 1 day late, this will have a knock-on effect and delay 600 and 800 by 1 day. Activity 400 started 1 day late and is estimated to finish 1 day late, this will delay 700 by 1 day. Finally the last activity 800 will be delayed 1 day because 600 is forecast to finish 1 day late.

Activity Number	Actual Start	Actual Finish	Percentage Complete	Remaining Duration
100	1 May	2 May	100%	-
200	2 May	4 May	100%	-
300	3 May	7 May	100%	-
400	4 May	6 May	100%	-
500	5 May	-	-	1
600	8 May	-	-	5
700	7 May	-	50%	-
800	-	-	-	-

Table 10: Data Capture at Timenow 8

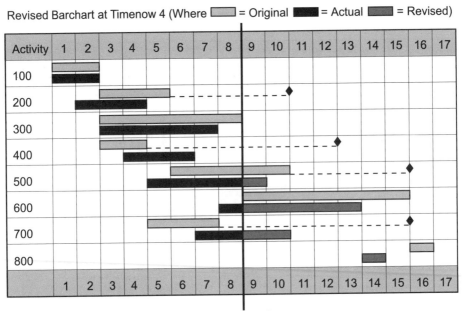

Revised Barchart at Timenow 4 (Where ▭ = Original ▬ = Actual ▤ = Revised)

Figure 10: Revised Barchart at Timenow 8

Timenow 8: The analysis shows activities 300 and 400 are now finished, 500 and 600 have a remaining duration of 1 and 5 days respectively, 700 is 50% complete which can be mathematically transposed to a remaining duration of 1.5 or round up to 2 days. Because 600 is forecast to finish early, 800 can also finish early on day 14, if the resources are available.

Appendix 3 will develop financial selection models from the *Project Selection* chapter. Consider the purchasing of a machine for $25,000 with the following cash-flow (see table 1):

Cash Flow Timing (Years)	Project Cash Flow ($)
0	($25,000)
1	$5,000
2	$7,000
3	$13,000
4	$16,000

Table 1: Cash-Flow

The solutions will be presented under the following headings:
- Payback period
- Return on investment
- Net present value (NPV) at 15%
- Internal rate of return (IRR)

Payback Period: If the project starts with a capital outlay of $25,000, the payback period is the time to recover this initial outlay from the cash-flow. In this case it will take 3 years (see table 2).

Table 2: Cash-Flow

Cash Flow Timing (Years)	Project Cash Flow ($)	Cash Flow Balance ($)
0	($25,000)	($25,000)
1	$5,000	($20,000)
2	$7,000	($13,000)
3	$13,000	$0

Return on Investment: The return on investment is determined from the following expression:

$$\text{Annual profit} = \frac{\text{Total gain - Total outlay}}{\text{Number of years invested}}$$

The total gain is the same as the total cash-flow during the life of the project;

$5,000 + $7,000 + $13,000 + $16,000 = $41,000.

The total outlay is the same as the initial investment = ($25,000). The number of years of the investment is 4 years.

$$\text{Annual profit} = \frac{\$41,000 - \$25,000}{4}$$

$$= \$4000$$

The annual return on investment is the annual profit expressed as a percentage of the initial investment.

$$\text{Annual return on investment} = \frac{\$4,000}{\$25,000} \times \frac{100}{1} = 16\%$$

Net Present Value (NPV): Using the proforma below, transfer the discount factor at 15% from the discount table (see *Project Selection* chapter), then multiply the cash-flow by the discount factor and sum the present values.

Table 3: Net Present Value (NPV)

Cash Flow Timing (Years)	Discount Factor (15%)	Project Cash Flow	Present Value
0		($25,000)	
1		$5,000	
2		$7,000	
3		$13,000	
4		$16,000	
		NPV	

Table 4: NPV Solution

Cash Flow Timing (Years)	Discount Factor (15%)	Project Cash Flow	Present Value
0	1.00	($25,000)	($25,000)
1	0.8696	$5,000	$4,348
2	0.7561	$7,000	$5,293
3	0.6575	$13,000	$8,548
4	0.5718	$16,000	$9,149
		NPV	$2,338

Internal Rate of Return (IRR): The IRR value is the same as the discount factor when the NPV is zero. The IRR figure is found by varying the discount factor until the NPV is zero. The first guess is often a stab in the dark, but it will indicate which way to go. If the NPV is positive increase the discount factor and if the NPV is negative decrease the discount factor.

Table 5: NPV DF 16%

Cash Flow Timing (Years)	Discount Factor (16%)	Project Cash Flow	Present Value
0	1.00	($25,000)	($25,000)
1	0.8621	$5,000	$4,311
2	0.7432	$7,000	$5,202
3	0.6407	$13,000	$8,329
4	0.5523	$16,000	$8,837
		NPV	$1,679

Table 6: NPV DF 17%

Cash Flow Timing (Years)	Discount Factor (17%)	Project Cash Flow	Present Value
0	1.00	($25,000)	($25,000)
1	0.8547	$5,000	$4,274
2	0.7305	$7,000	$5,114
3	0.6244	$13,000	$8,117
4	0.5337	$16,000	$8,539
		NPV	$1,044

Table 7: NPV DF 18%

Cash Flow Timing (Years)	Discount Factor (18%)	Project Cash Flow	Present Value
0	1.00	($25,000)	($25,000)
1	0.8475	$5,000	$4,238
2	0.7182	$7,000	$5,027
3	0.6086	$13,000	$7,912
4	0.5158	$16,000	$8,253
		NPV	$430

Table 8: NPV DF 19%

Cash Flow Timing (Years)	Discount Factor (19%)	Project Cash Flow	Present Value
0	1.00	($25,000)	($25,000)
1	0.8403	$5,000	$4,202
2	0.7062	$7,000	$4,943
3	0.5934	$13,000	$7,714
4	0.4987	$16,000	$7,979
		NPV	($162)

Solution: The discount factor is increased in 1% steps until the NPV value goes negative. The IRR, therefore, lies between 18% and 19%.

This appendix shows how to use a number of project management techniques to plan and control a house building project. From the scope of work and information given, perform the following *earned value* calculations:

- Draw a three level WBS and analyse the CPM
- Draw an ES barchart and resource histogram
- Track the project at timenow 4 and 8

Project Information: The scope of work includes the construction of a house, the outbuildings and landscaping the garden. The main house can be sub-divided into the principle trades: civil, carpenters/plumbers and electricians/painters. The outbuildings consist of a garage and a greenhouse, whilst the landscaping includes the grounds and the fencing. The civil work can be further sub-divided into: foundations, walls and roof. The carpenters and plumbers also includes the doors/windows and built in cupboards (bic's). The electricians and painters also includes the internal finishes.

Activity	Description	Duration	Resources	Costs (BAC)
100	Garage	3	2	$9,000
200	Greenhouse	2	2	$2,000
300	Foundations	1	3	$1,000
400	Walls	3	4	$12,000
500	Roof	5	2	$10,000
600	Doors	3	2	$6,000
700	Plumbing	2	2	$4,000
800	Bic's	3	1	$6,000
900	Wiring	4	1	$8,000
1000	Finishes	2	2	$4,000
1100	Painting	2	6	$6,000
1200	Driveway	2	3	$8,000
1300	Garden	4	2	$8,000
1400	Fence	4	2	$4,000
			Total	$88,000

Table 1: Activity Table

Table 2:
Logic Table
(house project)

Preceding Activity	Succeeding Activity	Preceding Activity	Succeeding Activity
Start	300	500	900
Start	1200	500	800
300	400	100	200
1200	400	200	1100
1200	100	1000	1100
1200	1400	900	1100
400	700	800	1100
400	600	1400	1300
400	500	1100	Finish
700	1000	1300	Finish
600	900		

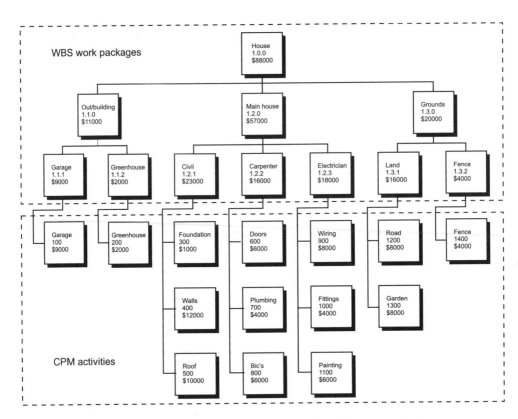

Figure 1: WBS work packages and CPM activities (house project)

Note: The numbering system for the WBS work packages and the activities are different. This will allow both numbering systems to operate linked and autonomously. One or more activities can be linked to a work package, this gives the planner more flexibility when developing the network logic.

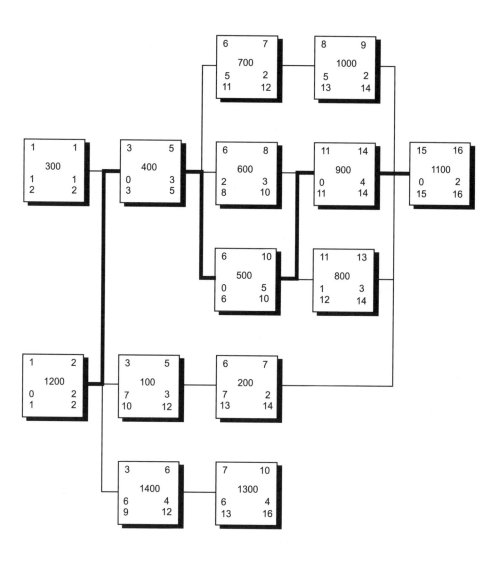

Figure 2: Network Diagram (house project)

Activity Table: The activity table collates the data from the *network diagram* (see figure 2) and presents it in a tabular format.

Activity Number	Description	Early Start	Early Finish	Late Start	Late Finish	Float
100	Garage	3 May	5 May	10 May	12 May	7
200	Greenhouse	6 May	7 May	13 May	14 May	7
300	Foundations	1 May	1 May	2 May	2 May	1
400	Walls	3 May	5 May	3 May	5 May	0
500	Roof	6 May	10 May	6 May	10 May	0
600	Doors	6 May	8 May	8 May	10 May	2
700	Plumbing	6 May	7 May	11 May	12 May	5
800	Bic's	11 May	13 May	12 May	14 May	1
900	Electrical	11 May	14 May	11 May	14 May	0
1000	Fittings	8 May	9 May	13 May	14 May	5
1100	Painting	15 May	16 May	15 May	16 May	0
1200	Road	1 May	2 May	1 May	2 May	0
1300	Garden	7 May	10 May	13 May	16 May	6
1400	Fence	3 May	6 May	9 May	12 May	6

Table 3: Activity Data (house project)

Early Start Barchart and Resource Histogram: The values from the activity data table (table 3) are transferred to the early start barchart (figure 3). The numbers in the barchart are the resources per day transferred from table 1. These values are added vertically to give the total daily resource requirement and is shown in the resource histogram (figure 3). The daily resource totals are then accumulated to give the running total which gives the characteristic S curve presentation (figure 4). Although this curve is for resources (because the figures were available) a similar curve can be drawn for costs. This curve (figure 4) is generally known as the budgeted cost for work scheduled (BCWS).

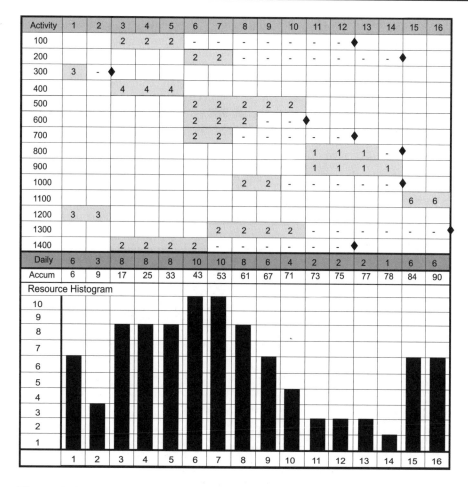

Activity	1	2	3	4	5	6	7	8	9	10	11	12	13	14	15	16
100			2	2	2	-	-	-	-	-	-	-	◆			
200						2	2	-	-	-	-	-	-	-	◆	
300	3	-	◆													
400			4	4	4											
500						2	2	2	2	2						
600						2	2	2	-	-	◆					
700						2	2	-	-	-	-	-	◆			
800											1	1	1	-	◆	
900											1	1	1	1		
1000								2	2	-	-	-	-	-	◆	
1100															6	6
1200	3	3														
1300								2	2	2	2	-	-	-	-	-	-	◆
1400			2	2	2	2	-	-	-	-	-	-	◆			
Daily	6	3	8	8	8	10	10	8	6	4	2	2	2	1	6	6
Accum	6	9	17	25	33	43	53	61	67	71	73	75	77	78	84	90

Figure 3: Early Start Barchart (showing resources) **and Resource Histogram** (showing the total daily resource and the accumulated running total)

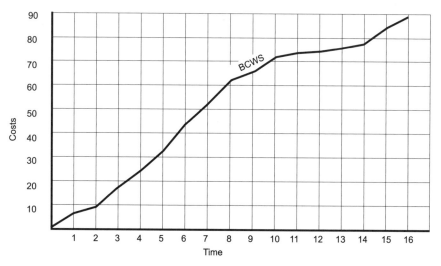

Figure 4: BCWS (accumulated resources against time - assume accumulated costs flow the same curve)

The *resource histogram* (figure 3) indicates the resource requirement per day. For the purpose of this exercise the available resources are assumed to be sufficient.

Expenditure Barchart and Expense Curves: The expenditure barchart assumes a linear cash-flow over the activities. The accumulation of the daily expenses will provide the basis for cost control. The BCWS is the integration of cost and time which forms the baseline plan to track the project's performance against (figure 4).

Earned Value	BCWP = PC * BAC
Scheduled variance	SV = BCWP - BCWS
Scheduled variance %	SV% = SV / BCWS
Cost variance	CV = BCWP - ACWP
Cost variance %	CV% = CV / BCWP
Estimate at completion	EAC = (ACWP / BCWP) * BAC

Table 4: Earned Value Equations (these equations will be used in the earned value analysis)

Data Capture at Timenow 4: The project has now started and the progress information is presented in the following format (table 5).

Activity Number	Actual Costs	Actial Start	Actual Finish	Percentage Complete	Remaining Duration
100	$8,000	3 May	-	67%	-
300	$0	1 May	2 May	100%	-
400	$3,500	4 May	-	33%	-
1200	$7,000	2 May	3 May	100%	-
1300	$1,000	-	-	-	-
1400	$0	4 May	-	25%	-

Table 5: Data Capture at Timenow 4

Earned Value at Timenow 4: The earned value table provides a simple format to compare the baseline plan with the progress. The partly completed proforma can be completed as a self-test.

Table 6: Earned Value proforma

Activity	BAC	BCWS	PC	BCWP	ACWP	SV	SV%	CV	CV%	EAC
100	$9,000		67%		$8,000					
200	$2,000		0%		$0					
300	$1,000		100%		$0					
400	$12,000		33%		$3,500					
500	$10,000		0%		$0					
600	$6,000		0%		$0					
700	$4,000		0%		$0					
800	$6,000		0%		$0					
900	$8,000		0%		$0					
1000	$4,000		0%		$0					
1100	$6,000		0%		$0					
1200	$8,000		100%		$7,000					
1300	$8,000		0%		$1,000					
1400	$4,000		25%		$0					
Totals	$88,000				$19,500					

Table 7: Earned Value at Timenow 4

Activity	BAC	BCWS	PC	BCWP	ACWP	SV	SV%	CV	CV%	EAC
100	$9,000	$6,000	67%	$6,000	$8,000	$0	0%	($2,000	(33.3%	$12,00
200	$2,000	$0	0%	$0	$0	$0	0%	$0	0%	$2,000
300	$1,000	$1,000	100%	$1,000	$0	$0	0%	$1,000	100%	$1,000
400	$12,00	$8,000	33%	$4,000	$3,500	($4,000	(50%)	$500	(12.5%	$10,50
500	$10,00	$0	0%	$0	$0	$0	0%	$0	0%	$10,00
600	$6,000	$0	0%	$0	$0	$0	0%	$0	0%	$6,000
700	$4,000	$0	0%	$0	$0	$0	0%	$0	0%	$4,000
800	$6,000	$0	0%	$0	$0	$0	0%	$0	0%	$6,000
900	$8,000	$0	0%	$0	$0	$0	0%	$0	0.00%	$8,000
1000	$4,000	$0	0%	$0	$0	$0	0%	$0	0%	$4,000
1100	$6,000	$0	0%	$0	$0	$0	0%	$0	0%	$6,000
1200	$8,000	$8,000	100%	$8,000	$7,000	$0	0%	$1,000	(12.5%	$7,000
1300	$8,000	$0	0%	$0	$1,000	$0	0%	($1,000	(100%)	$8,000
1400	$4,000	$2,000	25%	$1,000	$0	($1,000	(50%)	$1,000	100%	$4,000
Totals	$88,00	$25,00	22.7%	$20,00	$19,50	($5,000	($20%)	$500	2.5%	$88,50

359

Revised Barchart at Timenow 4: The revised barchart and the earned value table, contain complementary information. When calculating the revised barchart it is important to follow the activity logic through to completion (see network diagram figure 2).

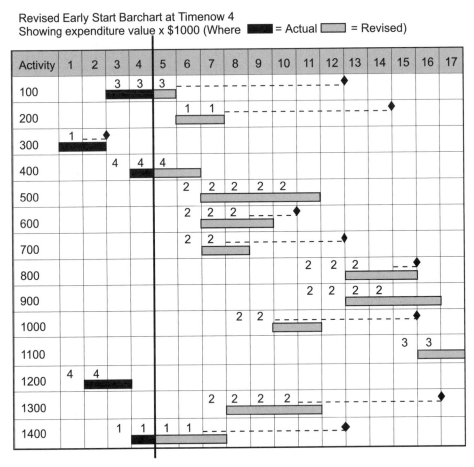

Figure 5: Revised Barchart at Timenow 4

Project Analysis at Timenow 4: The variance figures indicate that overall the project is late, but slightly under budget. The figures may be distorted, however, because activity 1300 costs have been reported, although there appears to be no progress. Similarly activity 300, progress is reported, but no costs. These are flags highlighting data that is conflicting and therefore needs to be checked.

Activity 400 is on the critical path and is 1 day late. The knock-on effect can be seen on the revised barchart. If this activity were crashed by 1 day this would bring the schedule back on course. The activity is under budget so there should be funds to cover any additional expenditure.

Activity Number	Actual Costs	Actual Start	Actual Finish	Percentage Complete	Remaining Duration
100	$11,000	3 May	6 May	100%	-
200	$2,000	7 May	8 May	100%	-
300	$2,000	1 May	2 May	100%	-
400	$11,500	4 May	6 May	100%	-
500	$7,000	7 May	(crash)	50%	2
600	$4,000	7 May	-	66.60%	-
700	$2,500	8 May	-	50%	-
1000	$1,500	8 May	-	50%	-
1200	$7,000	2 May	3 May	1	-
1300	$3,000	8 May	-	25%	-
1400	$3,500	4 May	7 May	100%	-

Table 8: Data Capture at Timenow 8 (the project has now progressed to timenow 8)

Activity	BAC	BCWS	PC	BCWP	ACWP	SV	SV%	CV	CV%	EAC
100	$9,000	$9,000	100%	$9,000	$11,000	$0	0%	($2,000)	(22.2%)	$11,000
200	$2,000	$2,000	100%	$2,000	$2,000	$0	0%	$0	0%	$2,000
300	$1,000	$1,000	100%	$1,000	$2,000	$0	0%	($1,000)	(100%)	$2,000
400	$12,000	$12,000	100%	$12,000	$11,500	$0	0%	50000%	(4.2%)	$11,500
500	$10,000	$6,000	50%	$5,000	$7,000	($1,000)	(16.6%)	($2,000)	(40%)	$14,000
600	$6,000	$6,000	66.60%	$4,000	$4,000	($2,000)	(33.3%)	$0	0%	$6,000
700	$4,000	$4,000	50%	$2,000	$2,500	($2,000)	(50%)	($500)	(25%)	$5,000
800	$6,000	$0	0%	$0	$0	$0	0%	$0	0%	$6,000
900	$8,000	$0	0%	$0	$0	$0	0%	$0	0%	$8,000
1000	$4,000	$2,000	50%	$2,000	$1,500	$0	0%	$500	25%	$3,000
1100	$6,000	$0	0%	$0	$0	$0	0%	$0	0%	$6,000
1200	$8,000	$8,000	100%	$8,000	$7,000	$0	0%	$1,000	12.50%	$7,000
1300	$8,000	$4,000	25%	$2,000	$3,000	($2,000)	(50%)	($1,000)	(50%)	$12,000
1400	$4,000	$4,000	100%	$4,000	$3,500	$0	0%	$500	12.50%	$3,500
Totals	$88,000	$58,000	58%	$51,000	$55,000	($7,000)	(12%)	($4,000)	(7.8%)	$97,000

Table 9: Earned Value at Timenow 8

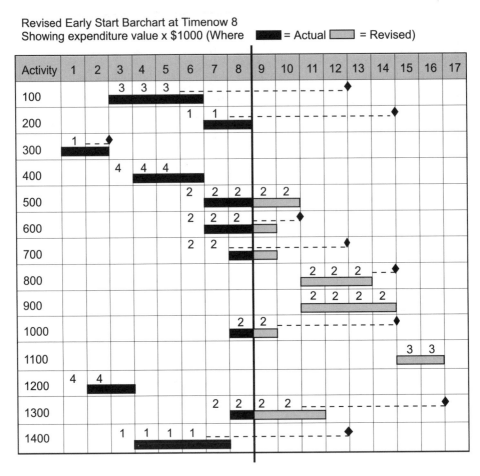

Revised Early Start Barchart at Timenow 8
Showing expenditure value x $1000 (Where ▅ = Actual ▭ = Revised)

Figure 6: Revised Barchart at Timenow 8

- **Project Analysis at Timenow 8:** From the schedule and cost variances, overall the project is still late, but now the budget is over spent. The trends indicate SV% improving from (20%) to (12%), but CV% deteriorating from 2.5% to (7.8%). This is flag to check productivity on activities 100, 500, 700 and 1300. They are either under performing, the estimate was too optimistic, or there are special circumstances.

  Although the SV is negative the revised barchart indicates that the project will finish on time. The discrepancy is caused by activities with float running late. The negative cost variance indicates a need to apply control on activities 500, 700 and 1300, to bring the project in on budget.

AOA: Activity-on-Arrow
AON: Activity-on-Node
ACWP: Actual Cost of Work Performed
APM: Association of Project Managers
BAC: Budget at Completion
BCWP: Budgeted Cost of Work Performed
BCWS: Budgeted Cost of Work Scheduled
BOK: Body of Knowledge
BOM: Bill of Materials
BOOT: Build Own Operate Transfer
BOT: Build Operate Transfer
CIF: Cost Insurance Freight
CV: Cost Variance
COD: Cash on Delivery
CPA: Critical Path Analysis
CPI: Cost Price Index
CPM: Critical Path Method
CV: Cost Variance

DCF: Discounted Cash-Flow
DDP: Delivered Duty Paid
DoD: Dept of Defence
EAC: Estimate-at-Competition
FF: Finish-to-Finish
FIFO: First In First Out
FRI: Forecast Rate of Invoicing
FS: Finish-to-Start
FOB: Free on Board
IPMA: International Project Management Association
IRR: Internal Rate of Return
JIT: Just-in-Time
LIFO: Last In First Out
MBE: Management by Exception
MBO: Management by Objectives
MRP: Material Requirement Planning
NCR: Non Conformance Report
NPV: Net Present Value
OBS: Organisation Breakdown Structure
PERT: Project Evaluation and Review Technique
PC: Percentage Complete
PDM: Precedence Diagram Method
PMBOK: Project Management Body of Knowledge
PMI: Project Management Institute
PMP: Project Management Professional
QCP: Quality Control Plan
ROI: Return on Investment
ROT: Refurbish Operate Transfer
SPI: Schedule Performance Index
SV: Schedule Variance
SF: Start-to-Finish
SS: Start-to-Start
TQM: Total Quality Management
WBS: Work Breakdown Structure

Adair, John., *Action-Centred Leadership*, Pan, 1989
Adair, John., *Effective Decision-Making*, Pan, 1985
Adair, John., *Effective Leadership*, Pan, 1988
Adair, John., *Effective Time Management*, Pan, 1988
Adair, John., *Team Building*, Pan
Adams, J., and **Campbell**, B., *Roles and Responsibilities of the Project Manager*, PMI
Ahuja, Hira., *Project Management: Techniques in Planning and Controlling Construction Projects*, Wiley, 1994
AS/NZS 4360:1995., *Risk Management*
Association of Project Managers (APM)., *Body of Knowledge (BOK)*

Barkley, Bruce., and **Saylor**, James., *Customer-Driven Project Management: A New Paradigm in Total Quality Implementation*, McGraw-Hill, 1994
Barnes, N., and **Wearne**, S., *The Future for Major Project Management*, International Journal of Project Management, Vol 11, No 3, August 1993, pp 135-142
Begg, D., *Economics*, McGraw-Hill, 1997
Belbin, M., *Management Teams*, Butterworth-Heinemann, 1996
Benedetto, R., *Matrix Management Theory in Practice*, Kendall Hunt
Bentley, C., *Configuration Management Within Prince,* 1993
Bolton, Robert., *People Skills,* Simon & Schuster, 1986
Bryans, P, **Cronin,** T., *Organisation Theory,* Core Business Studies, 1983
BS 5750 (1979), *Quality Management*
Burleson, C., *Effective Meetings*, Wiley

Caper, Richard., *A Project-By-Project Approach to Quality: A Practical Handbook for Individuals, Teams and Organizations*, Gower, 1997
Catapult., *Microsoft Project 98 Step by Step (Step by Step Series)*, 1997
Carnall, C., *Managing Change*, Prentice-Hall, 1990
Chapman, C., and **Ward**, Stephen., *Project Risk Management: Processes, Techniques and Insights*, Wiley, 1996

Charland, T., *Advanced Project Management Techniques Handbook*, 1990

Charoenngam, Chotchai., and **Popescu**, Calin., *Project Planning, Scheduling, and Control in Construction: An Encyclopedia of Terms and Applications*, Wiley, 1995

Child, J., *Organisations*, Sage, 1985

Clark, C., *Brainstorming*, Wilshire

Cleland, D., *Project Management Field Guide*, Van Nostrand Reinhold, 1997

Cleland, D., and **King**, W., *Systems Analysis and Project Management*, McGraw-Hill, 1983

Crosby, P.B., *Quality Without Tears*, McGraw-Hill, 1995

Crosby, P.B., *Quality is Free*, McGraw-Hill, 1987

Davidson Frame, J., *Managing Projects in Organizations: How to Make the Best Use of Time, Techniques, and People*, (Jossey-Bass Management Series), 1995

Davidson Frame, J., *The Project Office (Best Management Practices)*, Crisp,1998

Darnall, Russell., and **Thatcher**, John., *The World's Greatest Project: One Project Team on the Path to Quality (Perspective Series)*, Cambridge Interactive, 1996

Dinsmore, P., *Human Factors in Project Management*, Amacom

Dinsmore, Paul., (Editor) *The Ama Handbook of Project Management*, McGraw-Hill, 1993

Drigani, Fulvio., *Computerized Project Control*

Fellows, R., **Langford**, D and **Newcombe**, R., *Construction Management In Practice*, Construction Press

Fleming, Quentin., and **Koppelman**, Joel., *Earned Value Project Management*, PMIC, 1996

Forsberg, Kevin., *Visual Project Management,* 1993

Frank, M., *How to Run a Successful Meeting in Half the Time*, Corgi

Gibson, C.F., and **Nolan**, R.L., *Managing the Four Stages of EDP Growth*, Harvard Business Review, January 1974

Gido, J., and **Clements**, J., *Successful Project Management,* South Western College Pub, 1999

Goodworth, C., *Effective Delegation*, Business Books

Grey, Stephen., *Practical Risk Assessment for Project Management,* Wiley Series in Software Engineering Practice, 1995

Handy, C., *Understanding Organisations*, Penguin, 1993

Hans, J. **Thamhain** and **David,** L. **Wilemon.**, "*Conflict Management in Project-Oriented Work Environments*", Drexel Hill, Pennsylvania: Project Management Institute, 1974, p87

Harris, Jean., *Sharpen Your Team's Skills in Project Management*, McGraw-Hill, 1998

Haynes, Marion., *Project Management (Fifty Minute Book)*, Elaine Fritz, 1997

Heisler, Sanford., *The Wiley Project Engineer's Desk Reference: Project Engineering, Operations, and Management*, Wiley, 1994

Herzberg, F., *Work and the Nature of Man*

Institute of Chemical Engineers, *A Guide to Capital Cost Estimating*, 1988

Jain, R., and **Triandis**, Henry., *Management of Research and Development Organizations: Managing the Unmanageable*, (Wiley Series in Engineering and Technology Management), 1990

Johnston, Andrew., *A Hacker's Guide to Project Management*, Computer Weekly, 1995

Jones, Peter., *Handbook of Team Design: A Practitioner's Guide to Team Systems Development*, McGraw-Hill, 1997

Juran, Joseph., *Product Quality - A Prescription for the West*

Kerzner, H., *In Search of Excellence in Project Management*, Van Nostrand Reinhold, 1998

Kerzner, H., *Project Management A Systems Approach to Planning, Scheduling and Controlling*, Van Nostrand Reinhold, 1997

Kharbanda, O., and **Pinto**, Jeffrey., *What Made Gertie Gallop?: Lessons from Project Failures*, 1996

Kim, Steven., *Essence of Creativity: A Guide to Tackling Difficult Problems*, Oxford University Press, 1990

Kimbler, D., and **William**, Ferrell., *Tqm-Based Project Planning*, 1997

Knight, A and **Silk**, D., *Managing Information*, McGraw-Hill

Knutson, Joan., *Project Management: How to Plan and Manage Successful Projects*, Amacon, 1991

Kuhre, Lee., *ISO 14010s: Environmental Auditing: Tools and Techniques for Passing or Performing Environmental Audits*, Prentice-Hall, 1996

Lewis, James., *Project Planning, Scheduling & Control: A Hands-On Guide to Bringing Projects in on Time and on Budget*, McGraw-Hill, 1995

Lewis, James., *The Project Manager's Desk Reference: A Comprehensive Guide to Project Planning, Scheduling, Evaluation, Control & Systems*, Irwin, 1993

Lientz, Bennet., and **Rea**, Kathryn, *Breakthrough Technology Project Management*, Academic Press, 1998

Lock, D., *Project Management*, Gower, 1996

Lockyer, Keith., *Critical Path Analysis and Other Project Network Techniques*, Financial Times Pitman, 1991

Lockyer, Keith., *Production Management*, Financial Times Pitman, 1992

Lockyer, Keith, and **Gordon**, James., *Project Management and Project Network Techniques,* Financial Times Pitman, 1996

Lowery, G., *Managing Projects With Microsoft Project '98*, Van Norstrand Reinhold, 1997

Lysons, C., *Purchasing*, Financial Times Pitman, 1998

Maslow, A., *Motivation and Personality,* 1987

Meredith, J., and **Samuel**, J., *Project Management A Managerial Approach*, Wiley, 1995

Moody, P., *Decision-Making*, McGraw-Hill, 1989

Morris, Peter., *The Anatomy of Projects*, Thomas Telford, 1997

Morris, Peter., *The Management of Projects,* Thomas Telford, 1994

Mott, G., *Investment Appraisal for Managers*, Pan, 1982,

Mott, G., *Management Accounting*, Pan, 1987

Newbold, Robert., *Project Management in the Fast Lane: Applying the Theory of Constraints,* St. Lucie Press/Apics Series on Constraints Management, 1998

Obeng, Eddie., *All Change: Project Manager's Secret Handbook,* Financial Times Management, 1996

O'Connell, Fergus., *How to Run Successful Projects II: The Silver Bullet,* Prentice Hall, 1996

Oosthuizen, Pieter., *Goodbye MBA*, International Thomson, 1998

Palfreman, J., and **Swade**, D., *The Dream Machine*, BBC Books, 1993

Parkinson, C., *Parkinson's Law*, Buccaneer Books, 1993

Peace, A., *Body Language*, Sheldon Press, 1977

Pennypacker, James., *Project Management Forms*, Cambridge University Press, 1997

Phillips, Dwayne., *The Software Project Manager's Handbook: Principles that Work at Work*, IEE Computer Science Press, 1998

Pokras, Sandy., *Rapid Team Deployment: Building High-Performance Project Teams (Fifty-Minute Series)*, 1995

PMBOK Handbook Volume 6, *Project and Program Risk Management,* 1992

Pollalis, Spiro., *Computer-Aided Project Management: A Visual Scheduling and Management System*

Project Management Institute (PMI)., *The Global Status of the Project Management Profession*, PMI publication

Project Management Institute (PMI)., *A Guide to the Project Management Body of Knowledge (PMBOK), 1996*

Pyron, Tim., *Sams Teach Yourself Microsoft Project 98 in 24 Hours,* Sams

Pyron, Tim., *Special Edition Using Microsoft Project 98*, Sams, 1997

Raftery, John., *Risk Analysis in Project Management,* Routledge, 1993

Rakos, John., *Software Project Management for Small to Medium Sized Projects,* Prentice Hall, 1994

Rosenau, M., *Successful Project Management*, Van Nostrand Reinhold, 1998

Schuette, S., and **Liska**, W., *Building Construction Estimating* (McGraw-Hill Series in Construction Engineering and Project Management), 1994

Schuyler, John., *Decision Analysis in Projects*, Cambridge University Press, 1996

Sharp, John., and **Howard**, Keith., *The Management of a Student Research Project,* (second edition), Gower, 1996

Shaughnessy, Haydon., *Collaboration Management: New Project and Partnering Skills and Techniques*, Wiley, 1994

Simmons, Dick., *Software Measurement: A Visualization Toolkit for Project Control and Process Improvement*, Prentice Hall, 1997

Stephenson, Ralph., *Project Partnering for the Design and Construction Industry*, Wiley, 1996

Stuckenbruck, L., *The Implementation of Project Management: The Professional Handbook*, PMI

Toney, Frank., *Best Practices of Project Management Groups in Large Functional Organizations*, Addison-Wesley Longman, 1997

Turner, R., *Handbook of Project-Based Management*, McGraw-Hill, 1993

Turner, Rodney., *The Commercial Project Manager: Key Commercial, Financial, and Legal Skills for Project Managers*, McGraw-Hill, 1995

Verma, Vijay., and **Thamhain**, Hans., *Human Resource Skills for the Project Manager: The Human Aspects of Project Management Vol 2*, PMIC, 1996

Walker, Anthony., *Project Management in Construction*, Blackwell Science, 1996

Weiss, Joseph., and **Wysocki**, Robert., *5-Phase Project Management: A Practical Planning & Implementation Guide*, Perseus, 1992

Westney, Richard., *Computerized Management of Multiple Small Projects,* Marcel Dekker

Wild, R., *Production and Operations Management*, Holt, Rinehart and Winston, 1995

Wideman, Max., and **Dawson**, Rodney., *Project & Program Risk Management: A Guide to Managing Project Risks and Opportunities,* Vol 6, 1998

Wideman., *A Framework for Project and Program Management Integration*, PMBOK Handbook Series - volume 1, 1991

Van Der Waldt, Andre., *Project Management For Strategic Change and Upliftment*, International Thomson, 1998